EXCEL FOR REALTORS

Leslie Moxam

Reactive Publishing

CONTENTS

PREFACE

Imagine being able to transform endless rows of numbers into insights that drive smarter, faster decisions—insights that can not only enhance your day-to-day operations but also power up your career in real estate. Whether you're an experienced agent aiming to refine your strategy or a newcomer eager to learn the ropes, this book is your gateway to mastering Excel—the secret weapon behind many of the world's most successful real estate professionals.

In today's competitive real estate market, data is everything. From managing property listings and tracking client interactions to analyzing complex financial models and forecasting market trends, the power to harness data effectively can set you apart. This book, "Excel for Real Estate Agents: A Comprehensive Guide. Methods, Strategies and Executions," has been meticulously crafted to address every facet of your daily tasks, enabling you to work smarter, not harder.

Inside these pages, you will find a clear and structured approach designed specifically for the challenges and opportunities of the real estate industry. We start at the very beginning—getting comfortable with Excel's interface and basic functions—and gradually guide you into more specialized topics. You'll learn how to use essential formulas, create visually compelling charts, design custom dashboards, automate repetitive tasks with macros, and even integrate Excel with other industry software. No matter your current level of expertise, each chapter builds upon the previous one, ensuring a smooth learning curve as you steadily accumulate skills that are immediately applicable to your work.

But this isn't just another technical manual. It's an invitation to reimagine how you use technology to optimize every aspect of your business. Imagine being able to quickly generate a comprehensive financial analysis for a new listing, or effortlessly manage your CRM using customized templates— leaving you more time to focus on what truly matters: building relationships and closing deals. Each method, strategy, and execution detailed in this guide has been selected with your daily challenges in mind, aiming to simplify complex processes and elevate your performance.

We understand that as real estate professionals, you thrive on precision, agility, and results. This book is built around those pillars. You'll discover practical tips to handle property transactions seamlessly, analyze market trends with confidence, and collaborate with your team in ways that enhance productivity and accountability. The tools in this guide aren't just theoretical—they're battle-tested techniques that have helped countless agents achieve a competitive edge in the market.

Whether you decide to use this resource as a step-by-step workbook or a reference guide for tough questions on the job, know that the ultimate goal is your success. Excel is no longer just a spreadsheet program; it's an essential part of your professional toolkit, poised to revolutionize how you capture, process, and act upon the data that drives your business.

So, as you embark on this transformative journey, open your mind to new possibilities. Embrace the power of Excel, and let this book be your trusted companion in achieving excellence and exceeding your real estate goals. The future of your business is data-driven—let's harness that potential together!

Welcome to a new era in real estate. Welcome to the power of Excel.

CHAPTER 1: GETTING STARTED WITH EXCEL

Installing Excel and Initial Setup

E xcel is not just software; it's a powerful tool that can greatly enhance your effectiveness as a real estate agent. Your journey begins with installation and setting up Excel to meet your specific needs, laying the groundwork to fully leverage its capabilities in your daily activities.

Start by acquiring the software. Microsoft Excel is included in the Microsoft Office suite, which is available for both Windows and Mac users. If you don't already have it, head to the official Microsoft website to purchase or subscribe to Microsoft 365, which includes Excel. After your purchase, download the installer. For Windows users, installation is usually straightforward: double-click the downloaded file and follow the on-screen instructions. Mac users will follow a similar process by dragging the Excel icon into the Applications folder after downloading.

Once you have installed Excel, launch it for the first time. You'll likely encounter a welcome screen that prompts you to choose a template or create a new workbook. While it may be tempting to jump right into using templates, take a moment to explore your options. Familiarizing yourself with these choices can significantly influence how you utilize Excel in your practice. Whether you select a blank workbook or one of the pre-designed templates, this initial decision shapes your user experience going forward.

Now let's move on to customization, which is essential for maximizing efficiency. Begin by personalizing your interface; start with the Quick Access Toolbar located at the top left of your Excel window. Adding frequently used commands such as Save, Undo, and Redo will allow for quicker access. Simply right-click on any command you wish to add and select "Add to Quick Access Toolbar." This small adjustment can save valuable time in an industry where every minute counts.

Next, consider adjusting your view settings for optimal productivity. Switch between different viewing modes— such as Page Layout or Normal View—depending on your current task. For example, when entering data or performing calculations, Normal View provides a straightforward layout without distractions.

Once you're comfortable with the interface layout, take time to familiarize yourself with keyboard shortcuts that can greatly speed up your workflow. Take this example, using Ctrl + C to copy and Ctrl + V to paste are essential for quickly moving data around. Additionally, mastering shortcuts like Ctrl + Z for undoing actions or F2 for editing within a cell will make data management much smoother.

With these settings adjusted for enhanced efficiency, let's move on to some foundational tasks that will serve you well in real estate scenarios. Start by understanding how to enter and format data properly by creating a simple table for property listings:

1. Open a new workbook.

2. In cell A1, type "Property Address." In B1, enter "Price," C1 should read "Square Footage," and D1 "Bedrooms.

3. Below these headers, begin entering sample property data.

To format this table effectively:

- Highlight cells A1 through D1.

- Select "Bold" from the Home tab in the ribbon.

- Apply borders around this selection for clarity.

This organized layout will facilitate easy reference during analysis later on.

Don't forget the importance of saving your work regularly; try establishing a habit of saving every few minutes while working on significant projects or new listings. Use Ctrl + S frequently or enable auto-save features if you're using Microsoft 365 online.

Another vital aspect involves understanding Excel's various file formats beyond just .xlsx files—such as .csv (comma-separated values). This format is particularly useful when dealing with large datasets or importing/exporting data with other applications commonly used in real estate.

With installation complete and your initial setup finalized, you are now ready to harness Excel's functionalities effectively within real estate contexts—whether tracking properties, analyzing market trends, or managing client information efficiently.

These foundational skills will become an integral part of an extensive arsenal of tools at your disposal throughout your career as a real estate agent. Embrace this journey into data management; it's about more than just numbers; it's about transforming how you engage with every aspect of real estate transactions and client relations moving forward.

Exploring the Excel Interface

Mastering the Excel interface is crucial for enhancing your efficiency as a real estate agent. A solid understanding of the tools available will enable you to navigate complex data confidently and effortlessly. When you first open Excel, you might feel overwhelmed by the array of options presented, but with time and familiarity, this initial intimidation can turn into empowerment.

Essentially of Excel is the Ribbon—a collection of tabs at the top of your screen that organizes all available tools and commands. Each tab houses groups of related functions; for example, the Home tab provides essential formatting options such as font adjustments, alignment, and number formats. By familiarizing yourself with this layout, you will save valuable time when engaged in data entry or analysis.

Directly below the Ribbon lies the Formula Bar, which displays the contents of your currently selected cell and allows for direct editing. This feature is particularly important for entering formulas—whether calculating totals or averages— quickly and accurately. As a real estate agent managing numerous property listings and their associated figures, efficient use of the Formula Bar significantly enhances your data manipulation capabilities.

To further streamline your workflow, take advantage of Excel's customizable options. You can modify which commands appear on the Quick Access Toolbar—a small menu located above or below the Ribbon—for quick access to frequently used features like Print or Save. Simply right-click on any command in the Ribbon to add it to this toolbar; this small adjustment can greatly boost your productivity.

Navigating between worksheets also plays a vital role in optimizing your Excel experience. Each workbook can house multiple sheets, allowing you to organize information by property type, client, or market segment without cluttering your workspace. Utilize keyboard shortcuts such as Ctrl + Page Up/Page Down to swiftly switch between these sheets; this can be especially useful when comparing data across various properties or analyzing trends.

Excel's charting capabilities provide powerful visualization tools that can transform raw numbers into meaningful insights. While exploring property performance metrics or market trends, consider selecting your data range and using the Insert tab to experiment with different chart types —bar charts for price comparisons or line graphs for tracking market trends over time can yield valuable visual representations.

Should you encounter challenges while navigating Excel's functionalities, take advantage of its built-in help features. Pressing F1 opens contextual help directly related to what you're working on, providing detailed explanations and tutorials right within the application. This resource makes it easier to overcome obstacles without losing momentum in your tasks.

To deepen your understanding of Excel's interface, set aside time to practice creating sample spreadsheets relevant to real estate scenarios. For example, build a basic financial model estimating potential rental income from various properties based on different occupancy rates and rental prices. This exercise will not only familiarize you with formula creation but also reinforce practical skills that are essential when presenting financial analyses to clients.

Remember that mastery comes with regular use and exploration of new features as they emerge in updates or newer versions of Excel. Staying engaged with what Excel offers will keep you at the forefront of effective data management practices tailored specifically for real estate applications.

As you become more comfortable with these elements,

you'll find they not only enhance your personal efficiency but also elevate your professionalism in interactions with clients and stakeholders. A comprehensive understanding of the Excel interface will empower you as a real estate agent, providing clarity in decision-making supported by robust data management practices specifically designed for your field.

Understanding Worksheets and Workbooks

Understanding the difference between worksheets and workbooks is crucial for maximizing your efficiency as a real estate professional. In Excel, a workbook serves as a container for related data, while worksheets function as individual pages within that container. This organizational structure allows you to compartmentalize information, making it easier to analyze various aspects of your business without being overwhelmed by clutter.

A single workbook can contain multiple worksheets, each designed for specific tasks or datasets. For example, you might create one worksheet to manage property listings, another to track client interactions, and a third for analyzing market trends. This structured approach not only improves clarity but also makes it easy to navigate between different datasets.

When you start a new Excel file, you'll see a default workbook titled "Book1," which includes three blank worksheets named Sheet1, Sheet2, and Sheet3. To better reflect their contents, you can rename these sheets by right-clicking on the tab of any worksheet and selecting "Rename." Take this example, renaming Sheet1 to "Property Listings" immediately clarifies its purpose. This simple act of organization can save you significant time when searching for specific information later.

Efficiently managing your worksheets is essential for maintaining project clarity. You can easily rearrange them by clicking and dragging the tabs into your preferred order. For example, if you frequently analyze property sales data after reviewing client feedback, placing the "Sales Data" worksheet next to "Client Feedback" streamlines your workflow.

Excel also offers functionalities that enhance your experience with worksheets. The ability to group and ungroup sheets allows you to perform actions across multiple worksheets simultaneously. If you need a consistent layout or formula across various property types, grouping sheets can help you avoid repetitive tasks. To do this, select the first sheet, hold down Shift or Ctrl, and click on the other tabs you'd like to include; any actions—such as formatting or data entry—will apply to all selected sheets.

Data validation becomes an important consideration when working across different worksheets. Take this example, if you have a "Property Details" sheet with each row representing a different listing, ensuring that information like price or square footage adheres to specific formats is essential. By applying data validation rules—such as restricting price entries to numeric values—you enhance accuracy and reduce errors during data entry.

Excel's ability to link data between worksheets further enhances your analytical capabilities. If you're tracking expenses in one worksheet but need that information reflected in your primary "Dashboard" sheet for quick insights, use formulas that directly reference other sheets. Start your formula with an equal sign "=" followed by the target sheet's name, an exclamation mark, and then the cell reference (e.g., ='Expenses'!B2). This linking creates a dynamic workflow that updates automatically as changes are made.

Creating summary reports from multiple worksheets is another beneficial practice. Take this example, if you have separate sheets for sales data from different regions, functions like SUMIF or AVERAGEIF enable you to quickly consolidate performance metrics into one summary sheet. These consolidated views can be invaluable when presenting data-driven insights to clients or stakeholders.

As you become more comfortable navigating these features, consider exploring additional tools such as freezing panes within your worksheets for easier viewing of long lists of data. Freezing panes allows specific rows or columns to remain visible while scrolling through extensive datasets—ideal for reviewing client names alongside their properties or contact details.

Utilizing color coding within your worksheets also enhances readability significantly. For example, highlighting high-value properties in green while marking those needing urgent attention in red provides visual cues that accelerate decision-making processes.

By understanding how workbooks and worksheets interact, you can adopt a streamlined approach to real estate management tasks. As you cultivate this awareness through regular practice and experimentation with these features, you'll notice not only enhanced productivity but also increased confidence in handling complex datasets critical for success in real estate transactions.

Leveraging these tools will not only address your immediate needs but will also lay the groundwork for more sophisticated analyses in the future. Embracing these foundational elements equips you with practical skills that foster an organized and efficient workflow in your real estate career—allowing you to focus on what truly matters: effectively serving your clients and achieving results in an increasingly competitive environment.

Customizing the Excel Ribbon

Customizing the Excel Ribbon can significantly enhance your workspace, making it more efficient and tailored to your specific needs as a real estate professional. The Ribbon is the main interface for accessing various tools and functions in Excel, but its default layout may not reflect your priorities. By personalizing it, you can highlight frequently used features, creating a more intuitive and streamlined workflow.

To start customizing the Ribbon, simply right-click anywhere on it and select "Customize the Ribbon." This action opens a dialog box that displays the current layout alongside available commands. On the right side, you'll find a list of tabs such as Home, Insert, and Page Layout. Each tab can be expanded to reveal groups of related commands; for instance, the Home tab includes essential tools for font formatting and alignment—crucial for crafting polished presentations.

If you often use specific functions like VLOOKUP or conditional formatting, these may not be readily accessible in the default setup. You can create a new tab or group specifically for these functions to facilitate quicker access. Just click "New Tab" in the dialog box, rename it by clicking "Rename," and then drag relevant commands from the left column into this new section.

Additionally, consider removing commands that you rarely use. For example, if charts or pivot tables aren't part of your daily operations, eliminating them from view can help reduce distractions and allow for faster navigation to the tools that truly matter.

Excel also offers features that enhance productivity through Ribbon customization. One useful option is adding keyboard shortcuts to streamline repetitive tasks. After adjusting your Ribbon layout, you can assign shortcuts by selecting "Keyboard Shortcuts: Customize" at the bottom of the customization window. This feature is particularly beneficial for tasks like data validation or printing reports—functions you want to execute quickly.

Imagine you're frequently analyzing property market trends using charts; adding charting tools directly to your customized tab will save you valuable time when working with different datasets. You can easily drag these chart commands from their original locations into your custom tab.

Don't forget about Excel's built-in command search feature located at the top of the Ribbon—a powerful tool that helps you locate any command quickly if you forget its position. Just type what you're looking for in this search bar; it could range from basic arithmetic functions to advanced analytics options like creating dynamic dashboards with real-time data feeds.

Regularly reviewing your Ribbon setup is essential as your needs evolve in the ever-changing landscape of real estate analytics. With new Excel updates or as you expand into different areas—such as integrating financial analysis—it's wise to adjust your Ribbon configuration accordingly.

And, consider sharing your customized Ribbon with team members who may benefit from quick access to specific features. You can easily export your settings via the "Customize" menu by selecting "Import/Export," allowing others to adopt your efficient layout and saving them time while promoting consistency across collaborative efforts.

Lastly, think about how visual organization within the Ribbon can further enhance user experience. Grouping related tools together creates visual distinctions among commands—ensuring that whether you're tracking client interactions or analyzing property values across multiple metrics, you'll have an organized approach at your fingertips.

As real estate professionals adapt their strategies based on market demands, mastering customized tools in Excel provides greater flexibility and efficiency in daily operations. Tailoring the Ribbon goes beyond aesthetics; it's a strategic alignment of software capabilities with business goals—leading to improved data management and clearer insights that ultimately benefit client relations and drive success in transactions.

By incorporating these customization practices into your routine, navigating Excel will become second nature—enabling you to focus more on strategic decisions rather than getting lost in convoluted menus or searching endlessly for necessary functions. Embrace this transformation as a significant step toward greater productivity in your professional landscape.

Basic Excel Terminology

Understanding basic Excel terminology is essential for navigating the software effectively, especially in the fast-paced world of real estate. Being familiar with key terms not only enhances your communication with colleagues and clients but also boosts your overall productivity. Let's delve into some fundamental Excel concepts that will provide a solid foundation as you progress to more complex functions and features.

Essentially of Excel is the workbook, which serves as your project file where all your data is stored. Each workbook can contain multiple worksheets—imagine these as individual pages in a book. This structure allows you to organize different datasets or aspects of a project distinctly. Take this example, one worksheet might focus on property listings while another could be dedicated to financial projections. The ability to switch seamlessly between these sheets facilitates comprehensive analysis without cluttering a single page.

Within these worksheets are cells, the building blocks of your data. Each cell is identified by a unique reference made up of letters and numbers; for example, the cell located in column B and row 3 is known as B3. These cells can hold various types of data, including numbers, text, and formulas. Mastering how to navigate cell references is crucial when applying functions across datasets, particularly when analyzing dynamic property values or sales figures.

Formulas are expressions that perform calculations based on the data within your cells. They always start with an equals sign (=), followed by the operation or function you wish to execute. Take this example, if you want to calculate total sales from cell B2 to B10, you would write: =SUM(B2:B10). Understanding how to create and manipulate formulas is vital for generating meaningful insights from raw data—a skill that is indispensable for any real estate professional.

In addition to formulas, functions are predefined operations designed to simplify complex calculations. While a formula can add specific cells together, functions like AVERAGE or COUNT allow you to conduct broader analyses without manually entering each cell reference. Using functions effectively not only saves time but also reduces errors in your calculations, making them invaluable when working on property investment analyses or client reports.

Ranges refer to a selection of two or more cells, and they come into play when applying functions across multiple properties listed on your worksheet. For example, using the notation B2:B10 signifies all cells from B2 through B10 at once. This feature is crucial for generating comprehensive reports that require data from several entries without the hassle of selecting each one individually.

The type of data you enter into Excel plays a significant role in how it interprets that information. Common data types include text (strings), numbers (both integers and decimals), dates, and boolean values (TRUE or FALSE). Each data type behaves differently within Excel's functionalities; for instance, dates can be formatted for reporting timelines, while boolean values assist in logical tests throughout your datasets.

Formatting is another important concept that involves adjusting how cells appear to improve readability and presentation. You can format numbers as currency for clarity—an essential practice when discussing commission structures or rental prices with clients. Additionally, conditional formatting allows you to apply visual cues based on cell values; highlighting properties below a certain price point can facilitate quick decisions during negotiations.

Excel's interface comprises various components that help you interact with these terms effectively. Take this example, the Ribbon organizes commands into tabs like Home and Data, which streamlines navigation through the software when paired with your understanding of basic terminology.

Lastly, becoming familiar with keyboard shortcuts can significantly enhance your efficiency while working with Excel's extensive features. Simple keystrokes can quickly execute commands such as saving files (Ctrl + S) or copying selected cells (Ctrl + C), making repetitive tasks during data entry or report creation much more manageable.

Equipping yourself with this foundational terminology not only enables you to operate Excel confidently but also serves as a springboard into more advanced functionalities essential for tackling complex real estate analyses and reporting tasks. Each term interacts dynamically within Excel's environment, creating an interconnected system that reveals insights critical for making strategic decisions in your career.

As you master these concepts, remember that they are not just vocabulary but essential tools—key components in building a powerful arsenal for effectively managing real estate data.

Entering and Editing Data

To begin with data entry, consistency is key. When populating your spreadsheet with property listings or client information, make sure that each entry adheres to the same format. For example, when entering property prices, use numerical values without currency symbols or commas. This approach facilitates seamless calculations later on. You can always format the entire column as currency after inputting all the data, ensuring uniformity while allowing for precise financial reporting.

To streamline your data entry process, take advantage of Excel's AutoFill feature. If you have a list of consecutive dates for open house events starting from January 1st, simply input the first date in a cell and drag the fill handle (the small square at the bottom-right corner of the cell) down through the subsequent cells to auto-populate them. This method saves time and reduces errors compared to manual entry.

Editing data is just as crucial as entering it. If you spot an error in a property listing—such as a typo in an address or an incorrect price—you can quickly double-click the cell to enter edit mode. Alternatively, selecting a cell and pressing F2 allows for swift corrections without the need for double-clicking.

Excel's "Undo" function (Ctrl + Z) is invaluable when you make an unintended change. This feature can be a lifesaver during critical tasks like preparing client presentations, where every detail counts. Familiarizing yourself with other editing shortcuts can further enhance your workflow; for instance, Ctrl + D duplicates content from the cell above into the selected cell.

As your datasets expand, maintaining organization becomes increasingly important. Utilizing features like sorting and filtering enables you to effectively manage large volumes of information. Take this example, if you want to view properties listed above a specific price point or filter by location, simply click on the drop-down arrow in your header row after applying filters. This action provides quick access to relevant data without having to scroll through numerous entries.

Data validation is another essential aspect of ensuring accuracy from the outset. By setting up validation rules—such as restricting entries in a price column to numerical values —you can prevent erroneous data inputs that could skew analyses or reports later on. To implement this feature, select your desired range, navigate to Data > Data Validation, and choose the criteria you wish to enforce.

Beyond basic entries and edits, consider integrating comments and notes into your spreadsheet for added clarity and context. Right-clicking on a cell allows you to insert comments—perfect for adding explanations about specific properties or reminders about particular listings or clients.

Excel's Find and Replace function (Ctrl + F) simplifies updating repeated data throughout your sheets. For example, if you decide to update all references from "Downtown" to "Central District," this tool enables you to make those changes effortlessly, ensuring consistency across your document.

Additionally, knowing how to manage duplicates can significantly enhance data integrity within your spreadsheets. If you're working with client lists where some names may have been entered multiple times, using conditional formatting can help highlight these duplicates visually. You can set up rules by selecting your range and navigating to Home > Conditional Formatting > Highlight Cells Rules > Duplicate Values.

The interplay between entering and editing techniques lays a strong foundation for effective data management—a critical skill set for any real estate professional aiming for success in today's competitive market landscape. Each aspect of entering and refining data creates pathways for deeper analyses that transform mere numbers into actionable insights about properties or client interactions.

Saving and Sharing Workbooks

Saving and sharing workbooks in Excel is an essential step that not only protects your hard work but also enhances collaboration within your real estate team. As you gather data on properties, clients, and market trends, mastering the art of saving and sharing your insights can significantly boost your productivity and ensure effective communication.

To begin with, it's important to understand the various formats available for saving your workbooks. The default format, .xlsx, supports all Excel features, making it ideal for general use. However, when you need to export data for other applications or platforms, saving a copy as a .csv file can be particularly useful. This format is great for importing property listings into customer relationship management (CRM) systems or databases. To save in a different format, click on "File," select "Save As," and choose your desired format from the dropdown menu.

Creating backups is another critical practice when managing important documents. Regularly saving versions of your workbook can help prevent data loss due to unexpected crashes or errors. One effective way to do this is by using the "AutoRecover" feature found under "File" > "Options" > "Save." Here, you can adjust how frequently Excel saves backups of your files—setting it to a shorter interval, like every 5 minutes, can provide peace of mind during intense working sessions.

For sharing your workbook with colleagues or clients, Excel offers several options tailored to different needs. If collaboration is key, consider using Excel Online or OneDrive. By uploading your workbook to the cloud, you enable real-time co-authoring, allowing multiple users to view and edit the document simultaneously. This functionality is especially beneficial for team projects such as presentations or proposals, as it fosters an interactive work environment where changes are immediately visible.

If you're sharing via email or other platforms and need to protect sensitive information, implementing password protection can restrict access to only those who require it. This guarantees that confidential client data remains secure. To apply password protection, navigate to "File," click on "Info," then select "Protect Workbook." Choose "Encrypt with Password" and set a strong password that you will share only with trusted collaborators.

For scenarios where you want to provide read-only access while preventing any unwanted edits, consider saving your workbook as a PDF before sharing it. This way, recipients can view the information without the risk of altering it inadvertently. To create a PDF version, select "File," choose "Save As," and then select PDF from the file type options.

Enhancing communication when sharing workbooks is also essential. Excel's commenting feature allows you to clarify specific entries or raise questions directly within the context of the data presented. Simply right-click on a cell and select "Insert Comment." Your colleagues can respond within those comments if they have questions or additional insights.

Additionally, keeping track of changes made by collaborators is vital for maintaining data integrity. You can utilize Excel's "Track Changes" feature found under the "Review" tab. This function highlights modifications made by others and gives you the option to accept or reject these changes as necessary.

For extensive datasets that require periodic updates—such as property listings—consider establishing a shared link for direct access instead of sending files back and forth. This approach ensures everyone has access to the most current version without needing multiple copies scattered across different devices.

By mastering these techniques, you'll streamline your workflow while reinforcing teamwork in an industry where collaboration is crucial for success. Each method discussed builds upon fundamental principles of organization and communication that you've learned earlier in this guide regarding effective data entry and editing.

With practice and an understanding of these saving and sharing capabilities in Excel, you'll be better equipped to manage projects efficiently while keeping all relevant parties informed and engaged. This supports an environment where strategic decisions are driven by reliable data insights at every step of the process.

CHAPTER 2:
ESSENTIAL EXCEL
FUNCTIONS FOR
REAL ESTATE

Introduction to Functions and Formulas

F unctions and formulas in Excel are essential for effective data manipulation, particularly for real estate agents who rely heavily on metrics and insights. Although the interface may seem daunting at first, mastering these tools can transform raw data into actionable intelligence. Functions are predefined calculations that simplify complex tasks, while formulas enable you to create custom calculations tailored to your specific needs.

Let's explore some vital functions that are particularly beneficial in the real estate sector. The SUM function is a powerful yet straightforward tool that allows you to quickly calculate total sales figures or aggregate property values. For example, if you have sales prices listed in cells A1 to A10, entering =SUM(A1:A10) in another cell will instantly yield the total amount. This feature not only saves time but also minimizes the risk of manual errors when adding figures.

Moving beyond basic addition, the AVERAGE function is crucial for assessing performance metrics, such as average property prices or average days on the market. By inputting =AVERAGE(B1:B10), where B1 through B10 represent your sale prices, you gain valuable insights into pricing strategies and market conditions over time. Understanding these averages helps you make informed decisions about pricing properties competitively.

To further enhance your analytical capabilities, consider using the COUNT and COUNTA functions. COUNT tallies only numeric entries, making it ideal for quantifying sold properties or leads, while COUNTA includes all non-empty cells. Take this example, if you want to know how many properties you've sold within a specific timeframe, using =COUNT(C1:C20) will quickly provide that figure—an essential metric for tracking success and setting future goals.

One advanced function that can significantly influence decision-making is the IF statement. This logical function allows you to establish conditions based on specific criteria. Take this example, if you want to categorize properties by price range—labeling them as "affordable" or "luxury"—you could use =IF(D2<300000,"Affordable","Luxury"). This formula evaluates whether the value in D2 is less than 300,000; if true, it designates it as "Affordable," and otherwise as "Luxury." It's a practical way to analyze listings without extensive manual sorting.

When dealing with dates—a crucial component of real estate transactions—functions like TODAY and NOW provide real-time context. By using =TODAY(), you can automatically display today's date, which is helpful for tracking deadlines related to offers or listings. Alternatively, NOW displays both date and time, aiding in monitoring when data was last updated.

Text manipulation also contributes to creating user-friendly spreadsheets. The CONCATENATE function—or its newer alternative CONCAT—merges text from multiple cells into a single cohesive entry. Take this example, if column F contains clients' first names and column G contains their last names, using =CONCATENATE(F2," ",G2) seamlessly generates full names without extra effort.

Finally, accurate rounding of numbers is vital in financial documents or reports where precision is essential. The ROUND function ensures your figures reflect appropriate values without unnecessary decimal places—an important detail when presenting to clients or stakeholders. For example, =ROUND(H2,2) rounds the number in H2 to two decimal places.

By familiarizing yourself with these core functions and formulas in Excel, you're not just acquiring software skills; you're establishing a framework for effective data-driven decision-making in your real estate practice. Each function serves a purpose that aligns with overarching goals: improving efficiency, enhancing accuracy, and empowering informed choices based on solid numerical evidence.

As you integrate these foundational skills into your daily operations, remember that practice is key. Experiment with different combinations of functions and observe how they transform your dataset insights—this exploration will deepen your understanding and proficiency as a user of Excel in real estate scenarios.

Basic Arithmetic Operations

Mastering basic arithmetic operations in Excel is essential for real estate agents aiming to streamline their workflow and enhance their analytical skills. While functions like SUM, AVERAGE, and COUNT may seem straightforward, they serve as the foundation for effective data analysis. These operations enable agents to perform crucial calculations quickly, transforming raw numbers into valuable metrics that inform strategic decisions.

Take this example, imagine you need to assess total sales revenue from properties sold over the past quarter. By utilizing the SUM function, you can effortlessly aggregate these figures. If your sales data is recorded in cells A1 to A10, entering =SUM(A1:A10) in another cell will instantly provide the total revenue. This not only saves time but also minimizes the risk of human error associated with manual calculations.

In addition to summing values, calculating averages can yield deeper insights into market trends. For example, if you're evaluating the average price of properties sold, the AVERAGE function becomes indispensable. You might use =AVERAGE(B1:B10), where B1 through B10 represent your sales prices. Understanding these averages aids in establishing competitive pricing strategies and offers insights into market performance over time.

Efficient tracking of numeric data can be accomplished using the COUNT and COUNTA functions. The COUNT function specifically counts numeric entries, making it ideal for quantifying sold properties or leads generated. Conversely, COUNTA counts all non-empty cells, which is important for tracking various types of entries. For example, if you want to determine how many properties you've listed within a specific timeframe, using =COUNT(C1:C20) quickly provides that information.

An advanced application of these functions is found in the IF statement, which allows for conditional evaluations. Suppose you want to categorize your property listings based on price thresholds—labeling them as "affordable" or "luxury." This can be done with a formula like =IF(D2<300000,"Affordable","Luxury"). Here, Excel checks whether the value in D2 is less than 300,000; if so, it designates it as "Affordable"; otherwise, it classifies it as "Luxury." Such categorization simplifies inventory analysis without the need for tedious manual sorting.

As you work with larger datasets, VLOOKUP becomes invaluable for efficiently extracting specific information. Take this example, if you have a database of client preferences and want to quickly access details about specific listings, using =VLOOKUP(E2,A1:B100,2,FALSE) allows Excel to search for the value in E2 within the first column of range A1:B100 and retrieve corresponding information from the second column. This not only accelerates data retrieval but also enhances your ability to respond promptly to client inquiries.

Managing dates is another critical aspect of real estate transactions. The TODAY and NOW functions are useful for automatically displaying current dates—important for tracking deadlines related to offers or listings. For example, inputting =TODAY() will always show today's date, while NOW includes both date and time, which can be beneficial when monitoring updates.

Text manipulation also plays a vital role in creating clearer spreadsheets. The CONCATENATE function (or its updated version CONCAT) allows you to merge text from multiple cells seamlessly. Take this example, if columns F and G contain clients' first and last names respectively, using =CONCATENATE(F2," ",G2) generates a full name effortlessly. This functionality helps maintain professionalism in communications with clients.

Lastly, ensuring financial accuracy is crucial when preparing reports and documents. The ROUND function is essential here; it adjusts figures to reflect appropriate values without excessive decimal places—a detail that significantly matters during client presentations or financial analyses. For example, applying =ROUND(H2,2) rounds the value in H2 to two decimal places.

By familiarizing yourself with these basic arithmetic operations in Excel, you are establishing a strong foundation for more advanced analytical techniques tailored to your needs as a real estate professional. Each operation provides unique insights that can greatly enhance your efficiency and accuracy in managing data-driven decisions.

As you integrate these skills into your daily tasks, remember that practice will be your best ally. Experiment with various functions and observe their effects on your datasets; this hands-on experience will deepen your understanding and confidence in using Excel effectively within your real estate practice.

Using the SUM Function

The SUM function is a fundamental tool for effective data management in Excel, particularly for real estate agents who depend on numerical data to inform their decisions. This powerful function streamlines the process of adding multiple values, enabling agents to quickly calculate totals essential for analyzing property sales, revenue forecasts, and market trends.

To illustrate its utility, imagine you need to determine the total commission earned from property sales over a specific period. If your commission figures are listed in cells C2 through C15, simply enter =SUM(C2:C15) in another cell. The result will immediately show the total commission earned —an important figure that aids in financial planning and strategy. This straightforward method not only saves time but also minimizes the risk of errors that can occur with manual calculations.

The versatility of the SUM function extends beyond basic totals; it can be customized to meet specific criteria by integrating it with other functions. Take this example, if you want to sum only the commissions from properties sold above a certain price point, you can combine the SUM and IF functions in an array formula. Assuming your sales prices are in column A and commissions are in column B, you could write =SUM(IF(A2:A15>500000,B2:B15,0)). This formula calculates the total commissions for sales over (500,000, allowing for targeted financial assessments that highlight your performance in higher-value markets.

Understanding trends is crucial when analyzing property listings. The SUM function can help track cumulative sales across different categories—whether by month or property type. By organizing your data into structured tables and using the SUM function alongside filters or pivot tables, you can gain valuable insights into which property types are performing best during specific timeframes. This knowledge not only enhances your market intelligence but also empowers you to tailor your marketing strategies effectively.

Additionally, leveraging dynamic ranges with the SUM function further increases its utility. If you're frequently updating your sales data and want totals to adjust automatically without changing cell references manually each time new data is added, consider using named ranges or Excel tables. When you define a table by selecting your data range and using Insert > Table, Excel will automatically update formulas like =SUM(Table1[Commission]) as new rows are added.

The SUM function also proves invaluable for budgeting purposes. As a real estate agent managing various expenses— such as marketing costs or operational overhead—accurately summarizing these figures is essential for maintaining profitability. You can create an expense tracking sheet where all costs are recorded and then use =SUM(F2:F20) to quickly view total expenditures at any time. This insight supports budgetary discipline and informs future spending decisions.

Incorporating additional functions alongside SUM allows for even more nuanced analysis. For example, the AVERAGE function can complement SUM to assess average values across datasets. If you're analyzing monthly sales figures and wish to determine average monthly income from commissions over six months, you could combine both functions: =SUM(C2:C7)/COUNT(C2:C7). Understanding these averages enables you to set realistic targets and expectations moving forward.

As you become more proficient with these operations in Excel, you'll find that they form the foundation for advanced analytics techniques tailored specifically for real estate applications. The key is practice; regularly applying these functions will boost your confidence and efficiency when working with data.

In the end, mastering the SUM function is just one step on your journey toward becoming adept in Excel for real estate analysis. With each calculation performed using this tool, you're not merely crunching numbers; you're unlocking insights that drive informed decisions and contribute to your success as a real estate professional.

Utilizing AVERAGE for Property Analysis

Understanding property values and trends is essential for success in real estate. One of the most effective tools for this analysis is the AVERAGE function in Excel. This function enables you to quickly assess market data, evaluate property performance, and make informed decisions based on quantitative insights.

To leverage the AVERAGE function effectively, start by gathering relevant data about properties of interest, such as sale prices, rental rates, or even the average time properties remain on the market in a specific area. Take this example, if you're evaluating rental properties in a neighborhood, collect recent rental prices from listings or past transactions.

Once your dataset is organized in Excel, applying the AVERAGE function is straightforward. If your rental prices are listed from cell A2 to A10, you can calculate the average rent by entering =AVERAGE(A2:A10) into another cell. This formula will yield a single value representing the mean rent price for that range, providing immediate clarity on what tenants might expect to pay.

However, it's important to delve deeper into what these numbers indicate about your market. If you find that the average rent has significantly increased compared to previous years or neighboring areas, this could suggest rising demand or an improving neighborhood status—critical insights for shaping your pricing and marketing strategies.

Analyzing averages also proves beneficial when comparing different property types. For example, if you're assessing single-family homes versus multi-family units, calculating and comparing their average sale prices can reveal which option may yield better returns on investment in your area. If single-family homes are priced between)300,000 and (450,000 while multi-family units range from)200,000 to (350,000, computing their averages with =AVERAGE(B2:B10) for homes and =AVERAGE(C2:C10) for multi-family units will provide a clearer financial perspective to guide your investment strategy.

Another valuable application of the AVERAGE function is tracking performance over time. By maintaining a historical record of property sales or rental rates across months or years, you can identify trends that inform future projections. For example, if you have monthly sales prices recorded from January through December in column D (D2:D13), calculating an annual average using =AVERAGE(D2:D13) will reveal seasonal fluctuations and help predict sales strategies for upcoming months.

And, combining averages with other statistical measures enhances your analysis further. Pairing the AVERAGE with standard deviation calculations allows you to understand not only typical values but also variability around those values

—offering a more comprehensive view of market conditions. To calculate the standard deviation of your rental prices, use =STDEV.P(A2:A10), which highlights how much individual rents deviate from the average; significant variations may indicate niche markets within the broader area.

Beyond numerical analysis, visualizing this data through charts can transform raw figures into compelling narratives that engage clients during presentations. Creating line graphs to show average rents over time or bar charts comparing averages across property types enhances numerical data and reinforces your credibility as an informed expert.

Given that real estate is heavily influenced by local economic factors and trends, consistently utilizing Excel's AVERAGE function enables agents not only to keep pace with market changes but also to anticipate them proactively. This tool provides invaluable insights that become part of your arsenal when advising clients or making strategic decisions regarding buying or selling properties.

Effectively harnessing this tool transforms raw data into actionable intelligence—crucial for maintaining a competitive edge in today's fast-paced real estate environment. Whether you're accurately pricing listings or advising buyers about investment potential based on historical averages versus current asking prices, mastering this simple yet powerful function significantly sharpens your analytical capabilities as you navigate complex market landscapes.

COUNT and COUNTA for Data Sets

The COUNT and COUNTA functions in Excel are invaluable tools for real estate agents, helping to manage and analyze data effectively. Mastering these functions can streamline your workflow, enhance data accuracy, and yield critical insights into property listings and client interactions.

The COUNT function is specifically designed to tally the number of cells containing numerical values within a given range. For example, if you're tracking properties sold in a month and have sale prices listed in column B from cells B2 to B20, you would use the formula =COUNT(B2:B20) to determine how many of those properties resulted in sales. This formula will return the total number of sales recorded during that period.

In contrast, COUNTA counts all non-empty cells in a specified range, regardless of whether they contain numbers or text. This feature is particularly useful for tracking total listings or inquiries received. Take this example, if client inquiries are logged in column C from C2 to C30, applying =COUNTA(C2:C30) would provide the total number of inquiries, encompassing both successful contacts and unresponsive leads. Understanding the distinction between COUNT and COUNTA is essential, as it allows you to differentiate between quantitative sales data and qualitative aspects like client engagement.

Integrating these functions into your data management process significantly enhances your reporting capabilities. Consider preparing a monthly sales report for stakeholders or clients; by utilizing COUNT alongside other functions like SUM or AVERAGE, you can generate comprehensive insights. For example, calculating the average sale price while also showing the number of properties sold offers valuable context regarding your performance metrics—information that potential clients find beneficial.

For practical application, if you want to analyze your performance over several months, you can maintain a record of sales data across different sheets for each month and then consolidate this information in a summary sheet using the COUNT and COUNTA functions. This approach allows you to create a summary table that showcases the number of properties sold each month alongside the total inquiries received, presenting an easily digestible format that highlights trends over time.

Another effective strategy is to combine these counting functions with conditional formatting to visually emphasize key figures. By setting up rules that change cell colors based on sales numbers, you can quickly draw attention to months where performance exceeded expectations or fell short. This not only enhances clarity in your reports but also helps you stay attuned to emerging patterns.

Tracking various categories using COUNTIF or COUNTA can further refine your insights. If you categorize properties by type—such as residential, commercial, or industrial—applying =COUNTIF(A2:A50,"Residential") allows you to determine how many residential properties have been listed or sold over time. This capability enables you to develop targeted marketing strategies based on inventory levels and demand for specific property types.

Data integrity is another area where these counting functions excel. Regularly applying COUNT and COUNTA helps ensure that your databases remain clean and organized. If unexpected counts arise—for instance, significantly fewer sales than anticipated—this may indicate underlying issues that require immediate attention, such as missing entries or input errors.

These fundamental yet powerful tools empower real estate professionals not only to manage their data more efficiently but also to derive actionable insights that can inform strategic decision-making. By integrating COUNT and COUNTA into your routine practices—whether analyzing past performance or forecasting future trends—you significantly enhance your analytical capabilities.

In the end, mastering these functions lays a solid foundation for more advanced data analysis techniques. As real estate markets become increasingly competitive and data-driven decisions gain prominence, your ability to leverage Excel's COUNT and COUNTA effectively will not only boost your personal productivity but also contribute to the overall success of your real estate practice. Whether evaluating monthly performance metrics or ensuring data integrity across multiple listings, these functions are indispensable components of your Excel toolkit.

Using IF Statements for Decision Making

In the fast-paced world of real estate, making informed decisions is crucial to standing out from the competition. One effective way to enhance your decision-making process is by utilizing IF statements in Excel. These logical functions evaluate conditions and return specific values based on whether those conditions are met, providing a powerful tool for data analysis and strategic planning.

Consider a scenario where you need to evaluate properties based on their listing prices in relation to your client's budget. By employing an IF statement, you can streamline this analysis significantly. For example, if your client has a budget of)300,000 and you want to determine if the property listed in cell A2 falls within this limit, you could use the formula =IF(A2 <= 300000, "Within Budget", "Above Budget"). This formula instantly categorizes properties as either "Within Budget" or "Above Budget," allowing you to focus on viable options without manually reviewing each entry.

The versatility of IF statements extends beyond simple comparisons; they can be nested to accommodate multiple criteria. Take this example, if your client is looking for properties that not only fit their budget but also have at least three bedrooms, you can create a more complex formula: =IF(A2 <= 300000, IF(B2 >= 3, "Suitable", "Too Few Bedrooms"), "Above Budget"). In this case, the formula first checks if the price is within budget and then verifies the bedroom count. This layered approach gives you a clearer picture of which properties meet all of your client's specifications.

IF statements are also valuable in tracking commission calculations based on performance metrics. For example, if your agency offers a higher commission rate for sales exceeding (500,000, you can structure your formula like this: =IF(C2 > 500000, C2 * 0.05, C2 * 0.03), where C2 represents the sale price. This straightforward method automates commission calculations and ensures accurate predictions of earnings.

You might also consider combining IF statements with data validation techniques. Take this example, when collecting lead information through a form that requires agents to specify whether the property type is residential or commercial, an IF statement can prompt additional questions based on initial responses. This use of conditional logic creates an interactive experience that enhances lead gathering and supports precise follow-up inquiries.

The effectiveness of IF statements increases even further when paired with other Excel functions like VLOOKUP or SUMIF for more complex analyses. For example, if you want to assess total sales revenue while factoring in commissions that vary by property type, combining these functions allows for seamless integration of conditions into broader financial summaries.

In real estate transactions, data accuracy is paramount. Regularly applying IF statements helps maintain clarity and enables quick identification of anomalies—such as unusually high costs or missing data entries—prompting immediate corrective actions before they escalate into larger issues.

The true potential of using IF statements becomes apparent when automating reports for clients and stakeholders. Setting up dashboards with these logical functions reveals critical insights at a glance—whether presenting performance overviews or forecasting future sales based on historical trends influenced by various decision-making factors.

As you become proficient in crafting these logical formulas, consider documenting best practices or creating templates to standardize analyses across your team. This promotes consistency and fosters collaboration by making complex calculations accessible to all members involved.

By leveraging IF statements effectively, you transform raw data into actionable insights—streamlining processes while enhancing your analytical capabilities as an agent. As decision-making evolves alongside data-driven trends in real estate, mastering these functions will empower you to navigate complexities with confidence and precision.

In the end, harnessing the power of IF statements equips real estate professionals with essential tools for strategic analysis and sound decision-making—turning data from mere numbers into critical elements that guide successful outcomes in every transaction scenario encountered in this dynamic field.

VLOOKUP for Property Listings

In the world of real estate, quick access to relevant property information can significantly influence the success of closing a deal. One of the most effective tools at your disposal is VLOOKUP. This powerful function enables you to search for a specific value in one column and retrieve corresponding data from another, thereby streamlining your workflow and enhancing your ability to provide valuable insights to clients.

Consider a scenario where you have an Excel sheet listing properties with details such as addresses, prices, square footage, and the number of bedrooms. When a client inquires about a property based on its address, instead of manually sifting through rows of data, you can leverage VLOOKUP to swiftly locate and display that information. For example, if your property addresses are in column A and you want to retrieve the price from column B based on the address found in cell D1, you would use the formula: =VLOOKUP(D1, A:B, 2, FALSE). This formula searches for the address specified in D1 within column A and returns the corresponding price from column B.

The value of VLOOKUP increases significantly when managing multiple listings or assessing various properties for investment potential. If you're evaluating several properties based on their square footage and need to identify those that meet a specific threshold, you can employ VLOOKUP in conjunction with other functions like IF or conditional formatting to visually flag those that fall below your criteria. Take this example: =IF(VLOOKUP(D1, A:C, 3, FALSE) < 1500, "Below Average", "Meets Criteria"). This approach not only retrieves data but also facilitates active analysis.

In practice, VLOOKUP is particularly useful for cross-referencing different datasets—such as comparing current listings against historical sales data. If you maintain another table with past sale prices and wish to evaluate how current listings compare to previous values, VLOOKUP allows you to seamlessly integrate that information into a single view. For comparative analysis, where one table contains current listings and another displays past sales, using =VLOOKUP(A2, HistoricalSales!A:B, 2, FALSE) helps you pull historical prices next to your current listing price.

It's important to recognize some limitations of VLOOKUP. The function only searches for values in the leftmost column of your specified range and retrieves data from columns to its right. If your data structure doesn't align with this requirement—such as needing information from columns on the left—you may need to reconsider how you organize your spreadsheets or explore alternatives like INDEX-MATCH for more complex situations.

Maintaining accurate data is also crucial when using VLOOKUP effectively. Regular updates to property databases ensure that clients receive reliable information throughout their search process. Implementing data validation techniques can help maintain consistency across entries, preventing users from inadvertently inputting incorrect property details.

Combining VLOOKUP with named ranges can enhance clarity in complex spreadsheets. For example, if you've defined a named range "PropertyData" encompassing columns A through C on your worksheet where all properties are listed, you could use =VLOOKUP(D1, PropertyData, 2, FALSE). This not only improves readability but also simplifies formula management as it automatically adjusts when rows are added or removed.

One compelling application of VLOOKUP is generating reports directly from listings without extensive manual effort—an invaluable time-saver when preparing presentations for clients or stakeholders. By setting up dashboards that pull key metrics using VLOOKUP alongside charts summarizing these findings, you can transform raw numbers into digestible insights.

Additionally, leveraging Excel's conditional formatting capabilities together with VLOOKUP results allows you to instantly highlight key figures based on thresholds relevant for quick decision-making during showings or client meetings.

In the end, VLOOKUP serves as a foundational tool for efficient property management and analysis processes within Excel for real estate agents. Its versatility simplifies tasks and enhances client engagement by delivering timely insights tailored specifically to their needs—an essential aspect of exceptional customer service in today's competitive market.

As you become more adept at integrating this function into your daily practices and exploring its numerous applications across various scenarios in real estate operations—whether assessing potential investments or tracking market trends—you'll discover just how pivotal mastering it can be in achieving greater efficiency and accuracy in your role as an agent.

Using TODAY and NOW for Dates

Mastering date management in Excel can significantly enhance your efficiency, particularly in the fast-paced world of real estate. Two key functions that can streamline this process are TODAY and NOW. Each serves a distinct purpose, enabling you to automate date entries without manual input.

The TODAY function is simple yet powerful; it returns the current date each time your worksheet recalculates. For example, to display today's date in cell A1, you would enter =TODAY(). This function is especially helpful for tracking deadlines or indicating when a property was listed. If you're managing multiple listings and need to highlight those on the market for over 30 days, calculating the difference between TODAY and the listing date lets you quickly identify properties that may need price adjustments or increased marketing efforts.

To fully utilize this capability, you could set up a formula in another cell to calculate how long each property has been listed. Assuming your listing dates are in column B starting from B2, you would enter =TODAY()-B2 in column C. This calculation gives you the number of days since each property was listed. You can further enhance this by applying conditional formatting—color-coding properties based on how long they've been on the market: red for listings over 30 days, yellow for those between 15 and 30 days, and green for fresh listings under 15 days.

Conversely, the NOW function offers a similar but more specific capability by returning both the current date and time. This is particularly valuable when precise timing is crucial— such as recording when a client makes an inquiry or when an offer is submitted. To use it effectively, simply enter =NOW() into a cell. If you're preparing reports that require timestamps —like logging when offers are received—NOW provides an accurate record of these moments.

A compelling scenario emerges when you combine these two functions with data validation techniques. Take this example, if you want to ensure that all entry forms have valid dates before submission, you could create a validation rule that checks whether a date falls within acceptable parameters relative to TODAY or NOW—such as preventing future dates from being recorded for property availability or offer submissions.

Both functions are also instrumental in analyzing trends over time. If you're assessing how property prices change month-to-month, using TODAY with EOMONTH allows you to find the last day of the current month by entering =EOMONTH(TODAY(),0). This gives you a dynamic reference point that remains up-to-date.

Consider creating charts that visualize data trends over specific periods by utilizing dynamic ranges with these date functions. For example, if you'd like to display sales data from this year up to today, combining TODAY with other formulas will help filter your dataset accordingly.

You might also explore using arrays with these date functions for more complex analyses—such as calculating average days on market across various listings through an array formula that incorporates both TODAY and your listing dates dynamically.

One successful real estate agent I know attributes her streamlined weekly reports to her adept use of these date functions; automating date updates allows her more time to focus on strategic planning rather than manual calculations.

In the end, mastering TODAY and NOW equips real estate professionals with invaluable tools for efficient data management and insightful analysis. Whether keeping track of listing durations or capturing timely interactions with clients, these functions simplify tasks while ensuring accuracy —a vital element in maintaining competitiveness within the industry. As you integrate these techniques into your workflow, you'll likely notice enhancements not only in efficiency but also in clarity within your operations—an essential advantage for navigating the complexities of real estate transactions successfully.

CONCATENATE for Text Data

Using the CONCATENATE function in Excel can significantly improve how you manage and present text data, particularly in the fast-paced world of real estate. This function enables you to merge multiple pieces of text from different cells into one cohesive entry, which is essential for crafting complete property descriptions or compiling client information.

Consider a situation where property details are scattered across several columns: the address might be in column A, the city in column B, and the state in column C. To create a complete address in one cell, you would enter the formula =CONCATENATE(A2, ", ", B2, ", ", C2) into a new cell. This straightforward formula combines the three components with commas and spaces for clarity, resulting in something like "123 Main St, Springfield, IL." This polished output is not only informative but also easy to read.

You can take this a step further by incorporating additional text or formatting. If your agency wants to create engaging promotional descriptions based on features listed in separate cells—such as "3 bedrooms," "2 bathrooms," and "swimming pool"—you could use CONCATENATE like this: =CONCATENATE("Featuring: ", D2, ", ", E2, ", and ", F2). This generates an enticing phrase that captures attention.

It's important to note that Excel 2016 and later versions offer a more flexible alternative: the ampersand operator (&). This method provides simpler syntax and improved readability. For example, instead of using CONCATENATE, you might write =A2 & ", " & B2 & ", " & C2 to achieve the same result more intuitively.

In practical applications within real estate operations, imagine preparing a client list where each entry includes personalized greetings or reminders for follow-ups. By combining first names from one column with a default message stored elsewhere—like ="Hello " & G2 & ", don't forget our meeting next week!"—you can quickly generate tailored messages without manually adjusting each entry.

To deepen your understanding of CONCATENATE's capabilities, consider scenarios involving numbers or dates alongside text. Take this example, if you're including property prices or listing dates in your descriptions—such as "Listed at)250,000 on March 5th"—your formula might look like this: =CONCATENATE("Listed at \(", TEXT(H2,"#,##0"), " on ", TEXT(I2,"mmmm d")). Here, the TEXT function formats numbers and dates appropriately to integrate seamlessly into your output.

While CONCATENATE is effective for basic tasks of merging text strings, it has limitations when dealing with longer strings or complex operations involving multiple items. In such cases, where data sets expand and efficiency is paramount, Excel's newer TEXTJOIN function (available from Office 365) becomes invaluable. For example: =TEXTJOIN(", ", TRUE, A1:A10) automatically merges all entries from A1 to A10 while skipping any empty cells—a useful feature when managing extensive lists.

As you integrate these techniques into your daily routines, you'll discover enhanced efficiency not just in creating cohesive outputs but also in managing larger datasets with greater ease. Well-structured presentations of text data can lead to better client relationships and more streamlined processes throughout various stages of real estate transactions.

By effectively applying these methods—whether crafting comprehensive property descriptions or customizing client communications—you position yourself as a professional who knows how to leverage data for impactful interactions within the market. Embracing these tools transforms routine data management tasks into opportunities for creative expression and strategic marketing—key elements in building lasting relationships in real estate.

Using ROUND for Financial Precision

Using the ROUND function in Excel is vital for maintaining financial precision, particularly in the real estate sector. Given that transactions frequently involve substantial sums of money, presenting figures accurately is crucial for building client trust and facilitating informed decision-making. The ROUND function allows you to control the number of decimal places shown in your financial reports, enhancing their clarity and professionalism.

Consider a scenario where you've calculated a property's selling price based on various expenses and commissions. If your formula generates a result like)250,000.568, it might raise concerns rather than inspire confidence. By utilizing the ROUND function, you can present this figure in a more digestible format. Take this example, if your total price calculation is in cell A1, you can use the formula =ROUND(A1, 0) to round it to (250,001—a figure that feels precise and approachable.

Let's delve deeper into how the ROUND function interacts with different types of numbers. In real estate, you often encounter rental rates or commission fees where even cents can make a difference. For example, if the monthly rent is)1,245.678 and you wish to present this amount rounded to the nearest cent, you would use =ROUND(A2, 2), resulting in (1,245.68. This level of detail not only respects your clients' perspectives but also aligns with industry standards.

Beyond enhancing clarity, the ROUND function is also crucial in budgeting scenarios. Suppose you're preparing a budget sheet for an upcoming property project, where estimates may vary among contractors or suppliers. By applying ROUND, you ensure that your total projected costs are consistent when communicating with stakeholders. Take this example, if you're summing various cost estimates across cells B2 through B10, you could use =ROUND(SUM(B2:B10), 0), yielding a single rounded total that's easy to reference.

When presenting financial forecasts or investment analyses, clarity is essential. You can enhance data representation by using ROUND alongside other functions. For example, if you're calculating projected returns on investment (ROI) over time with varying cash flows listed in column C, applying =ROUND(C2/C3 * 100, 2) will provide the ROI percentage rounded to two decimal places—offering potential investors a clear and professional snapshot.

In more complex situations involving multiple financial calculations—such as amortization schedules—combining ROUND with other Excel functions like PMT or FV can be advantageous. For example, if you're calculating monthly payments on a mortgage loan found in cell D1 at an interest rate in E1 over a specified period in F1 months, your formula might look like this: =ROUND(PMT(E1/12,F1,D1), 2). This not only ensures clarity but also guarantees that outputs are ready for use without further adjustments.

Navigating real estate transactions often involves negotiations around pricing or financing options; thus, providing rounded figures fosters an environment of transparency and professionalism. Clients appreciate straightforwardness, and presenting well-rounded numbers can eliminate confusion while building trust.

It's also important to recognize when to apply rounding versus maintaining raw data for effective reporting practices. In internal analyses where precision is prioritized over presentation—such as tracking costs—you might opt to display raw data while summarizing findings with rounded values for client-facing documents.

Mastering the ROUND function in Excel not only boosts your accuracy but also enhances your reputation as a meticulous professional who values detail and clarity in communication. Integrating these techniques into your workflow empowers you to manage financial data confidently and effectively, ultimately strengthening relationships with clients and colleagues alike.

The significance of precise financial reporting cannot be overstated; it enhances your credibility and demonstrates an understanding of nuanced client needs while paving the way for informed decision-making throughout the real estate transaction process.

CHAPTER 3: DATA ORGANIZATION AND MANAGEMENT

Structuring Data for Real Estate

Effectively structuring your data in Excel is crucial for real estate agents aiming to streamline their workflow and enhance their analytical capabilities. Proper organization not only simplifies navigation but also supports more informed decision-making. Let's delve into some practical strategies to optimize your real estate data for maximum impact.

Begin by establishing a clear framework for your datasets. Take this example, when tracking property listings, create a dedicated worksheet with specific columns for essential details such as property type, location, price, square footage, and status. Each property should occupy its own row, ensuring distinct records that promote clarity and facilitate easier sorting and filtering when analyzing subsets of your data.

To illustrate this, imagine you're tracking 50 properties. Your columns might be organized as follows:

- A: Property ID

- B: Address
- C: City
- D: Price
- E: Status (Active/Under Contract/Sold)
- F: Listing Date

With this setup, adding new listings becomes a straightforward task; simply enter each new property in a new row beneath the existing entries. This method prevents duplication and helps maintain the integrity of your records.

Next, enhance your organization by leveraging Excel's table feature. By converting your data range into a table using the shortcut Ctrl + T, you gain access to useful features like filtering and sorting without needing to reapply these settings every time you update your data. This dynamic tool simplifies analysis and allows for seamless management of large datasets.

For example, if you have several properties under contract, applying a filter enables you to quickly isolate those entries without scrolling through all records. This capability to manipulate views on-the-fly is particularly beneficial during client meetings, where quick access to relevant information can help you present compelling insights.

Another vital aspect of structuring your data is standardizing entries wherever possible. Consistency is key to maintaining a clean dataset. Take this example, always use uniform formats for property types (e.g., "Condo," "Single Family," "Townhouse") and ensure prices are consistently entered as currency. This uniformity not only enhances readability but also minimizes errors during calculations or analyses.

Consider incorporating drop-down lists for specific fields using Excel's Data Validation feature. By setting predefined options for entries like status or property type, you reduce the likelihood of variations in spelling or terminology that could complicate future analysis.

When analyzing financial metrics related to these properties —such as commission calculations or return on investment —keep related financial data adjacent to your listings. For example, if each property has an associated commission rate or estimated monthly rental income, placing those figures next to the corresponding property can significantly streamline calculations.

Let's say you're calculating commissions based on sales prices listed in column D and commission rates stored in column G. If G2 contains the commission rate for the first property (e.g., 0.06), you can compute the commission in H2 using the formula =D2*G2. Dragging this formula down will automatically apply it across all listings, saving you time and reducing errors.

In summary, structuring your real estate data effectively not only boosts operational efficiency but also enhances analytical capabilities. With organized information at your fingertips, producing insightful reports or presentations becomes effortless. This level of preparation empowers you to respond swiftly to client inquiries or market changes while ensuring that your business decisions are grounded in reliable information.

Investing time in structuring your Excel datasets will yield significant returns throughout your career as a real estate agent. It lays a strong foundation for everything from daily operations to complex analyses. When organized well, your data transforms from mere numbers into actionable insights that drive success in your real estate endeavors.

Using Tables to Organize Data

Using tables in Excel can significantly enhance the organization and management of real estate data. Properly structured datasets not only improve clarity but also accelerate trend analysis and informed decision-making. Let's delve into how you can utilize Excel's table feature to optimize your real estate operations.

To start, converting your dataset into a table simplifies various aspects of data management. Highlight your data range and use the shortcut Ctrl + T to create a table. This action opens the Create Table dialog box—make sure to check the "My table has headers" option if your data includes headers. Once you've created the table, Excel will format your range, providing a clear visual distinction that enhances readability.

One of the key benefits of tables is their automatic expansion when new data is added. As you list more properties, there's no need to redefine your range; the table adjusts dynamically. For example, if you add another property listing to an existing 50 entries, the table will incorporate it seamlessly.

Additionally, tables come equipped with built-in filtering options right in the header row. Suppose you want to assess properties by their status—active, under contract, or sold. Simply click the drop-down arrow in the header to quickly filter properties based on these statuses. This feature is particularly valuable during client meetings, where quick access to specific information can significantly impact discussions.

Sorting capabilities within tables also surpass those of standard ranges. You can easily sort by any column with just a couple of clicks. If you're interested in identifying properties with the highest prices or determining which listings have been active the longest, you can sort directly from the table header without navigating through multiple menus.

Another notable advantage is that when you apply formulas within a table, Excel uses structured references instead of traditional cell references. Take this example, when calculating total commission on sales prices for various properties listed in your table, you would write a formula like =[@Price]*[@CommissionRate] rather than using standard references like D2*G2. This approach enhances readability and makes it clearer what each part of the formula represents.

If you're maintaining a column for estimated monthly rental income alongside sales prices and commission rates, adding a new calculated column within your table using structured references allows for seamless updates as new data comes in.

And, consider leveraging conditional formatting within tables to visually emphasize important information at a glance. For example, if you want to highlight properties priced above)500,000, conditional formatting can automatically apply color coding based on these criteria. This not only creates an appealing visual layout but also draws attention to high-value listings effortlessly.

As we increasingly rely on technology in real estate management, tracking changes over time becomes essential. Tables make it easy to utilize Excel's built-in version history feature when collaborating on shared documents stored in cloud services like OneDrive or SharePoint. You'll have immediate access to previous versions and edits made by team members whenever needed.

In summary, integrating tables into your Excel workflow fundamentally transforms how you manage and analyze real estate data. They provide structure and organization that lead to improved efficiency and insightful analysis. With features that simplify filtering and sorting, dynamic expansion capabilities, and enhanced formula applications through structured references, tables are indispensable tools for any serious real estate agent seeking success.

By embracing this structured approach today, you're not only setting yourself up for better organization but also for more impactful analyses in the future—ensuring that every decision is backed by well-organized data and strategic foresight.

Sorting and Filtering Property Listings

Sorting and filtering property listings in Excel can turn a vast amount of data into actionable insights, significantly enhancing your decision-making process. By mastering these features, you can quickly identify relevant information—an essential skill in the fast-paced real estate market.

To start sorting your data, click on the header of the column you wish to organize. Take this example, if you're sorting by property price, select that column's header. A small drop-down arrow will appear, revealing sorting options that allow you to arrange the data from lowest to highest or vice versa. This straightforward action can greatly clarify your listings. For example, if you need to present properties within a specific price range to a potential buyer, just a few clicks will give you a neatly organized list ready for discussion.

Filtering complements sorting perfectly by allowing you to narrow down your listings to only those that meet specific criteria. If you want to view only active listings, click the drop-down arrow in the status column header and uncheck all options except "Active." Instantly, your focus shifts to properties that are currently available, streamlining your interactions with clients.

Combining sorting and filtering can yield exceptional results. Imagine filtering your listings to show only single-family homes under (400,000. After applying this filter, you might sort these entries by square footage to identify the most spacious options within that price range. This powerful combination enables you to provide tailored insights to clients with specific requirements.

Excel's Table feature further enhances the functionality of sorting and filtering. When your data is formatted as a table, applying filters becomes more intuitive. Each column header includes an automatic filter drop-down menu that is visually distinct from standard data ranges. As you filter within a table format, Excel retains these settings when new data is added, meaning you won't have to reset filters every time your property list updates.

Consider how this could work in practice: if you receive new property information weekly, you could set up a system where new listings seamlessly integrate into your existing table without disrupting previous sorting and filtering settings. This efficiency saves time spent managing your database while allowing for continuous updates without losing track of essential views.

Beyond organization, filtering helps keep potential buyers engaged by providing focused options based on their preferences. If clients express interest in specific features—like waterfront views or recent renovations—you can quickly filter your listings to highlight those properties.

For more complex needs, Excel's Advanced Filter feature simplifies creating multiple criteria setups. For example, if you're looking for properties priced between)300,000 and (500,000 with at least three bedrooms and two bathrooms, Advanced Filter allows you to define these conditions easily and simultaneously.

Visual appeal also plays an important role; consider implementing conditional formatting alongside your sorted and filtered data. If you've sorted property prices in descending order but want high-value homes highlighted for quicker identification during client meetings, conditional formatting enables those properties to stand out through color coding or bold text.

Being proficient in sorting and filtering not only sharpens your analytical skills but also showcases professionalism when interacting with clients or colleagues. It signals that you're prepared and knowledgeable about your listings—an advantage in negotiations and discussions.

In summary, mastering the art of sorting and filtering property listings in Excel empowers you to manage extensive datasets efficiently while presenting clear information tailored to client needs. The ability to swiftly adjust views based on current market dynamics is crucial for agile decision-making—an essential trait for success in real estate.

As you continue refining these skills within Excel's robust framework, you'll increasingly leverage data not just as numbers on a spreadsheet but as strategic tools driving engagement and informed decisions in real-time scenarios.

Data Validation for Input Accuracy

Data validation is essential for maintaining the accuracy and integrity of your data in Excel. In the real estate sector, where precise information can significantly influence business decisions, implementing effective data validation techniques is crucial. These methods ensure that the data you input accurately reflects reality and adheres to specific criteria.

To begin, select the cells or range you wish to validate. Then, navigate to the "Data" tab on the Excel ribbon and click on "Data Validation." This action opens a dialog box where you can set rules regarding what type of data can be entered. Take this example, if you're tracking property prices, you may want to limit entries to numerical values above zero. In the settings tab, choose "Decimal" from the drop-down menu under "Allow," and specify a minimum value of 0. This precaution prevents accidental entries of negative numbers or erroneous values, which could lead to significant miscalculations in financial analyses.

Consider a scenario where you are managing a list of rental properties with specific criteria for the number of bedrooms. You can establish a validation rule that permits only integers between 1 and 5 in the bedrooms column. With this setup, if someone attempts to enter "three and a half," Excel will prompt an error message, preventing incorrect data from entering your system. This control is vital for maintaining robust datasets that inform client decisions and internal reports.

Another effective application of data validation is through the use of drop-down menus for validating lists. If you often input property types—such as residential, commercial, or industrial —you can create a defined list to ensure consistency. Within the Data Validation dialog box, select "List" under "Allow," and specify the source as a range containing your property types. This allows users to select from pre-defined options when entering property details, significantly reducing errors from misspellings or variations in terminology.

For more complex scenarios, consider using custom formulas for validation. For example, if you're tracking closing dates that must occur after today's date, you can create a formula like =A1>TODAY(). This rule effectively prevents past dates from being entered in the closing date field, ensuring that all records remain valid and relevant.

To further enhance your data validation efforts, you can incorporate conditional formatting to visually reinforce compliance with your established rules. After setting up your validations, apply conditional formatting to highlight cells that violate these rules. Take this example, if an invalid entry appears in a property price column due to a manual error, conditional formatting can change its color to red, drawing immediate attention for quick corrections.

Reflecting on my experience in real estate, I recall working with a client whose spreadsheet was riddled with errors regarding property square footage due to inconsistent manual entries from different team members. This confusion during client presentations not only wasted time but also jeopardized a significant deal. After implementing strict data validation protocols—along with drop-down menus for common metrics —we saw a dramatic improvement in the accuracy of our reports. This simple change enhanced client trust and streamlined our operations.

It's important to thoroughly test your validation rules after setting them up. Create sample entries to observe how Excel responds; this step is critical for ensuring your validations function as intended without introducing unforeseen issues down the line.

By using data validation effectively, you position yourself as a professional who prioritizes accuracy. This not only enhances your credibility but also optimizes workflow efficiency by reducing the time spent correcting errors later on.

To wrap things up, mastering data validation provides you with powerful tools for maintaining accuracy within your datasets. Given that real estate transactions often hinge on precise details and timely responses to market changes, leveraging these techniques fosters trust among clients and ensures decisions are based on reliable information. Embracing these practices will elevate your proficiency with Excel and solidify your role as a knowledgeable resource in the real estate landscape.

Highlighting Duplicates and Gaps

Managing large datasets in Excel presents a significant challenge, particularly when it comes to identifying and addressing duplicates and gaps. In the real estate sector, where precision is crucial, overlooking these discrepancies can result in flawed analyses, incorrect client information, and missed opportunities. Therefore, mastering the techniques for highlighting duplicates and filling gaps is essential for maintaining data integrity.

Let's begin by exploring how to find duplicate entries within your dataset. Suppose you have a list of property addresses or client names that require review. Start by highlighting the relevant range of cells and navigating to the "Home" tab on the Excel ribbon. From there, click on "Conditional Formatting," select "Highlight Cells Rules," and then choose "Duplicate Values." A dialog will appear, allowing you to choose a formatting style—such as a light red fill with dark red text—to make duplicates easily identifiable at a glance. Once applied, any duplicate entries will be highlighted instantly, enabling you to take appropriate action.

Take this example, if you're compiling a list of leads from various sources and discover that several clients appear multiple times due to overlapping data collection methods, highlighting these duplicates can help streamline your outreach efforts. A clear visual representation of repeat entries allows you to consolidate contact information or eliminate redundancies effectively.

Next, let's focus on addressing gaps in your dataset. Missing values can disrupt analyses and mislead decision-making processes. To identify these gaps effectively, use conditional formatting once again. Select your range and choose "New Rule" under Conditional Formatting. Opt for "Use a formula to determine which cells to format," then enter a formula like =ISBLANK(A1), adjusting it for your specific range. This rule highlights any cell without an entry in a distinct color—let's say yellow—to draw attention to missing data points.

Consider tracking listings for properties where certain fields —like square footage or price—are left blank. These details are critical for client presentations or market analysis. Highlighting these gaps ensures that all essential information is captured before finalizing reports or making decisions.

In addition to visual formatting, Excel functions such as COUNTIF for duplicates and COUNTA for tracking non-empty cells can further enhance your data management efforts. For example, placing =COUNTIF(A:A,A1) in an adjacent column will count occurrences of each entry in column A. If this count exceeds one, you've identified a duplicate without relying solely on visual cues.

Once you've identified gaps, it's important to take strategic action based on your specific needs—whether that means entering default values or reaching out for necessary information. Take this example, if certain properties lack descriptions due to incomplete input from team members, establishing standard operating procedures for data entry can ensure consistent updates moving forward.

Reflecting on my own experiences in real estate analytics, I recall a project where we discovered numerous gaps during our quarterly review of rental listings due to inconsistent reporting from various agents across our office. By implementing mandatory fields that required completion before submission—supported by validation rules and regular audits—we significantly reduced missing information in future datasets.

Regularly monitoring your datasets not only enhances their quality but also builds trust with clients who rely on accurate information when making investment or property transaction decisions. Your commitment to maintaining clean data reinforces your professional reputation within the industry.

As we explore more data management techniques throughout this guide, keep in mind that highlighting duplicates and filling gaps are foundational steps toward creating robust datasets that empower informed decision-making in real estate transactions. Mastering these skills positions you as a knowledgeable agent who leverages technology efficiently while ensuring accuracy at every level of operation.

Creating Drop-down Lists

Creating drop-down lists in Excel is a valuable technique that can significantly improve data entry efficiency and accuracy, especially for real estate agents who often manage standardized information like property types, client preferences, and status updates. By using drop-down lists, agents can select from predefined options—such as "Residential," "Commercial," or "Pending"—rather than typing repetitive entries. This not only minimizes input errors but also saves time.

To get started, prepare your list of entries, which can be located on the same sheet or a different one. For example, if you want to create a list of property types, you might set it up on Sheet2 by entering values like "Residential," "Commercial," "Industrial," and "Land" in a separate column. Having a well-defined reference list is essential; it simplifies the drop-down creation process and ensures consistency across your data.

Once your list is ready, head back to your main data entry sheet where you'd like to implement the drop-down feature. Select the cell or range of cells for which you want to enable the drop-down. With the desired cells highlighted, go to the "Data" tab on the ribbon and click on "Data Validation." This action will bring up a dialog box.

In the dialog box under the "Settings" tab, choose "List" from the "Allow" dropdown menu. Next, specify the location of your list in the "Source" field. Take this example, if your entries are located in cells A1 through A4 on Sheet2, you would enter =Sheet2!A1:A4 here. Alternatively, if you prefer to input items directly without referencing another sheet, you can type them in manually, separated by commas: Residential, Commercial, Industrial, Land.

After setting up your source list, click OK. You should see a small arrow appear next to any cell within your selected range —this indicates that a drop-down menu is now available for selection.

Consider how this feature streamlines tasks when filling out a property listing form. Instead of repeatedly typing "Residential," agents can simply select it from the drop-down menu, saving time while ensuring consistent and accurate categorization of each listing. This uniformity proves beneficial during data analysis since consistent entries make sorting and filtering much more effective.

To further enhance user experience, consider adding an input message that guides users on how to complete the fields correctly. Within the Data Validation dialog box, navigate to the "Input Message" tab and check "Show input message when cell is selected." Then fill in fields like Title (for example: "Select Property Type") and Input message (such as: "Choose from the drop-down list"). This small addition can prevent mistakes by clearly outlining expectations for anyone using your spreadsheet.

When utilizing Excel's features like this one, it's essential to prioritize usability—particularly when dealing with larger datasets or multiple users entering information simultaneously during events such as open houses. Clarity can greatly enhance overall efficiency.

After creating your drop-down lists, it's important to maintain them as changes occur in the real estate market. If new property types emerge or older categories become outdated, updating your source list keeps everyone informed and avoids introducing confusion into reports or analyses.

Reflecting on collaborative projects with fellow agents highlights how clear categorization can streamline communication and reduce unnecessary back-and-forth clarifications about property statuses or types—especially across teams with varying levels of technical expertise.

In summary, implementing drop-down lists not only increases operational efficiency but also enhances data quality management—a crucial aspect when generating reports for clients who rely on precise insights into market trends and property evaluations. By mastering this skill early in your Excel journey, you're laying a strong foundation for advanced data management practices that will be invaluable throughout your real estate career.

In the end, utilizing drop-down lists transforms mundane data entry tasks into streamlined processes that promote accurate decision-making and boost productivity across various facets of real estate operations.

Importing and Exporting Data

Importing and exporting data in Excel can significantly enhance the efficiency of real estate professionals who regularly manage large volumes of information. Whether transferring property listings from a CRM system or sharing analysis reports with clients, mastering data movement is essential for accuracy and productivity. This skill is particularly important when juggling multiple data sources or collaborating with colleagues.

To begin importing data, first identify the format of the incoming information. Excel supports various formats, including CSV, TXT, and data from other Excel workbooks. For example, if you receive a CSV file containing property listings, open Excel and go to the "Data" tab on the ribbon. Click on "Get Data," select "From File," and then choose "From Text/CSV." This action will open a dialog box where you can locate your file.

Once you've selected the file, Excel will present a preview of your data. This step is crucial as it allows you to spot any inconsistencies before incorporating the information into your workbook. You can adjust settings like delimiters—commonly commas for CSV files—or change the data types for each column if necessary. After verifying that everything looks correct, click "Load." Your imported data will appear in a new worksheet, ready for further analysis.

Exporting data follows a similar but reversed process. Imagine you've compiled a list of properties to share with potential buyers or partners that includes specifications and current market values. To export this information, navigate to the worksheet with your finalized list, select the relevant range, then return to the "File" menu and click on "Save As." Here, you can choose your preferred format; CSV is often favored for its compatibility across different systems.

Before saving, consider what format would be most beneficial for your audience. If they require detailed formatting and formulas to remain intact, saving as an Excel Workbook (.xlsx) might be preferable. Conversely, if they are importing the file into another system that doesn't need formatting, opt for CSV. It's also wise to name your file descriptively to reflect its contents—this helps keep your records organized.

Take this example, suppose you are managing an annual report that highlights market trends and property sales within a specific neighborhood. You could import quarterly sales data from various agents into one master file using the steps outlined above. After analyzing this consolidated data in Excel —applying functions like AVERAGE or SUM—you can then export the results as a PDF report for stakeholders or clients.

Also, proficiency in importing and exporting data greatly streamlines collaboration among teams. Consider a scenario where multiple agents need access to updated property information while working on joint projects; importing shared files ensures that everyone is aligned with the latest figures without redundancy. This approach allows team members to focus on high-impact tasks instead of sifting through outdated or inconsistent records.

Another practical aspect involves integrating external databases or systems like CRM software that many real estate agents use daily. With tools like Microsoft Power Query built into Excel, you can connect directly to these databases for real-time updates rather than manually inputting information—a significant time-saver.

It's also crucial not to overlook maintaining clean datasets after importing; regularly check for duplicates or errors that may have occurred during the transfer process. Utilizing features such as conditional formatting to highlight duplicates can be invaluable in this regard.

To wrap things up, mastering data import and export

techniques equips you with essential skills necessary for effective real estate management. The ability to accurately transition between different datasets not only boosts personal productivity but also supports informed decision-making based on reliable information—critical factors in today's fast-paced real estate landscape. By honing these processes early in your career, you're positioning yourself for ongoing success in an ever-evolving market environment where timely insights often dictate competitive advantage.

CHAPTER 4:
ADVANCED EXCEL
FORMULAS FOR
REAL ESTATE

Nesting Functions for
Complex Calculations

Nesting functions in Excel opens up a realm of complex calculations, allowing real estate agents to analyze data with greater efficiency and precision. By combining multiple functions into a single formula, you gain deeper insights while keeping your spreadsheet organized and free from excessive formulas. For example, when assessing the profitability of various properties based on projected income and expenses, nesting functions can streamline your calculations significantly.

Imagine you're trying to determine if a property's expected monthly rental income covers its mortgage payment. If the rental income is in cell A1 and the mortgage payment is in cell B1, a straightforward way to compare these values is by using an IF function: =IF(A1>B1, "Profitable", "Not Profitable"). This simple formula provides a clear answer. But what if you also need to consider potential maintenance costs?

This is where nesting becomes particularly useful. By incorporating maintenance costs from cell C1 into your formula, you can create a more comprehensive assessment: =IF(A1>(B1+C1), "Profitable", "Not Profitable"). This enhanced formula checks whether the rental income not only covers the mortgage but also includes maintenance costs, giving you a fuller picture of profitability.

As you evaluate multiple properties with differing incomes and expenses, nested functions can make your analysis much more manageable. Suppose you have rental incomes listed in column A and total expenses in column B. In cell C2, you could implement the following nested formula: =IF(A2>B2, A2-B2, 0). By dragging this formula down the column, you quickly calculate net profits for all properties, providing an immediate snapshot of which ones are genuinely profitable.

The true power of nesting lies in its versatility; it allows you to incorporate additional functions within your IF statements or combine them with others like SUM or AVERAGE for even greater depth. Take this example, if you want to calculate the average net profit across multiple properties while considering only those that are profitable (returning zero for unprofitable ones), your formula in cell D2 could be:

=AVERAGE(IF(A2:A10>B2:B10, A2:A10-B2:B10, 0)).

This array formula focuses solely on profitable properties while ignoring those that don't meet the criteria.

Nesting extends beyond financial calculations; it can also simplify data analysis tasks such as market comparisons or client assessments. For example, if you're tracking how many residential properties sold above a certain price point within a specified range, nested COUNTIF functions can help. Your formula might look like this:

=COUNTIF(A2:A100, ">500000") - COUNTIF(B2:B100, "<200000").

This counts how many residential properties sold above)500,000 while subtracting those that sold below (200,000—offering valuable insight into market performance for specific segments.

While working with nested functions may seem intimidating at first, practice will build your confidence. Start with simpler formulas and gradually incorporate more complexity as you become comfortable. Each time you nest a function within another, consider what information you're seeking or what decision you're trying to inform. This approach not only clarifies your intentions but also enhances your analytical skills.

Additionally, remember that Excel provides tools to help identify errors in nested functions. If a calculation doesn't yield the expected result, utilize the formula auditing tools found in Excel's "Formulas" tab to troubleshoot issues. With time and exploration of nested functions, you'll find they become an invaluable part of your Excel toolkit.

By mastering these advanced techniques, you'll harness Excel's true potential in real estate—transforming raw data into actionable insights that support strategic decision-making and ultimately drive success in your endeavors.

Using INDEX and MATCH for Lookup

The use of the INDEX and MATCH functions in Excel significantly enhances how real estate agents conduct lookups, surpassing the limitations of simpler functions like VLOOKUP. These two functions work together seamlessly, providing both flexibility and precision when retrieving data from extensive datasets—a necessity in real estate where quick and accurate cross-referencing of information like property prices, client details, and market trends is essential.

To illustrate the synergy between INDEX and MATCH, imagine you have a table listing properties along with their details —such as location, price, and square footage. If you want to determine the price of a specific property by name, this combination allows for an efficient solution.

Take this example, let's say your property names are in column A and their prices are in column B. To find the price of a property called "Oceanview Villa," you would start with the MATCH function to identify its row number with the following formula:

=MATCH("Oceanview Villa", A:A, 0)

This formula searches column A for "Oceanview Villa" and returns the corresponding row number. Next, you would use this result within an INDEX function to pull the price from column B. Your complete formula would be:

=INDEX(B:B, MATCH("Oceanview Villa", A:A, 0))

This combined formula instructs Excel to look in column B (where the prices are stored) and return the value found at the row identified by MATCH. The real advantage of this method lies in its adaptability; whether you change the property name or rearrange your data, the structure of your formula remains robust.

INDEX and MATCH become particularly advantageous with larger datasets, especially since VLOOKUP requires that the lookup column be to the left of the return column. With INDEX and MATCH, any arrangement is possible. For example, if your data includes property IDs in column A, names in column B, and prices in column C, you can still retrieve prices using:

=INDEX(C:C, MATCH("Oceanview Villa", B:B, 0))

This flexibility can greatly enhance your efficiency when analyzing diverse datasets.

Another practical application is quickly identifying properties within a specific price range. Suppose you have a table listing properties with their associated prices and want to find all properties priced below)300,000. By combining IF statements with INDEX and MATCH, you can generate results dynamically.

If your properties are organized from A2 to C100, with names in column B and prices in column C, you could create an array formula like this:

=IFERROR(INDEX(B\(2:B\)100, SMALL(IF(C\(2:C \)100<300000, ROW(C\(2:C\)100)-ROW(C\(2)+1), ROW(1:1))), "")

This formula uses IFERROR to manage any potential errors from unmatched conditions while SMALL retrieves row numbers for properties under)300,000 sequentially as you drag down. Each drag generates another result without cluttering your worksheet with multiple formulas.

Utilizing these functions opens new avenues for deeper data insights. Take this example, if you're analyzing how many properties sold above a certain threshold across various neighborhoods or regions, combining these functions can provide actionable insights to inform your marketing strategies or pricing decisions.

While mastering INDEX and MATCH may seem challenging at first, focusing on practical applications in your daily tasks will build your confidence. Start with straightforward lookups and gradually incorporate more complexity as you become comfortable. As you practice these techniques, take a moment to reflect on their impact—consider how they streamline your processes or enhance your ability to analyze data effectively.

In the end, mastering INDEX and MATCH not only equips you with advanced Excel skills but also empowers you to make data-driven decisions that can greatly influence your success in real estate transactions. This combination transforms how you navigate data landscapes, turning challenges into opportunities for insightful analysis.

Applying Conditional Formatting to Insights

Conditional formatting is a powerful tool in Excel, especially for real estate professionals who need to make quick, data-driven decisions. This feature allows users to apply visual cues that highlight critical trends and anomalies in their datasets, making it easier to understand the data at a glance. By leveraging conditional formatting, you can uncover insights about property values, sales performance, and client engagement that might otherwise go unnoticed.

Consider a dataset filled with various property listings and their respective prices. It's easy to feel overwhelmed by the numbers, but conditional formatting can help you focus on properties that exceed a specific price threshold. This not only saves time but also directs your attention toward high-value assets or potential red flags in the market.

To get started, select the range of cells you wish to format. Take this example, if you want to highlight all properties priced above (500,000, navigate to the "Home" tab on the Excel ribbon. Click on "Conditional Formatting," then choose "New Rule." From there, select "Format cells that contain" and set the rule to "greater than" 500,000. Choose your preferred formatting style—like filling those cells with green—and click OK. Instantly, all properties that meet this criterion will be visually distinguished.

This straightforward technique streamlines your decision-making process. Whether you're evaluating potential investment opportunities or preparing reports for clients, these visual indicators enhance your ability to communicate findings effectively. Stakeholders can quickly identify which properties merit further exploration based on their price points instead of sifting through extensive numerical data.

The benefits of conditional formatting extend beyond simple price thresholds; you can also establish dynamic rules based on various criteria such as property type or days on the market. For example, if you're monitoring how long listings remain active before being sold, color-coding those cells according to time intervals—like yellow for properties over 30 days and red for those over 90 days—can offer immediate insights into market trends.

Imagine managing a portfolio of rental properties where you want to visualize units underperforming relative to expected occupancy rates. By applying conditional formatting rules that highlight any unit with an occupancy rate below a certain percentage—say 80%—you gain quick access to properties that may require strategic marketing adjustments or additional attention from your team.

And, combining conditional formatting with data validation tools enhances its effectiveness even further. By setting up dropdown lists for status updates (e.g., "Available," "Under Offer," "Sold") alongside automatic color-coded statuses, you create an interactive dashboard right within your spreadsheet.

As you explore these features, remember to use the "Manage Rules" option within the Conditional Formatting menu for ongoing adjustments. This flexibility allows you to make real-time changes as your criteria evolve or as new listings arise.

While conditional formatting greatly enhances visualization and comprehension of data at first glance, it's essential to use it judiciously; excessive highlighting can lead to confusion instead of clarity. Strive for simplicity and relevance when choosing colors and conditions to ensure clear communication without overwhelming viewers with visual noise.

By mastering conditional formatting in Excel, you not only acquire technical skills but also gain a strategic advantage in swiftly and accurately analyzing real estate data. This capability positions you as a proactive agent ready to respond decisively based on concrete insights derived from well-structured data analysis rather than relying solely on instinct or guesswork.

In the end, effective use of conditional formatting enhances understanding while streamlining communication in the fast-paced world of real estate transactions. It empowers agents like you to surface insights that foster better decision-making and contribute significantly to success in navigating this competitive field.

Using AND, OR in Logical Tests

Logical tests in Excel can greatly enhance your analytical capabilities, especially when dealing with complex real estate datasets. The AND and OR functions enable you to evaluate multiple conditions at once, giving you a deeper understanding of your data. This functionality becomes particularly valuable when filtering listings, assessing market trends, or generating targeted reports.

The AND function returns TRUE only when all specified conditions are met. Take this example, if you want to identify properties priced above)300,000 with at least three bedrooms, you would create a formula like this: =AND(A2>300000, B2>=3). In this example, A2 represents the price and B2 indicates the number of bedrooms. If both criteria are satisfied, the formula yields TRUE; otherwise, it returns FALSE.

By using this formula effectively, you can create dynamic filters. For example, you might set up a new column to evaluate these conditions across your entire dataset. By dragging the fill handle down, you can apply the same logic to multiple rows, swiftly pinpointing properties that meet your criteria without the need to sift through data manually.

Conversely, the OR function provides flexibility by returning TRUE if any one of several conditions is met. For example, if you're searching for properties located in a specific neighborhood or priced above (500,000, your formula would look like this: =OR(C2="Downtown", A2>500000). This functionality is particularly useful for generating targeted marketing lists or identifying high-value properties in desirable areas.

Combining AND and OR can further enhance your analysis. Take this example, if you want to find properties that either meet both criteria (price above)300,000 and three bedrooms) or are located in an exclusive neighborhood, you might nest these functions like this: =OR(AND(A2>300000, B2>=3), C2="Luxury Estates"). This approach allows for more strategic decision-making by broadening your exploration of options based on varying criteria.

Excel's logical functions can be even more powerful when paired with conditional formatting. After applying your logical tests using AND and OR, you can set up rules that highlight cells based on these evaluations. Take this example, you might color-code all properties over (500,000 that have three bedrooms. This visual cue makes it easier to spot desirable listings during client presentations.

As you integrate these logical formulas into your workflow, consider using named ranges for improved clarity and organization. Instead of directly referencing specific cell coordinates like A2 or B2, define meaningful names such as "Price" or "Bedrooms." This practice simplifies your formulas and minimizes errors when managing large datasets.

Additionally, advanced users can leverage Excel's ability to handle arrays. By creating an array formula that evaluates multiple rows simultaneously based on your AND/OR criteria —simply pressing Ctrl + Shift + Enter after typing your formula—you can process batches without dragging formulas down through hundreds of rows.

While incorporating these logical testing techniques into your real estate practices, it's crucial to maintain data accuracy. Remember that logical tests are only as effective as the data they analyze; incorrect inputs can lead to misleading conclusions. Regular audits of your dataset are essential to ensure integrity.

To wrap things up, mastering the AND and OR functions provides you with powerful tools to refine your analyses in Excel. These logical tests empower real estate agents to make informed decisions by streamlining data filtering processes and enhancing visibility into key trends within property listings. The ability to evaluate multiple conditions opens new pathways for strategic insights—enabling you to serve clients with precision and confidence in today's competitive market landscape.

Creating Dynamic Ranges with OFFSET

Creating dynamic ranges in Excel with the OFFSET function can significantly enhance your management and analysis of real estate data. OFFSET enables you to define a cell range that automatically adjusts based on specific criteria, which is particularly beneficial for handling the fluctuating datasets typical in real estate markets. Whether you're tracking property prices, client information, or sales metrics, using OFFSET can streamline your data analysis and make it more efficient.

Consider a scenario where you're compiling a report on sales over time and adding new properties weekly. Instead of manually updating your reports each time new data arrives, you can create dynamic charts that automatically include only recent data points using OFFSET. For example, if your sales figures are recorded from A1 through A1000 and you're interested in visualizing just the last three months of data, your OFFSET formula might look like this: =OFFSET(A1, COUNT(A:A)-90, 0, 90). This not only keeps your reports up-to-date but also saves valuable time when preparing for client meetings or team discussions.

Another powerful application of OFFSET is its combination with functions like SUM or AVERAGE for calculating values across dynamic ranges. Take this example, if you want to calculate the average price of properties sold within the last month, you could use =AVERAGE(OFFSET(A1, COUNT(A:A)-30, 0, 30)). This formula adjusts automatically based on how many entries are present in your dataset without requiring constant manual updates. As new sales are recorded in your spreadsheet, this approach ensures that your average calculations remain accurate.

Enhancing clarity and usability further involves creating named ranges with OFFSET. Instead of referencing complex nested formulas directly within your worksheets—which can lead to confusion—you can define a named range like "RecentSales" based on your OFFSET formula. By doing this through Formulas > Name Manager > New Name (for example), you can easily refer to "RecentSales" in other calculations or charts without repeatedly rewriting intricate formulas.

While implementing these strategies can greatly improve efficiency and accuracy when handling property listings or transaction data, it's important to monitor performance as well. Excel may experience lagging issues if you work with excessively large datasets or overly complicated formulas that recalculate frequently. To maintain responsiveness when dealing with significant amounts of data—while ensuring smooth operation—consider limiting dynamic ranges when possible or opting for simpler formulas.

Incorporating OFFSET into your Excel toolkit not only simplifies routine tasks but also enables you to generate insightful reports efficiently. By embracing this capability alongside logical functions such as AND and OR—discussed previously—you position yourself for deeper analyses that facilitate informed decision-making in real estate endeavors.

In the end, dynamic ranges created through OFFSET offer real estate agents increased versatility when analyzing ever-changing datasets. By automating parts of your reporting process and establishing connections between various data points within Excel spreadsheets—you empower yourself with powerful insights ready to be delivered confidently during presentations or decision-making sessions.

Using CHOOSE for Flexible Calculations

The CHOOSE function in Excel offers remarkable flexibility for calculations, making it an invaluable tool for data analysis and reporting, especially in the fast-paced real estate sector. This function allows you to select a value from a list based on a specified index number, enabling dynamic responses and calculations that adjust according to user input or other variables.

The syntax of the CHOOSE function is simple: CHOOSE(index_num, value1, [value2], ...). Here, index_num determines which value to return from your provided list. For example, if you have a list of properties with their corresponding statuses—such as "Available," "Under Contract," or "Sold"—you can use CHOOSE to display a specific status based on a given index. If "Available" is the first item in your list, the formula =CHOOSE(1, "Available", "Under Contract", "Sold") will return "Available.

This functionality is particularly beneficial when analyzing different property types or categories. Consider evaluating various property features like size, location, and price. With CHOOSE, you can dynamically adjust calculations based on user selections. Imagine a drop-down menu in your spreadsheet where selecting an option automatically updates key figures; this interactivity enhances the relevance of your analysis.

Take this example, suppose you want to calculate potential commission earnings based on property prices across different tiers—such as low-end, mid-range, and high-end properties. Using CHOOSE allows you to quickly apply varying commission rates based on the selected property tier. If tier 1 corresponds to low-end properties with a 3% commission rate, tier 2 for mid-range at 5%, and tier 3 for high-end at 7%, your formula could be structured like this:

=CHOOSE(A1, B1*0.03, B1*0.05, B1*0.07)

In this scenario, A1 holds the tier number chosen by the user (with 1 representing low-end properties). If B1 contains the sale price of the evaluated property, this formula will correctly calculate the commission based on the selected tier.

And, combining CHOOSE with other functions can enhance its utility even further. For example, integrating it with IF statements allows for more complex decision-making scenarios:

=IF(B2 > 500000, CHOOSE(A2, "High-End", "Mid-Range", "Low-End"), "")

In this case, if B2 represents a property's sale price exceeding)500K and A2 indicates its category using similar indices as before, this formula will dynamically classify it as "High-End," "Mid-Range," or "Low-End." This streamlines your classification process without requiring repetitive manual entries.

Another practical application is in creating dashboards where users can toggle between different views or metrics using interactive controls linked directly to CHOOSE functions. By employing data validation lists alongside CHOOSE, you can effortlessly switch between visualizing sales data by region or property type without needing multiple complex charts.

While leveraging CHOOSE within your Excel toolkit significantly enhances flexibility and interactivity, it's essential to avoid overcomplicating formulas. Each added layer should simplify analysis rather than confuse users who may not be familiar with nested functions.

With these insights into harnessing the power of CHOOSE

for flexible calculations in Excel, you're equipped to elevate your real estate analytics. The ability to adapt calculations dynamically not only boosts efficiency but also provides deeper insights that empower strategic decision-making during critical moments—be it client presentations or internal reviews.

Embracing such tools strengthens your capabilities as a data-driven real estate professional, allowing you to navigate complex datasets with ease while consistently delivering impactful results.

Power Query for Real Estate Data

Power Query has revolutionized data management in Excel, particularly for real estate agents who often juggle numerous datasets from various sources. This powerful tool simplifies the process of importing, cleaning, and transforming data, eliminating the need for complex formulas or programming expertise. With its intuitive interface, Power Query is both accessible and feature-rich, significantly enhancing analytical capabilities.

Consider the scenario where you receive a large CSV file containing property listings from multiple agents. Instead of spending hours sorting and filtering this information manually in a traditional spreadsheet, Power Query allows you to connect directly to the file and load it into Excel with ease. In just a few clicks, you can remove unnecessary columns, adjust data types, and filter out irrelevant rows. This immediate access transforms a once cumbersome task into a streamlined process, saving you valuable time that can be better spent on client engagement or market research.

To begin using Power Query, head to the Data tab in Excel and select "Get Data." You can choose your data source—be it an Excel workbook, text file, or online database. Take this example, if you're importing property data from an online listing service, select "From Web" and enter the URL. Power

Query will retrieve the data and present it in its editor interface.

Inside the editor, you have a wealth of options at your disposal. If you want to remove duplicates from your listings, simply select the column containing property IDs or addresses and click "Remove Duplicates." The result is immediate: your dataset becomes cleaner without the need for manual checks. Additionally, the "Transform" menu lets you change data types—such as converting text-based prices into numeric formats for financial calculations—ensuring that all entries are properly formatted for analysis.

Another invaluable feature is "Merging Queries," which allows you to combine datasets effectively. Take this example, if one dataset contains property details while another holds owner information, merging them based on a common column like Property ID creates a comprehensive view of each listing in one table. To merge queries, navigate to the Home tab in the Power Query Editor and select "Merge Queries." You will be prompted to choose which tables to merge and on which fields; this capability enhances your ability to create detailed reports with minimal manual effort.

Transforming data extends beyond simple operations; you can create calculated columns within Power Query using custom formulas tailored to your needs. For example, if you're looking to calculate potential rental yields based on purchase prices and estimated rents, you could add a calculated column that divides expected monthly rent by the property price multiplied by 12 (to annualize it). The formula would look like this:

Rental Yield = Estimated Rent / (Property Price * 12)

Once your transformations are complete, loading the cleaned data back into Excel is straightforward. Just click "Close & Load," and your modified dataset will appear in either a new worksheet or an existing one of your choice. This functionality not only saves time but ensures that your analyses are based on reliable and current information.

Using Power Query alongside Excel's analytical tools opens up new possibilities for insightful reporting. With each dataset linked through Power Query's established connections, updating analyses becomes as simple as refreshing those connections whenever new data is available. Imagine preparing for a quarterly review; instead of manually updating figures across multiple spreadsheets, you can refresh your Power Query connections to instantly reflect the latest property listings.

This ability to automate tasks greatly enhances efficiency while minimizing errors typically associated with manual data entry. It liberates precious hours that can be redirected toward building client relationships or exploring new market opportunities.

As you explore the full potential of Power Query in your real estate practice, you'll discover its capacity for managing complex datasets not only boosts efficiency but also empowers strategic decision-making through accurate analytics. By mastering this tool, you position yourself as a skilled analyst capable of navigating intricate datasets effortlessly—an invaluable asset in today's competitive real estate landscape.

Embracing such advanced tools signifies not just an enhancement of skills but an evolution in how real estate professionals approach their work; no longer bound by tedious processes but propelled forward by smart technology integration designed for modern demands.

CHAPTER 5:
FINANCIAL ANALYSIS
WITH EXCEL

Calculating Mortgage Payments

C alculating mortgage payments is an essential skill for real estate agents, enabling them to provide clients with accurate financial information crucial for informed decision-making. Mastering this calculation not only enhances your service offerings but also strengthens your credibility in client interactions.

At the heart of mortgage payment calculations are three key components: the loan amount, interest rate, and loan term. The most commonly used formula for determining monthly mortgage payments is:

[M = (P[r(1 + r)^n] / [(1 + r)^n – 1])]

Where:

- (M) represents the total monthly mortgage payment.
- (P) is the principal loan amount.
- (r) is the monthly interest rate (annual interest rate

divided by 12).

- (n) is the total number of payments (loan term in years multiplied by 12).

Let's illustrate this with a practical example. Imagine a client interested in purchasing a property priced at (300,000, planning to make a)60,000 down payment. This leads to a principal loan amount ((P)) of (240,000. If the annual interest rate is set at 4% and the loan term spans 30 years, we can begin calculating the monthly payment.

First, convert the annual interest rate into a monthly rate:

$[r = (4\% / 100)/12 = 0.003333]$

Next, calculate (n):

$[n = 30$ years 12 months/year $= 360$ payments $]$

Now, substitute these values into the formula:

$[M = (240000[0.003333(1 + 0.003333)^{360}] / [(1 + 0.003333)^{360}) - 1]]$

This simplifies to:

$[M \backslash)1,145.80]$

Thus, your client can expect to pay approximately (1,145.80 each month toward their mortgage.

To further aid clients in grasping their long-term financial commitments, consider creating an amortization schedule using Excel. This schedule provides a detailed breakdown of each payment over time, illustrating how much goes toward principal versus interest—offering transparency and clarity.

Here's how to set up an amortization schedule in Excel:

1. Create a worksheet with headers: Month, Payment, Principal Paid, Interest Paid, Remaining Balance.

2. Input your initial values for principal and interest.

3. For each month (starting from Month 1), use

formulas to calculate:

4. Interest Paid: Remaining Balance * Monthly Interest Rate

5. Principal Paid: Monthly Payment - Interest Paid

6. Remaining Balance: Previous Remaining Balance - Principal Paid

7. Drag these formulas down for each month until you reach the end of your loan term.

Take this example:

- In cell B2 (Month 1), enter the total monthly payment ()1,145.80).

- In cell C2 (Principal Paid), use =B2-(A2*Monthly_Interest_Rate).

- In cell D2 (Interest Paid), use =Remaining_Balance*Monthly_Interest_Rate.

- In cell E2 (Remaining Balance) should equal =Initial_Principal-Cumulative_Principal_Paid.

By replicating these calculations throughout your table using relative references and dragging down formulas, you'll create a comprehensive view of how payments are allocated over time.

Utilizing Excel's capabilities not only streamlines calculations but also enhances client presentations with visually appealing graphs that represent amortization schedules or total interest paid over the life of the loan.

Equipped with these insights, you can empower your clients as they navigate their purchasing decisions—whether determining affordability or comparing different financing options based on varying rates or terms.

Incorporating this knowledge into your client interactions fosters trust and positions you as an invaluable resource in their real estate journey. Your ability to communicate complex mortgage-related concepts clearly will resonate with buyers' needs—a crucial element in securing sales and building lasting relationships.

As you refine your skills in calculating mortgage payments and effectively presenting this information through Excel tools, you'll likely see an increase in client satisfaction as they gain clarity about their financial commitments and options available in today's market landscape.

Using NPV and IRR for Investment Analysis

Investment analysis is a fundamental aspect of real estate practice, and grasping the metrics of Net Present Value (NPV) and Internal Rate of Return (IRR) is essential for making informed investment decisions. These financial concepts enable real estate agents to assess potential investments, compare various properties, and ultimately provide sound advice to clients.

Essentially of NPV is the focus on the value of future cash flows generated by an investment, which are discounted back to their present value. The formula for NPV is expressed as:

$[NPV = ((\text{Cash Flow\_t} / (1 + r)^t)) - \text{Initial Investment}]$

In this equation:

- (Cash Flow_t) refers to the cash inflow during period (t),
- (r) represents the discount rate or the required rate of return, and
- (t) signifies each time period in years.

To illustrate how NPV works, consider a client evaluating an investment property that generates annual cash flows of (20,000 over five years, with an initial purchase cost of)80,000 and a discount rate of 10%.

Let's break down the NPV calculation step by step:

1. Year 1: (Cash Flow_1 = (20,000 / (1 + 0.10)^1) = 18,181.82)

2. Year 2: (Cash Flow_2 = (20,000 / (1 + 0.10)^2) = 16,528.93)

3. Year 3: (Cash Flow_3 = (20,000 / (1 + 0.10)^3) = 15,020.48)

4. Year 4: (Cash Flow_4 = (20,000 / (1 + 0.10)^4) = 13,656.80)

5. Year 5: (Cash Flow_5 = (20,000 / (1 + 0.10)^5) = 12,505.28)

Next, we sum these present values and subtract the initial investment:

[

Total NPV = (18,181.82 + 16,528.93 + 15,020.48 + 13,656.80 + 12,505.28) - 80,000

]

This leads to a Total NPV of approximately -(4,107.69, indicating that this investment does not meet the client's desired return based on their expectations.

Now let's turn our attention to IRR, which identifies the discount rate that brings the NPV to zero. This metric offers insights into potential profitability without needing to preset a specific rate.

In Excel, calculating IRR is straightforward using its built-in function:

1. Start by listing your cash flows in one column, beginning with the initial investment as a negative value (-)80,000), followed by the positive annual cash flows ((20,000).

2. Use the formula =IRR(A1:A6) where A1:A6 includes all listed cash flows.

Excel will calculate the IRR based on these inputs and provide you with a percentage reflecting how well this investment might perform compared to other options.

Referring back to our earlier example: if Excel indicates an IRR of approximately 8%, this suggests that while the property may generate income over time, it falls short of the required return of 10%. This analysis enables you to guide your clients in deciding whether to proceed with this purchase or explore alternative investments that may offer better returns.

Presenting both NPV and IRR calculations during client consultations—perhaps utilizing charts generated in Excel—creates a visual narrative that contrasts potential profits against associated costs in any transaction.

To enhance your analysis further in Excel:

- Consider creating a summary worksheet that highlights key figures such as total cash flows over time alongside calculated NPV and IRR.
- Employ data visualization techniques like graphs or dashboards to enrich your presentations; demonstrating how variations in discount rates impact your calculations can lead to insightful discussions about risk management and investment strategies.

By mastering these concepts, you not only guide your clients effectively but also establish yourself as an expert capable of transforming complex data into actionable insights. This ability resonates with both seasoned investors and first-time buyers alike.

In the end, mastering these financial analyses elevates your practice beyond mere transaction facilitation; it strategically influences investment choices—an invaluable skill set for any ambitious agent aiming for long-term success in the field.

Creating Amortization Schedules

Creating an amortization schedule is essential for real estate agents aiming to provide clients with clear insights into loan repayment structures. By understanding how loans are paid off over time, agents can better guide clients in selecting the most suitable financing options for their property investments. An amortization schedule details each payment, breaking it down into principal and interest, which helps clients grasp the financial commitments involved in real estate transactions.

To begin constructing an amortization schedule in Excel, gather key information: the loan amount, interest rate, and loan term. Take this example, let's consider a scenario where a client wishes to finance a property with a loan amount of)200,000 at an annual interest rate of 4% for 30 years.

Start by calculating the monthly payment using Excel's PMT function:

1. Open Excel and select a new worksheet.

2. In cell A1, input your loan amount: 200000.

3. In cell A2, input your annual interest rate: 0.04.

4. In cell A3, input your loan term in years: 30.

Next, you can calculate the monthly payment in cell A4 using the following formula:

```excel
=PMT(A2/12, A3*12, -A1)
```

This formula divides the annual interest by 12 to obtain the monthly interest rate and multiplies the loan term by 12 to determine the total number of payments. After entering this formula, you'll find that the monthly payment is approximately (954.83.

Now that you have your monthly payment figured out, let's create a detailed amortization schedule starting in cell A6:

1. Column Headers: In row 6 (cells A6 through E6), label your columns as follows:

2. A6: "Payment Number

3. B6: "Payment

4. C6: "Interest

5. D6: "Principal

6. E6: "Remaining Balance

7. Payment Number: In cell A7, enter 1 for the first payment number. In cell A8, enter =A7+1 and drag this formula down until you reach 360 (for a 30-year loan).

8. Monthly Payment: In column B (starting from B7), enter =A\)4 to consistently reference your calculated monthly payment throughout.

9. Interest Calculation: In cell C7, calculate the interest for the first month using:

```excel
=A(1*(A)2/12)
```

1. Principal Calculation: In D7, determine how much principal is paid off with:

```excel
=B7-C7
```

1. Remaining Balance: Finally, in E7 calculate:

```excel
```

```
=A(1-D7
```
` ` `

For E8 and below, use:

` ` `excel

```
=E7-D8
```
` ` `

Now drag down all formulas in columns C through E from row 7 to row 366 (to cover all payments).

Once you've populated these cells correctly:

- Column C will show decreasing amounts as less interest is owed over time.

- Column D will gradually increase as more principal is paid off.

- Column E will display how much of the original loan remains after each payment.

This creates a comprehensive view of how each payment affects both principal and interest over the life of the loan.

To enhance comprehension, visualize this data by creating a chart:

- Highlight your Payment Number alongside Remaining Balance from columns A and E.

- Insert a line chart to illustrate how quickly clients pay down their debt compared to how much they owe over time.

This schedule not only clarifies financial responsibilities for your clients but also highlights important milestones— such as when they'll own their property outright or how fluctuations in interest rates might impact overall costs if refinancing becomes necessary.

Having this schedule readily available not only boosts your credibility as an agent but also fosters trust with clients by demonstrating transparency regarding one of their most significant financial commitments—the mortgage.

To wrap things up, crafting an amortization schedule equips you with valuable insights that benefit both your clientele and your own expertise as a knowledgeable advisor in real estate finance. It serves as an essential tool for successful negotiations and client satisfaction in today's competitive market landscape.

Using Goal Seek for Financial Planning

Mastering Excel's Goal Seek function can significantly enhance your financial planning capabilities, particularly in the dynamic realm of real estate. This powerful tool enables agents to analyze various financial scenarios by adjusting a single input value to achieve a desired outcome. This way, it becomes easier to assess how changes in key variables—such as interest rates or loan amounts—affect overall financial obligations, ultimately leading to more informed decisions.

Imagine advising a client on their home purchase. They might wonder how different down payment amounts will impact their monthly mortgage payments. To explore this, you'll need to gather some essential information: the current loan amount, interest rate, and loan term. Take this example, let's say your client has decided on a purchase price of)300,000 with a 20% down payment and a fixed interest rate of 4% over 30 years.

Start by setting up your initial spreadsheet:

1. Open Excel and create a new worksheet.

2. In cell A1, type "Purchase Price" and enter 300000 in cell B1.

3. In cell A2, type "Down Payment Percentage" and

enter 0.20 in cell B2.

4. In cell A3, type "Loan Amount," and in B3 use the formula:

```excel
=B1*(1-B2)
```

1. In cell A4, type "Annual Interest Rate" and enter 0.04 in B4.

2. In cell A5, type "Loan Term (Years)" and enter 30 in B5.

Next, calculate the monthly mortgage payment using the PMT function based on the loan amount:

1. In cell A6, write "Monthly Payment" and in B6 enter:

```excel
=PMT(B4/12, B5*12, -B3)
```

This initial setup gives your client an estimate of their monthly mortgage payment based on their chosen parameters.

Now, let's utilize Goal Seek to determine what down payment percentage would result in a target monthly payment—let's say (1,200.

1. Click on cell B6 where you calculated the Monthly Payment.

2. Navigate to the "Data" tab on Excel's ribbon.

3. Click "What-If Analysis," then select "Goal Seek."

4. In the Goal Seek dialog box:

5. Set "Set Cell" to B6 (the Monthly Payment).

6. Set "To Value" to 1200.

7. Set "By Changing Cell" to B2 (the Down Payment Percentage).

8. Click "OK."

Excel will adjust the value in B2 until it identifies an appropriate down payment percentage that results in a monthly payment close to)1,200.

Once you click OK and Excel completes its calculations, take note of the adjusted value that appears in B2; this indicates what your client needs to put down upfront to meet their desired monthly payment.

Goal Seek not only delivers precise answers but also enhances your ability to explore various financing strategies tailored to clients' diverse needs and goals. It fosters deeper conversations about financial readiness while helping you craft customized solutions that align with your clients' circumstances.

To further maximize this tool for practical applications within your business:

- Use Goal Seek during client meetings as an interactive feature—invite clients to suggest figures while observing real-time adjustments.

- Document different scenarios within your spreadsheets; consider calculating alternative percentages or varying terms which can facilitate quicker decision-making.

The true power of Goal Seek lies beyond simple adjustments; it stimulates discussions around affordability thresholds while reinforcing trust through transparency about potential costs associated with property purchases.

As you integrate these advanced techniques into your practice, remember that Excel is not merely a spreadsheet tool— it serves as a strategic partner that can help you navigate complex financial landscapes effectively while instilling confidence in your clients throughout their real estate journey.

By leveraging Goal Seek effectively, you distinguish yourself as an agent who doesn't just present options but actively engages clients in shaping their financial futures through informed choices—an essential aspect of building long-lasting relationships rooted in expertise and trustworthiness within the real estate industry.

Understanding Financial Ratios

Understanding financial ratios is crucial for real estate agents who want to analyze properties effectively and make informed investment decisions. These ratios act as key indicators of a property's performance, enabling agents to evaluate profitability, assess risk, and compare various investments. Let's explore the essential financial ratios every real estate agent should know and how they can be applied in practice.

One of the most fundamental ratios is the Gross Rent Multiplier (GRM). This ratio provides a quick estimate of a property's value based on its rental income. To calculate GRM, simply divide the property's price by its gross annual rental income. For example, if a property costs (400,000 and generates)40,000 annually in rent, the GRM would be:

[GRM = (Property Price / Annual Rental Income)]

[GRM = (400,000 / 40,000) = 10]

This indicates that it would take approximately ten years of rental income to cover the property purchase price. A lower GRM typically suggests a more attractive investment; however, it's important to combine this metric with additional analyses for a comprehensive evaluation.

Next is the Net Operating Income (NOI) ratio. This metric reveals the income a property generates after deducting operating expenses from gross income. To calculate NOI:

1. Determine your Gross Rental Income.

2. Subtract total operating expenses (excluding mortgage payments).

Take this example, if your property generates (60,000 in rental income with operating expenses of)20,000:

[NOI = Gross Rental Income - Operating Expenses]

[NOI = 60,000 - 20,000 = 40,000]

That means after covering operational costs, you have (40,000 available for debt service or profit.

Another important ratio is the Capitalization Rate (Cap Rate), which assesses an investment's potential return based on NOI relative to its purchase price or current market value. The Cap Rate can be calculated as follows:

[Cap Rate = (NOI / Current Market Value)]

Using our previous example where NOI is)40,000 and the market value of the property is (500,000:

[Cap Rate = (40,000 / 500,000) = 0.08 or 8\%]

An 8% Cap Rate suggests that if conditions remain constant, you could expect an annual return of 8% on your investment. This benchmark can vary significantly depending on location and property type.

As we delve into leverage considerations in investments, we encounter the Debt Service Coverage Ratio (DSCR). This ratio determines whether a property can comfortably cover its debt obligations using its net income. DSCR is calculated as follows:

[DSCR = (NOI / Total Debt Service)]

If our earlier property has an annual debt service (total mortgage payments) of)30,000:

[DSCR = (40,000 / 30,000) 1.33]

A DSCR above 1 indicates sufficient income to cover debts

comfortably; lenders typically favor a DSCR of at least 1.25.

Another vital metric is the Return on Investment (ROI) calculation, which evaluates overall profitability over time. ROI measures the gain or loss generated relative to investment costs using this formula:

[ROI (\%) = ((Gain from Investment - Cost of Investment / Cost of Investment)) * 100]

Take this example, if you sold your property for (500,000 after purchasing it for)400,000 (excluding operational costs), your gain would be calculated as follows:

[

ROI = ((500,000 - 400,000 / 400,000)) * 100 = 25\%

]

This indicates that you've achieved a solid return of 25% on your initial investment.

To effectively utilize these financial ratios in your practice as a real estate agent requires familiarity with tools like Excel for data analysis and visualization. Begin by creating an organized spreadsheet to input key figures such as purchase prices, annual rents collected, operating expenses, and mortgage amounts—all linked dynamically so that updates reflect across all calculations instantly.

For example:

- In Column A: List properties.

- In Column B: Enter Purchase Prices.

- In Column C: Record Gross Rental Income.

- In Column D: Input Operating Expenses.

- Formulas in subsequent columns will automatically compute GRM, NOI, and Cap Rate—providing instant insights at your fingertips.

This approach not only simplifies tracking but also allows you to run "what-if" scenarios quickly when assessing new opportunities or advising clients—a fundamental skill set that enhances trustworthiness.

In summary, mastering these financial ratios equips you with actionable insights necessary for driving success in real estate transactions while effectively communicating value propositions to clients and stakeholders alike. By integrating these practices into your workflow through Excel or other innovative tools within real estate analytics platforms— the power lies firmly within your hands to make smarter investment decisions with confidence and clarity moving forward.

Performing Break-even Analysis

Performing a break-even analysis is an essential skill for real estate agents, as it offers valuable insights into the financial viability of property investments. This analysis helps determine the point at which total revenues equal total costs— indicating that there is neither profit nor loss. Understanding your break-even point is crucial for making informed decisions about pricing, investment strategies, and identifying when a property becomes profitable.

To start, you need to gather some key data: fixed costs, variable costs per unit (such as maintenance or management expenses), and revenue per unit (like rental income). Let's consider an example of evaluating a rental property with the following figures:

- Fixed Costs: (30,000 per year (including property taxes, insurance, and mortgage payments)

- Variable Costs:)500 per month (covering maintenance and repairs)

- Rental Income: (2,000 per month

First, calculate your annual revenue from the rental income:

[Annual Revenue = Monthly Rent 12]

[Annual Revenue = 2,000 12 = 24,000]

Next, you'll need to determine your total annual costs by adding both fixed and variable costs together. Start by converting your variable costs into an annual figure:

[

Annual Variable Costs = 500 12 = 6,000

]

Now, add the fixed costs:

[

Total Annual Costs = Fixed Costs + Annual Variable Costs

]

[

Total Annual Costs = 30,000 + 6,000 = 36,000

]

With these calculations in hand, you can find your break-even point in terms of the monthly rental income required to cover all costs:

[

Break-even Point (BEP) = (Total Annual Costs / Monthly Rent)

]

[

BEP = (36,000 / 2,000) = 18

]

This indicates that you would need to rent out the property for at least 18 months to cover your total costs. If you're considering different rental prices or wish to quickly evaluate potential changes in operating expenses or revenues, Excel can be an invaluable tool.

By setting up a simple Excel model, you can adjust values dynamically. In one column, enter various scenarios for monthly rent alongside different fixed and variable costs. Use Excel's formula capabilities to automatically recalculate the break-even point based on these inputs.

For example:

1. Column A: Monthly Rent

2. Column B: Fixed Costs

3. Column C: Variable Costs

4. Column D: Break-even Point Formula

In Cell D2, input:

```excel
= (B2 + (C2 * 12)) / A2
```

Dragging this formula down will allow you to analyze various rent levels quickly.

If you want to explore how increasing rent affects profitability, simply change values in Column A and observe how quickly you reach profitability according to your calculated BEP in Column D.

However, understanding break-even analysis goes beyond just numbers; it provides persuasive arguments when negotiating with clients or stakeholders about pricing strategies and investment viability.

Consider a scenario where market conditions shift—perhaps due to economic changes or new competition affecting demand. Regularly revisiting your break-even analysis enables you not only to adapt but also to effectively forecast potential changes in cash flow.

Finally, consider visualizing this data using charts within Excel. You might create line graphs that plot revenue against total costs over time or bar charts that display how different scenarios impact your break-even point. Such visual representations can simplify complex data relationships for clients who may not be financially savvy but require clear guidance on investment performance.

In the end, mastering break-even analysis through practical applications like Excel equips real estate professionals with critical insights necessary for steering investments towards profitability. By integrating these tools and techniques into your workflow, you'll be better prepared to navigate the financial landscape of real estate with confidence.

Cash Flow Modeling

Cash flow modeling is essential for real estate agents who want to grasp the financial health of their investments. Unlike basic profit or loss calculations, cash flow modeling provides a comprehensive perspective on how income and expenses may vary over time. It involves tracking the inflow and outflow of cash, which directly influences your investment strategy and overall financial success.

To create an effective cash flow model in Excel, start by identifying all potential income sources related to the property. This includes rent, additional income from services like parking or laundry, and even tax credits or rebates. For example, if you manage a multifamily rental property, your income might look like this:

- Monthly Rent from Units:)5,000
- Additional Income (Parking Fees): (200
- Annual Tax Rebate:)1,500

First, calculate your total monthly income:

1. **Total Monthly Income = Rent + Additional Income

2. Monthly Income = 5,000 + 200 = 5,200

Next, turn your attention to outgoing cash flows. These typically consist of fixed costs such as mortgage payments, property taxes, and insurance, along with variable costs like maintenance and utilities. Here's a breakdown of these expenses:

- Mortgage Payment: (2,000/month
- Property Taxes:)300/month
- Insurance: (150/month
- Maintenance Costs:)400/month
- Utilities: (250/month

Now, let's calculate your total monthly expenses:

1. **Total Monthly Expenses = Mortgage + Property Taxes + Insurance + Maintenance + Utilities

2. Total Expenses = 2,000 + 300 + 150 + 400 + 250 = 3,100

With both total monthly income and expenses established, you can now determine the property's monthly cash flow:

1. **Monthly Cash Flow = Total Monthly Income - Total Monthly Expenses

2. Monthly Cash Flow = 5,200 - 3,100 = 2,100

This calculation shows that after covering all expenses, you would generate a positive cash flow of)2,100 each month.

To visualize this cash flow over time—perhaps across a year—set up a straightforward model in Excel. You might structure it as follows:

1. Column A: Month (January through December)

2. Column B: Total Monthly Income

3. Column C: Total Monthly Expenses

4. Column D: Monthly Cash Flow

For January, input the following formulas:

In Cell B2:

```excel
=5000+200
```

In Cell C2:

```excel
=2000+300+150+400+250
```

In Cell D2:

```excel
=B2-C2
```

Once you've established these formulas for January, drag them down through December in their respective columns to observe how your cash flow evolves month-to-month.

If you anticipate fluctuations—such as increased maintenance costs due to aging appliances—consider creating scenarios within your model. You can add new columns to input various expense estimates and analyze their impact on overall cash flow.

Visual aids enhance comprehension; generating charts in Excel can effectively illustrate monthly cash flows. A line graph showing monthly revenues against expenses provides a quick overview of trends throughout the year. Such visuals serve not only as analytical tools but also as compelling presentation assets when discussing finances with potential investors or clients.

Accurately modeling cash flows empowers real estate professionals to make informed decisions regarding acquisitions or sales while offering critical insights into investment sustainability. By utilizing Excel for detailed cash flow analysis and scenario planning, you'll gain confidence in managing your portfolio towards profitability.

These tools go beyond mere number crunching; they are fundamental in developing a resilient strategy capable of adapting to market shifts or unexpected expenses. Staying attuned to your cash flows enables a proactive approach—an essential trait for successful real estate agents navigating uncertainty.

In the end, investing time in mastering cash flow modeling will yield significant benefits for your career growth and client satisfaction. As you refine these skills through practical applications in Excel, you'll find yourself equipped with not just numbers but compelling narratives that illustrate the potential profitability and risks of your investments.

CHAPTER 6:
CREATING CHARTS
AND GRAPHS

*Benefits of Visual Data
Representation*

V isual data representation is not just a tool; it's a powerful means of communicating complex information in an easily digestible format. For real estate agents, the ability to present data visually can greatly enhance client interactions and streamline decision-making processes. Imagine entering a meeting equipped with not just numbers, but vibrant charts and intuitive graphs that narrate the market story at a glance. The impact of this approach is profound.

One of the standout benefits of visual data representation is its ability to uncover trends and insights that might be overlooked in raw data tables. Take, for instance, a simple line graph showing property price trends over several years. Rather than wading through columns of figures, clients can instantly recognize upward or downward trends, making market dynamics easier to understand. This visual clarity encourages informed discussions and strategic planning, allowing agents to offer nuanced advice based on observable patterns.

And, visual representations cater to varying learning styles and preferences. Many clients may find raw numbers daunting or confusing; however, a well-designed pie chart illustrating market share or a bar graph comparing property values can make that same information much more accessible. When clients can see their options laid out visually, they often become more engaged and willing to discuss their choices. For example, using heat maps to showcase property density or average sale prices enables clients to quickly identify neighborhoods that meet their needs.

Visual aids can also enhance presentations during open houses or listing meetings. Imagine showcasing a well-crafted infographic that highlights the key features of a property alongside its market comparables. This approach not only captures attention but also reinforces your professionalism and expertise as an agent who effectively utilizes modern tools. Clients tend to engage more when they can visualize what you're explaining; they feel like active participants in the conversation rather than passive recipients of information.

Incorporating visuals into your reports and proposals benefits not just your clients but also streamlines your workflow. Instead of spending hours verbally explaining complex metrics, you can let visuals do much of the heavy lifting. For example, creating dynamic dashboards in Excel allows you to compile multiple datasets into one cohesive presentation that updates in real time as new data is entered. This not only saves time but ensures you are always presenting the most accurate information possible.

Additionally, aesthetically pleasing visuals can enhance your brand image. When clients receive materials that are visually appealing and professionally presented, it reflects positively on you as an agent and demonstrates your commitment to quality service. You distinguish yourself in a crowded marketplace by presenting information clearly and attractively.

To maximize the effectiveness of your visual data representation, consider integrating storytelling elements into your visuals. Each chart or graph should support a narrative that logically guides clients through their choices and decisions. Take this example, when discussing investment potential across various properties, use visuals that showcase projected growth alongside historical performance data—helping clients connect past trends with future opportunities.

Embracing visual data representation will transform how you engage with clients and interpret data yourself. It empowers you not only to share insights but also to cultivate lasting relationships rooted in transparency and understanding—cornerstones of any successful real estate practice. Through visual storytelling grounded in solid data analysis, you position yourself as an invaluable asset in your clients' decision-making journeys.

Creating Column and Bar Charts

Creating column and bar charts in Excel can greatly enhance your ability to communicate complex real estate data. These visual tools transform numerical information into a format that's easy to understand, enabling clients to make informed decisions quickly. Let's explore the step-by-step process of creating these charts and their application in real estate.

Begin by organizing your data into a clear table format. For example, if you're analyzing property prices across various neighborhoods, structure your data with columns for Neighborhood Names, Average Prices, and any additional metrics such as Number of Sales or Year Built. A well-organized dataset serves as the foundation for effective chart creation.

Once your data is set, select the range of cells you want to visualize. In this case, highlight the cells containing

Neighborhood Names and their corresponding Average Prices. This selection informs Excel about the specific information you wish to convert into a chart.

Next, navigate to the "Insert" tab on the Ribbon. Here, you'll find various chart options within the Charts group. To create a column chart, click on the Column Chart icon and choose your preferred style from the dropdown menu. Clustered column charts are particularly effective for comparing categories like neighborhood prices.

After inserting your chart, you'll see it alongside your data on the worksheet. This is the perfect time to refine it for clarity and aesthetics. Click on the chart title to rename it—consider something descriptive like "Average Property Prices by Neighborhood." This will help viewers immediately grasp what they are looking at.

You can also customize your chart's colors by selecting different sections of the bars or columns and choosing a color scheme that aligns with your branding or highlights specific data points. Take this example, if one neighborhood has significantly higher prices than others, using a distinct color can emphasize that important insight.

To further improve readability, consider adding data labels directly onto your columns or bars. Right-click on any bar within your chart and select "Add Data Labels." This feature displays actual figures above each bar, ensuring viewers can easily interpret trends without guessing at numbers.

Having created a basic column chart, let's turn our attention to bar charts, which serve a similar purpose but are particularly useful for comparing values when dealing with long category names or numerous entries that might clutter vertical space.

To create a bar chart using the same dataset of average property prices across neighborhoods, follow similar steps: select the range of cells again and return to the "Insert" tab. This time, opt for the Bar Chart option instead of Column

Chart from the dropdown menu.

Once inserted, adjust its orientation if necessary—bar charts often provide better readability for long neighborhood names because they allow for horizontal spacing rather than vertical stacking. Just like with column charts, customize titles and colors while adding relevant data labels for clarity.

As these visuals take shape, consider how they can be utilized during client presentations or marketing materials. When showcasing properties at open houses or meetings with potential buyers or sellers, having these visuals readily available can significantly enhance discussions about pricing strategies or market trends.

Take this example, if you're presenting investment opportunities in different areas using bar charts that depict price growth over recent years alongside predicted future values, you can effectively illustrate potential returns for clients interested in investment properties.

Finally, remember that Excel also offers features like trendlines within these graphs, which help illustrate market directions more comprehensively. This is particularly useful when discussing long-term investment prospects with clients seeking reassurance about their financial decisions.

In summary, mastering column and bar charts in Excel not only enriches your presentations but also equips you with powerful tools that enhance client understanding and engagement—key components in building trust within real estate relationships. As you become proficient in creating these visual representations of data insights, you'll find them invaluable in facilitating informed decision-making processes for both you and your clients alike.

Understanding Line and Area Charts

Understanding line and area charts is essential for real estate professionals looking to convey trends and comparisons effectively. While column and bar charts work well for categorical data, line and area charts excel in displaying information over a continuous range. This makes them particularly suited for visualizing changes in property values over time and analyzing market trends.

To create a line chart in Excel, begin by organizing your data. For example, suppose you are tracking the price fluctuations of a specific property type over several years. Your dataset should include columns for Year and Average Price, structured like this:

| Year | Average Price |

| 2018 | (300,000 |

| 2019 |)320,000 |

| 2020 | (310,000 |

| 2021 |)350,000 |

| 2022 | (400,000 |

After organizing your data, select the range of cells that includes both the Year and Average Price columns. With the data highlighted, navigate to the "Insert" tab on the Ribbon. In the Charts group, click on "Insert Line or Area Chart" and choose the "Line" option from the dropdown menu.

Once your chart appears on the worksheet, it's important to customize it for clarity. A well-defined title is crucial; click on the default title to edit it. Consider using a title like "Average Property Prices Over Time" to help viewers quickly grasp what they are analyzing.

To further enhance readability, add data markers to your line chart. Right-click on the line itself and select "Add Data Labels." This feature displays specific values at each point along the line, allowing clients to see exact figures without having to estimate based on the graph alone.

Area charts can be especially useful when you want to

emphasize volume or magnitude alongside trends. They function similarly to line charts but fill the area beneath the line with color. To create an area chart using your dataset, repeat the selection process and choose "Insert Area Chart" from the dropdown menu instead of Line Chart.

As with line charts, customization is vital for making area charts effective communication tools. Consider changing colors for better visibility or using contrasting colors for different datasets. Take this example, if you're comparing two property types over time—like single-family homes and condos—you can assign distinct colors to each category's area.

If you're comparing datasets with significantly different scales —such as average home prices alongside average rental rates— consider utilizing secondary axes. To add a secondary axis:

1. Select one of your data series.

2. Right-click and choose "Format Data Series.

3. In the Format Data Series pane that opens on the right side of Excel, select "Secondary Axis.

This adjustment ensures both datasets are displayed clearly without misrepresentation due to scale differences.

Another powerful feature in Excel is adding trendlines to your charts, which can be particularly beneficial when forecasting future prices based on historical trends. Right-click on any data series within your chart and select "Add Trendline." You can choose from various options like linear or exponential, depending on which best fits your dataset.

Take this example, if you're showing how property prices have steadily increased but recently experienced volatility due to market fluctuations, an exponential trendline might illustrate potential future increases more accurately than a linear one would.

Using line and area charts can greatly enhance client

presentations by providing clear visual evidence of market trends and price trajectories. During meetings or open houses focused on investment potential or pricing strategies, these visuals support claims with hard data that resonates more powerfully than numbers alone.

By mastering these types of charts in Excel and understanding their proper applications, you equip yourself as a real estate agent with persuasive tools that help clients visualize complex information quickly and intuitively. Presenting dynamic market changes compellingly builds trust and enhances decision-making processes for both you and your clients.

As you explore Excel's capabilities with visualizations like line and area charts, remember that these tools not only refine your presentations but also elevate your professional image as someone proficient in both real estate markets and analytical tools—an invaluable combination in today's competitive landscape.

Pie and Doughnut Charts for Visualizing Shares

Pie and doughnut charts are invaluable tools for real estate agents looking to present data in a clear and compelling way. These chart types excel at illustrating proportional relationships, making them particularly effective for analyzing market shares, property type distributions, or client demographics. By using these charts, agents can quickly convey how different segments contribute to the overall picture, providing crucial insights for any real estate professional.

Creating a pie chart in Excel is a simple process. Start by organizing your data in a straightforward format. Take this example, if you're examining the distribution of property types sold in your area over the past year, your dataset might look like this:

| Property Type | Number Sold |

| Single-family Home | 150 |

| Condo | 75 |

| Townhouse | 50 |

| Multi-family | 25 |

Once your data is structured, select the range that includes both the property types and their corresponding sales numbers. Next, go to the "Insert" tab on the Ribbon, click on "Insert Pie or Doughnut Chart," and choose "Pie Chart" from the dropdown options.

After inserting the pie chart, it's important to customize it for clarity and impact. Start by adding a descriptive title, such as "Distribution of Properties Sold in 2023," which will help viewers immediately understand what they are looking at.

To enhance your pie chart's informational value, consider adding data labels that display percentages alongside the sales figures. You can do this by right-clicking on any section of the pie chart and selecting "Add Data Labels." For greater clarity, you might prefer to show percentages instead of raw numbers, allowing viewers to easily grasp each category's contribution to total sales.

Doughnut charts follow a similar process but feature a hollow center that can be used for additional information or even another dataset. This characteristic is especially useful when you want to display two related datasets side by side, such as comparing property sales from one year to another.

For example, if you wish to illustrate property sales from 2022 alongside those from 2023 using a doughnut chart, organize your data like this:

| Property Type | Sales 2022 | Sales 2023 |

| Single-family Home | 120 | 150 |

| Condo | 60 | 75 |

| Townhouse | 30 | 50 |

| Multi-family | 20 | 25 |

Highlight the entire dataset and insert a doughnut chart just as you would with a pie chart. To create two concentric rings representing each year's sales figures, use Excel's formatting options to adjust the number of doughnuts displayed.

Color customization in both pie and doughnut charts is crucial for maintaining viewer engagement and understanding. Use contrasting colors for different segments to ensure clarity. For example, assign warm tones to one year's sales data and cool tones to another year's data in your doughnut chart for quick visual differentiation.

Another powerful aspect of these charts is their ability to highlight significant changes over time or between categories. If you notice that single-family homes have seen a substantial increase in sales compared to other categories, consider using a larger slice or emphasizing that segment with bolder colors to draw immediate attention.

When presenting this information in meetings with clients or colleagues, pie and doughnut charts serve not just as aesthetic visuals but also as strategic tools that facilitate discussions about market dynamics. Clients often respond more positively to visual representations than raw data; these charts help them grasp complex information effortlessly.

While these charts can greatly enhance your presentations, it's essential to avoid overcrowding them with too many categories. Aim to limit your pie chart segments to five or six at most; otherwise, clarity may suffer as viewers struggle to interpret smaller slices.

By utilizing pie and doughnut charts effectively, you can elevate your analytical capabilities in real estate. Presenting insights clearly and engagingly not only builds client trust but also reinforces your position as a knowledgeable professional capable of translating complex data into actionable strategies for success. Each time you employ these visualizations in your practice, remember they represent not just statistics but opportunities—opportunities for growth and informed decision-making in an ever-evolving market landscape.

Scatter Plots for Comparative Analysis

Scatter plots are a vital tool for real estate agents seeking to analyze and visualize relationships between two variables. These graphs allow you to plot data points based on their values, making it easier to identify trends, correlations, and outliers within your datasets. Take this example, a scatter plot can effectively illustrate the relationship between property prices and square footage, revealing how these variables interact across various listings.

To create a scatter plot in Excel, start by organizing your data into two columns. If you want to explore how property sizes affect sale prices, your dataset might look like this:

| Square Footage | Sale Price |

| 1500 | 300000 |

| 1800 | 350000 |

| 2200 | 420000 |

| 2500 | 500000 |

| 3000 | 600000 |

With your data structured, select the range for both columns. Then, go to the "Insert" tab in the Ribbon and choose "Scatter Chart" from the chart options. Excel will generate a scatter plot that positions each property according to its square footage on the X-axis and sale price on the Y-axis.

To enhance clarity and understanding, it's essential to add chart elements. By clicking on the "Chart Elements" icon next to your chart, you can include axis titles and a chart title that clearly conveys what your scatter plot represents. For example, labeling the X-axis as "Square Footage (sq ft)" and the Y-axis as "Sale Price ())" enables viewers to quickly grasp the information being presented.

One of the most powerful features of scatter plots is their ability to reveal trends through trendlines. To add a linear trendline, right-click on any data point within your scatter plot and select "Add Trendline." This line visually represents the overall direction of your data points—whether they cluster around an upward or downward slope. In real estate analysis, an upward trend may indicate that larger homes typically command higher prices, which is crucial information when pricing properties or advising clients.

Additionally, adjusting the formatting of your data points can improve readability. You might consider changing their colors or shapes based on additional criteria such as property type or region. For example, using different shapes for single-family homes versus condos allows viewers to distinguish between categories at a glance while still observing overall trends.

Scatter plots also serve as a practical tool for identifying outliers—data points that significantly deviate from others in your dataset. If one property's size is much larger than typical for its price point, this could signal a unique opportunity or a potential risk for buyers. By highlighting such outliers with distinct colors or markers, you draw attention to critical factors that may warrant further investigation.

The combination of visual representation and analytical insights is invaluable in discussions with clients or stakeholders. Effectively using scatter plots simplifies complex information and fosters informed conversations about market dynamics. Clients often prefer clear visuals over raw numbers; presenting them with easy-to-understand graphics not only enhances your professionalism but also showcases your analytical skills.

While scatter plots offer substantial insights, it's important to handle data ranges carefully; ensure that both variables are accurately represented without any gaps in information. Misleading graphs can undermine trust and credibility.

By employing scatter plots effectively, you can significantly elevate your real estate analysis capabilities. Visualizing relationships between factors such as size and price uncovers valuable insights that empower strategic decision-making. Each time you incorporate scatter plots into your practice, recognize their potential not just as representations of data but as gateways to deeper understanding—insights that translate into successful transactions and satisfied clients navigating a complex marketplace landscape.

Using Sparklines for Quick Data Insights

Sparklines are a powerful yet often underutilized feature in Excel, offering quick visual insights into data trends without cluttering your spreadsheets. These miniature charts fit neatly within a single cell, making them ideal for summarizing large datasets at a glance. For real estate agents, sparklines can provide immediate visual cues about market trends, property performance, and sales fluctuations over time.

To create sparklines, start by selecting the cells where you want to display these visual summaries. For example, if you're tracking monthly sales figures for various properties, your dataset might look like this:

| Property Name | January | February | March | April | May |

| House A | 250000 | 270000 | 300000| 290000| 320000 |

| House B | 150000 | 160000 | 170000| 180000| 190000 |

| House C | 350000 | 360000 | 370000| 380000| 390000 |

Once your data is organized, highlight the cells where you want to add sparklines. Navigate to the "Insert" tab in the Ribbon and select "Sparklines." You will then be prompted to choose the data range corresponding to each property's sales figures. After clicking "OK," Excel will generate sparklines right next to your selected properties.

These small charts effectively communicate trends. Take this example, if House A demonstrates a consistent upward trajectory in sales over the months while House B remains relatively flat, it quickly indicates which property is performing better in the market. This information can be crucial when advising clients on investment opportunities or pricing strategies.

To further enhance the effectiveness of your sparklines, customize their appearance using options available in the Sparkline Tools Design tab. You can modify colors to indicate performance—using green for increases and red for decreases —or add markers for significant data points like peaks and troughs. These enhancements enable you to convey even more information at a glance.

Consider placing sparklines alongside other key metrics such as average sale prices or inventory levels in your reports. For example, if you have monthly inventory levels displayed in one column, adding corresponding sparklines will help visualize whether inventory is increasing or decreasing relative to sales over time.

Integrating sparklines into dashboards that summarize overall market conditions can also be beneficial. Picture a dashboard showcasing various properties with their corresponding sales trends depicted through sparklines; this layout allows stakeholders to quickly grasp complex market dynamics without having to sift through extensive numbers.

While sparklines provide immediate insights, it's essential not to overlook context. Always accompany them with brief explanations that highlight what these trends mean for real estate decisions. Take this example, a sharp increase in sales for a particular neighborhood, as shown by sparklines, may warrant further investigation into local factors driving demand—such as new amenities or schools that have recently opened.

Be mindful of the limitations of sparklines; they lack detailed labels and axes, meaning they should complement rather than replace comprehensive data presentations. Use them strategically alongside more extensive analyses when presenting to clients or stakeholders who may desire deeper insights into specific numbers.

Incorporating sparklines into your Excel toolkit enhances your ability to present data clearly and effectively. They offer an immediate snapshot of trends that not only aids personal analysis but also fosters clearer communication with clients and colleagues alike. As you continue to utilize these tools, recognize how they empower you to synthesize information quickly—transforming complex datasets into intuitive visuals that can drive strategic decision-making in real estate transactions.

Mastering the effective use of sparklines will undoubtedly set you apart as an agent who not only knows their numbers but also understands their implications on market behavior and client needs—a valuable combination in today's competitive real estate landscape.

Customizing Chart Elements

Customizing chart elements in Excel is essential for enhancing the clarity and impact of your data visualizations. A thoughtfully designed chart not only conveys information but also tells a story, highlighting key insights and making data more accessible. By adjusting various elements—such as titles, labels, colors, and styles—you can turn ordinary charts into powerful communication tools that truly engage your audience.

Start with the title of your chart. A clear, descriptive title immediately informs viewers about the data being represented. Instead of using a generic title like "Sales Data," opt for something more specific, such as "Monthly Sales

Trends for Residential Properties in 2023." This not only captures attention but also provides context. To change the title, simply click on the existing text in your chart and type in your new title. You can further enhance it by modifying the font style or size to make it stand out.

Next, pay attention to your axis labels. These labels are crucial for providing context about what the data points represent. For example, when comparing property sales over several months, label your X-axis as "Months" and your Y-axis as "Sales Amount (()." You can edit these labels by selecting the desired axis and accessing the "Axis Options" menu, where you can customize font size, color, and orientation to improve readability.

Colors also play a vital role in how viewers interpret data. When designing charts, choose a color palette that aids understanding rather than complicating it. Take this example, using shades of green to represent sales increases and shades of red for decreases can intuitively convey trends. To modify colors in Excel, click on the chart element you wish to change —whether it's bars, lines, or slices—and select "Format" from the context menu. You can choose solid fills or gradients that align with your branding or personal preference.

Legends are another important element that should not be overlooked. They clarify what different colors or patterns signify within your chart. If you're displaying multiple datasets—such as various properties or time periods—ensure your legend is clear and easy to understand. Position it where it does not obscure the chart while keeping it prominent enough for quick reference.

Gridlines can help viewers track values across a chart; however, too many can clutter your visualization. Consider simplifying them by reducing their number or changing their color to a lighter shade for less distraction. You can adjust these settings through the "Format Gridlines" option by right-clicking on them.

Another effective customization technique is adding data labels directly onto your chart elements. These labels provide immediate access to specific data points without requiring viewers to reference axes. For example, in a bar chart showing sales per property, labeling each bar with its exact sales figure enhances clarity. Simply right-click on any bar or point in your chart and select "Add Data Labels" from the menu to display values alongside corresponding graphical elements.

If you want to emphasize particular data points—such as record-high sales—consider using callouts or annotations. This approach draws attention directly to significant insights within the broader dataset. Take this example, if one month shows an unusually high number of sales due to a new development in the area, use an arrow or callout box pointing to that point with a brief note explaining why this spike occurred.

Lastly, strive for consistency in style across all charts you create for reports or presentations. A cohesive visual style reinforces professionalism and makes it easier for clients or colleagues to digest information across multiple charts. Maintaining similar colors, fonts, and layout styles creates a unified look that enhances overall comprehension.

With these strategies for customizing chart elements at your fingertips, you're ready to present data in ways that captivate and inform effectively. By transforming basic charts into polished visual narratives, you enhance not only your reports but also facilitate better decision-making among stakeholders. As you hone these skills, remember that every detail counts; each customized element contributes to building a clearer picture of complex datasets—one that resonates deeply with those seeking insights in today's competitive real estate market.

Choosing the Right Chart Type

Choosing the right chart type for your data is essential for effectively conveying insights. In real estate, where information can range from property prices to market trends, selecting the most appropriate chart can significantly enhance your message. A well-chosen chart not only improves comprehension but also highlights the critical elements of your analysis.

Begin by evaluating the nature of your data. Take this example, if you want to illustrate trends over time—such as fluctuations in property prices over several months—a line chart is typically the best choice. This format allows viewers to visualize changes easily and identify patterns. To create a line chart in Excel, simply highlight your data set, go to the "Insert" tab, select "Line Chart," and pick your preferred style. This will provide a clear representation of how property values have changed, facilitating quick analysis of market dynamics.

When comparing quantities across different categories, bar charts are particularly effective. They offer straightforward visual comparisons that enable viewers to quickly discern which properties are performing better than others. To build a bar chart, select your data range, click on "Insert," and then choose "Bar Chart." You can further customize it by adjusting colors and labels for improved clarity.

If your goal is to illustrate proportions—such as the share of various property types sold within a year—a pie chart may be beneficial. While pie charts can be criticized for lacking precision compared to other types, they excel at providing a quick visual representation of parts relative to a whole. To create one in Excel, select your data and choose "Pie Chart" from the "Insert" menu. Remember to limit the number of slices; too many categories can complicate interpretation.

Scatter plots are another powerful tool for analyzing relationships between two variables. For example, you might explore how square footage correlates with selling price across different properties. By plotting this data on a scatter plot, you can visually assess any correlations or trends that emerge. To create a scatter plot, select both variable sets and click on "Insert," followed by "Scatter." This will help you determine whether larger homes tend to command higher prices or if there's variability within certain price ranges.

Area charts are also worth considering when you want to emphasize changes in volume over time while displaying multiple datasets simultaneously. This is particularly useful for illustrating total sales figures alongside average prices in an overlapping format. Area charts effectively combine elements of line and bar charts; just ensure that each dataset remains distinct through appropriate color differentiation.

Audience engagement is another critical factor when choosing a chart type. If you're presenting data to clients or stakeholders, consider their familiarity with various visualizations. Simpler formats like bar or pie charts often resonate better with non-technical audiences compared to more complex scatter plots or line graphs filled with technical jargon.

Don't overlook the importance of interactivity in modern presentations. Tools like Excel allow you to create dynamic charts that respond to user inputs or filters—enabling viewers to explore data tailored specifically for their needs without overwhelming them with information all at once.

In the end, selecting the right chart type hinges not only on what best represents your data but also on how well it aligns with your audience's understanding and interests. Take time during your preparation phase to experiment with different visualizations for the same dataset; this practice will clarify what works best before sharing insights with others.

As you develop this skill set, keep in mind that each type of chart has its strengths and weaknesses. The key lies in matching those characteristics with the story you wish to tell through your data visualization efforts. By mastering this process, you'll be able not only to present numbers but also to foster meaningful discussions driven by clear insights and informed decisions within the competitive landscape of real estate.

CHAPTER 7: UTILIZING PIVOTTABLES FOR REAL ESTATE DATA

Introduction to PivotTables

PivotTables in Excel are a powerful feature that can significantly simplify data analysis for real estate professionals. As you explore the intricacies of your market data, PivotTables will become invaluable tools for summarizing and organizing complex datasets without the burden of manual calculations. They enable you to transform raw data into insightful reports, allowing you to easily identify trends, compare properties, and assess market conditions at a glance.

To begin mastering this tool, start with a well-structured dataset. Ideally, your data should be organized in rows and columns with clear headers. For example, consider a dataset containing property sales details such as sale price, location, square footage, and agent names. This structured layout is essential because it allows Excel to process the information accurately.

Creating your first PivotTable is straightforward. Begin by highlighting the range of cells containing your data. Next, navigate to the "Insert" tab on the Excel ribbon and select "PivotTable." A dialog box will appear, prompting you to choose whether to place the PivotTable in a new worksheet or an existing one. Opting for "New Worksheet" typically provides more space for analysis and visualization. After clicking "OK," Excel will generate a blank PivotTable field list on the right side of your screen, ready for customization.

With your PivotTable set up, it's time to populate it with relevant data fields. Drag and drop fields from your dataset into different areas—Rows, Columns, Values, and Filters—in the field list. Take this example, if you want to analyze sales by location, drag the "Location" field into Rows. To display total sales figures, place the "Sale Price" field in Values. Excel automatically summarizes this data for you, calculating totals or averages based on your specifications.

One of the key strengths of PivotTables is their flexibility. You can easily rearrange fields to explore various aspects of your data without starting from scratch each time. For example, if you want to examine how property sizes relate to selling prices across different locations, simply move the "Square Footage" field into Columns while keeping "Location" in Rows. Instantly, you'll gain insights into which property sizes perform best in various regions.

Filtering options further enhance your ability to refine your analysis. You can use filters to focus on specific property types or price ranges that interest you most. By dragging fields like "Property Type" or "Price Range" into the Filters area of the PivotTable field list, you can dynamically adjust which subset of data is displayed based on relevant criteria at any given moment.

To illustrate this functionality: suppose you're examining

high-end properties in a particular neighborhood. Applying a filter enables you to concentrate solely on luxury listings above a certain price threshold while excluding lower-priced properties from view. This focused analysis empowers decision-making regarding marketing strategies or investment opportunities tailored specifically for high-value segments.

Visual representation also plays an important role when using PivotTables for reporting purposes; integrating charts alongside your table enhances clarity and engagement when presenting findings to clients or colleagues. Once you've generated insights within a PivotTable, contextually relevant charts can be created by selecting any cell within it and navigating back to "Insert" to choose from line charts or bar graphs that best convey what you've discovered.

By mastering these techniques, you'll not only streamline your workflow but also develop a deeper understanding of how real estate dynamics function through visible data patterns —providing you with an advantage during negotiations and enabling effective communication of trends to stakeholders seeking actionable insights from today's evolving markets.

As you continue exploring this powerful feature of Excel along with other analytical tools throughout our journey together here, embracing its capabilities will yield substantial rewards in navigating the complexities inherent in real estate while fostering better outcomes both personally and organizationally!

Creating PivotTables from Real Estate Data

Creating a PivotTable from your real estate data is an essential skill that can significantly enhance your ability to analyze market trends and performance metrics. By understanding how PivotTables function, you can transform raw datasets into actionable insights specifically designed for real estate analysis.

Begin by preparing your data. Picture a spreadsheet filled with property sales information, including columns for sale prices, locations, square footage, and agent names. A well-structured dataset is critical, as it enables Excel to interpret and summarize the information accurately. If your data contains empty rows or inconsistent headers, now is the perfect time to tidy it up.

To create a PivotTable, start by highlighting the entire range of your dataset, including the headers. Next, navigate to the "Insert" tab in the Excel ribbon and select "PivotTable." A dialog box will prompt you to choose where you want to place your new PivotTable: in a new worksheet or an existing one. Opting for "New Worksheet" provides a clean slate for detailed analysis without distractions.

After clicking "OK," Excel will display a blank PivotTable field list on the right side of your screen. This is where the real work begins. You can start dragging fields into various areas —Rows, Columns, Values, and Filters—to build your analysis framework. For example, if you're interested in sales figures by location, drag the "Location" field into Rows. To calculate total sales for each location, move the "Sale Price" field into Values. Instantly, Excel compiles this data for you.

What makes PivotTables particularly powerful is their flexibility. You can effortlessly rearrange fields to examine different aspects of your dataset without needing to recreate anything from scratch. Take this example, if you want to explore how square footage correlates with sale prices across locations, simply drag "Square Footage" into Columns while keeping "Location" in Rows. This adjustment provides immediate insights into which property sizes yield higher sales in specific regions.

Additionally, filters enhance the functionality of PivotTables by allowing you to narrow down data based on specific criteria. By dragging fields like "Property Type" or "Price

Range" into the Filters area of the field list, you can customize what data appears according to your current focus. For example, if you're analyzing luxury homes, applying a filter lets you isolate properties above a certain price point while excluding more affordable listings.

To visualize this process: imagine filtering down to high-end properties within a particular neighborhood that might attract potential investors. With just a few clicks, you can concentrate solely on these listings, gaining insights into market demand and pricing strategies that align with the expectations of affluent buyers.

And, enhancing your PivotTable with visual aids can greatly improve clarity when presenting findings. After deriving insights from your data table, consider creating charts to visually represent these trends for clients or team members. To do this effectively, click on any cell within your PivotTable and return to the "Insert" tab. Choose chart types such as bar graphs or line charts that best illustrate your findings.

By embracing these techniques, you not only streamline your workflow but also sharpen your analytical skills in real estate dynamics. This knowledge equips you with valuable insights during negotiations and discussions with stakeholders who rely on informed decision-making based on current market conditions.

Sorting, Filtering, and Grouping

Sorting, filtering, and grouping data in Excel are vital skills for real estate agents who want to enhance their analysis and decision-making processes. By organizing your data effectively, you can uncover valuable insights that drive strategic actions in your business. These techniques enable you to manage large datasets efficiently, allowing you to identify trends and patterns that might otherwise remain hidden.

Let's begin with sorting. This straightforward yet powerful

tool allows you to quickly organize your data. Take this example, if you have a list of properties detailing their location, sale price, and square footage, you can sort the data by selecting the column header you want to focus on—let's say "Sale Price." By navigating to the "Data" tab in the Excel ribbon and clicking either the "Sort A to Z" or "Sort Z to A" button, you can easily rearrange your listings from lowest to highest price or vice versa. Sorting by sale price is particularly beneficial for identifying affordable options for first-time homebuyers or highlighting high-value listings that may attract luxury buyers.

Next, filtering takes your analysis a step further by enabling you to view specific subsets of your data. Imagine you're interested in properties within a certain price range or in particular neighborhoods. By clicking on the filter icon in the column header, you can access dropdown menus for each column. For example, if you want to see properties priced between)300,000 and (500,000, simply set those parameters within the "Sale Price" filter. Excel will then hide all other rows that don't meet your criteria, allowing you to concentrate solely on the listings that align with your current needs.

Grouping can be particularly useful when working with extensive datasets that require summarization. Suppose you want to analyze sales performance over different months or quarters. Start by selecting your dataset and navigating back to the "Data" tab. Choose "Group," and then specify how you want to group your data—whether by month or another time frame. This process condenses detailed listings into summarized views that display total sales for each month, giving you an at-a-glance perspective of market trends over time.

For maximum effect, consider applying these techniques together. After sorting and filtering your properties by type and price range, you can group them by neighborhood to gain deeper insights into local markets. This layered analysis not only reveals which properties are available but also highlights where specific types of homes are concentrated, enabling targeted marketing efforts.

The combination of sorting, filtering, and grouping creates a dynamic environment for data exploration. For example, when preparing a report for a client interested in investment opportunities across various neighborhoods, these tools allow you to present organized information clearly and efficiently. You can illustrate potential growth areas based on historical sales data combined with current market conditions.

To further enhance your findings, consider creating charts after your analysis. Take this example, after filtering for high-demand areas with properties under)400,000, you could generate a bar chart that displays average sale prices in these neighborhoods. Such visual representations help clients quickly grasp market dynamics and make your presentations more persuasive during discussions.

As real estate transactions rely heavily on accurate data interpretation and timely decision-making, mastering these skills can significantly improve your efficiency and effectiveness in this role. With well-sorted and filtered data at your fingertips, you'll be better positioned to seize opportunities as they arise while delivering exceptional value to your clients.

In summary, sorting allows for quick organization of datasets; filtering provides focused insights into specific categories; and grouping aggregates information for clearer trend analysis —all essential components of effective real estate data management. As you continue honing these skills within Excel's framework, consider how each technique complements the others to create a comprehensive view of your real estate landscape.

Utilizing Slicers and Timelines

Slicers and timelines significantly enhance your data analysis capabilities in Excel, transforming how you engage with complex datasets. As a real estate agent, these tools enable intuitive filtering of information, allowing you to present insights to clients and stakeholders more effectively. By incorporating slicers and timelines into your workflow, you can create an engaging user experience that simplifies data exploration.

Let's start with slicers. Think of them as interactive visual buttons that simplify the process of filtering data. For example, if you have a table that lists properties along with various attributes such as location, price range, and property type, a slicer can help you isolate specific categories without navigating through multiple menus. To add a slicer, select your data table and go to the "Insert" tab in the Excel ribbon. Click on "Slicer" and choose the fields you want to filter by—let's say "Property Type." A window will appear, allowing you to select the property types (e.g., single-family homes or condos) that you want to include in your view. Once inserted, the slicer will display as a separate panel on your worksheet.

After adding the slicer, clicking any button within it instantly updates your data view to reflect your selections. Take this example, if you're presenting options to a client who is interested only in condos within a specific price range, they can simply click on "Condos" in the slicer while you apply price filters through another method. This immediacy fosters more informed discussions and quicker decision-making.

Timelines are another powerful feature, specifically designed for analyzing date-related data. Imagine you have property sales data spanning several years with seasonal fluctuations. To analyze these trends effectively, insert a timeline by selecting your date field from the same "Insert" tab where you accessed slicers. Timelines appear as horizontal bars that allow users to filter data by days, months, quarters, or years at a glance.

For example, if you're assessing quarterly sales performance over the last three years for different neighborhoods, dragging the timeline slider will dynamically adjust your dataset to reflect only the selected dates. This capability facilitates swift comparisons across time periods; you might want to demonstrate how sales surged during certain seasons or declined at others—insights that are crucial for planning future marketing campaigns.

The true power of slicers and timelines emerges when they are used together. Consider preparing a comprehensive market analysis report where potential buyers are interested in properties based not only on type but also on availability within specific time frames. By filtering by property type with a slicer and adjusting timelines for relevant quarters or years, you can effortlessly showcase trends that highlight market changes over time.

To further visualize your findings and enhance presentations for clients or team meetings, consider combining filtered results with charts or graphs. Take this example, illustrating average sale prices over quarters alongside property type distribution can provide compelling insights into market dynamics.

Let's walk through a practical example: You've created a dataset containing several properties across various neighborhoods, with their sale dates and types (single-family homes versus condos) listed. The first step? Insert both a slicer for "Property Type" and a timeline based on "Sale Date." Now imagine conducting an analysis focused on condos sold between January 2021 and December 2022 in specific neighborhoods—this combination empowers you to deliver highly relevant insights quickly.

In summary, these tools work together seamlessly: Slicers offer an interactive way to visually filter categories while timelines facilitate focused examination of date-based trends.

Mastering these techniques not only enhances your personal efficiency but also positions you as an authority capable of clearly and confidently interpreting complex datasets in front of clients. Embrace these features within Excel; they are essential tools for elevating your presentations and overall business strategy in the competitive real estate landscape.

PivotCharts for Dynamic Data Visualization

Creating PivotCharts in Excel opens up new avenues for data visualization, especially for real estate agents aiming to convey complex information in a clear and engaging manner. These dynamic visualizations not only enhance your data analysis capabilities but also empower you to present findings that resonate with clients and stakeholders.

A PivotChart is closely linked to a PivotTable, allowing you to visualize the summarized data from your table in a graphical format. This powerful combination helps reveal patterns and trends that might otherwise go unnoticed in raw data. For example, if you've created a PivotTable summarizing property sales by neighborhood and price range, transforming this into a PivotChart enables you to quickly identify which neighborhoods are performing best.

To create a PivotChart, start by generating a PivotTable from your dataset. Select your data range, navigate to the "Insert" tab on the ribbon, and choose "PivotTable." Once your table is set up, click anywhere within it, return to the "Insert" tab, and select "PivotChart." You will then be prompted to choose the chart type that best represents your data—options include bar charts, line graphs, pie charts, and more.

Take this example, if you want to illustrate the average sale price of properties across different neighborhoods over the past year, set "Neighborhood" as rows in your PivotTable and "Sale Price" as values. With this structure in place, opting for a clustered column chart for your PivotChart allows viewers to easily compare price fluctuations across various areas.

One of the standout features of PivotCharts is their dynamic interactivity. When you adjust the underlying data or filter criteria in your associated PivotTable—using slicers or timelines—the chart updates automatically. This real-time interaction enhances clients' understanding of changes or trends during presentations.

Imagine presenting sales data at an open house event. By having a live connection between your PivotChart and its source data via slicers that filter by property types or price ranges, prospective buyers can see real-time market trends as they inquire about specific areas or types of homes. This responsiveness not only engages clients but also fosters trust through transparency.

Another powerful aspect of PivotCharts is their ability to display multiple metrics simultaneously without overwhelming viewers. For example, you could create a combination chart that shows average sale prices as columns while displaying sales volume as lines on the same graph. This dual representation allows clients to grasp not just how much properties are selling for but also how many units are moving within specific time frames—a critical insight when advising them on market conditions.

To illustrate this further, suppose you've collected quarterly sales figures from various neighborhoods over two years. After crafting your initial PivotTable summarizing these figures, you can insert a combined chart where sales volume appears as line markers above each quarter's respective bar representing average prices. This visualization effectively communicates both market activity and pricing trends simultaneously, providing clients with deeper insights into their buying or selling strategies.

Customizing your charts can further enhance their effectiveness; adjusting colors for different neighborhoods improves clarity during presentations or reports. Additionally, incorporating titles and labels directly on charts helps convey key takeaways quickly without requiring extensive explanation.

In the end, mastering PivotCharts equips agents with invaluable skills that can distinguish them in their marketing efforts. By integrating these visual tools into your analytical process, you can distill complex datasets into accessible narratives that guide client decisions confidently and effectively.

Embrace these capabilities within Excel; they will not only streamline your workflow but significantly elevate how you represent essential market insights in real estate transactions. The journey toward becoming an influential expert in your field begins with leveraging these powerful visualization tools —transforming raw numbers into compelling stories that inspire action.

Customizing Calculations in PivotTables

A key first step in customizing PivotTable calculations is to utilize calculated fields. These fields allow you to create new data points derived from existing fields in your dataset. For example, if you want to calculate total commissions based on property sales, you can create a calculated field that multiplies the sale price by the commission rate. Here's how to do it:

1. Select your PivotTable and navigate to the "PivotTable Analyze" tab.

2. Click on "Fields, Items & Sets," then choose "Calculated Field."

3. In the dialog box, give your new field a name—let's say "Total Commission.

4. In the formula box, enter = Sale Price * Commission Rate.

5. Click "OK," and your new field will appear in the

PivotTable.

This feature allows you to dynamically analyze commissions as you filter or adjust your dataset. Take this example, if you want to quickly identify which properties generated the highest commissions over the last quarter, having this calculated field in place enables you to manipulate filters easily and see updated results without needing additional calculations elsewhere.

In addition to calculated fields, value field settings provide further customization for how data is displayed in your PivotTable. If you're analyzing property sales and wish to see not just totals but also averages or percentages of totals, you can achieve this with just a few clicks:

1. Right-click on the value you wish to modify within your PivotTable.

2. Select "Value Field Settings."

3. Here, you'll find options like "Sum," "Average," "Count," and more.

4. Choose the desired function—let's say "Average" for average sale price—and click "OK."

With this adjustment, your PivotTable will now reflect average sale prices instead of totals. This flexibility allows for more nuanced presentations of data, which can be critical when discussing performance metrics with clients or team members.

Another effective way to customize calculations is by grouping dates within your data. For example, if you're analyzing property sales over several years and want to observe trends by quarter rather than by individual months or years, Excel makes this process straightforward:

1. Right-click on any date field within your PivotTable.

2. Select "Group."

3. Choose how you want to group your data—by months, quarters, or even years.

4. Click "OK," and watch as your data reorganizes itself into more meaningful intervals.

By grouping dates effectively, you can uncover trends that may not be immediately visible with raw monthly data alone.

It's also important to consider filtering data before it enters the PivotTable calculations themselves. If you're focusing exclusively on residential properties within a mixed dataset (including commercial properties), filtering out non-residential entries before running your analysis can streamline your insights:

1. Click on any dropdown arrow next to Row Labels or Column Labels.

2. Uncheck any categories that don't apply—in this case, commercial properties.

3. Your PivotTable will now reflect only residential transactions.

This targeted approach ensures that all subsequent calculations remain relevant and focused on what truly matters for your analysis.

Finally, utilizing slicers offers an interactive way for users to engage with PivotTable data while maintaining calculation integrity. Slicers provide a user-friendly interface for dynamically filtering data without requiring repeated navigation through menu options:

1. With your PivotTable selected, go to the "PivotTable Analyze" tab.

2. Click on "Insert Slicer.

3. Select the fields you'd like slicers for—such as property type or location—and click "OK.

Adding slicers allows anyone reviewing the PivotTable to filter results effortlessly through a simple click interface without altering the underlying calculations directly.

By mastering these customization techniques within PivotTables, you'll not only enhance your analytical capabilities but also improve how effectively you communicate insights drawn from complex datasets. The ability to tailor these calculations provides clarity and relevance—both essential for making informed real estate decisions in today's competitive market landscape.

Integrating External Data Sources

One of the easiest ways to integrate external data is by importing it from different file formats. If you receive property listings, sales figures, or market analyses in formats such as CSV or TXT files, bringing that information into Excel is straightforward. To get started:

1. Open Excel and go to the "Data" tab on the Ribbon.

2. Click on "Get Data," then select "From File" and choose "From Text/CSV."

3. Browse to find your file, select it, and click "Import."

4. Follow the prompts in the import wizard to adjust how your data is displayed, ensuring each column aligns correctly.

By efficiently importing data, you consolidate crucial information and enhance your analyses without the burden of manual entry. For example, if you regularly receive a CSV file containing updated market trends from a real estate database, integrating this directly into Excel allows for automatic updates to your reports and visualizations whenever you refresh the data.

In addition to static files, real-time data connections can be incredibly valuable. Many real estate agents utilize online databases or APIs (Application Programming Interfaces) to access live market information or property management systems. Excel's built-in functionality makes establishing these connections easy:

1. In the "Data" tab, click "Get Data" and choose "From Online Services."

2. Depending on the service you wish to connect to—such as Microsoft Azure or other web-based APIs—follow the prompts to authenticate your account.

3. Once connected, specify which datasets you'd like to pull into your workbook.

Imagine having immediate access to up-to-date housing market statistics right within your analysis spreadsheets; this capability not only saves time but also enhances accuracy in your decision-making processes.

Another powerful method for integrating external data is through Microsoft Power Query, which simplifies connecting, combining, and refining data from different sources before loading it into Excel:

1. Under the "Data" tab, select "Get Data" and then "From Other Sources," choosing "Blank Query."

2. In the Power Query Editor window that appears, enter your source URL or connect to another database as needed.

3. Use Power Query's interface to filter, sort, and transform your data into a usable format before loading it into Excel.

Take this example, if you're compiling sales data from multiple sources—like an MLS (Multiple Listing Service) along with a personal database of past clients—Power Query can help merge these datasets while allowing you to clean up inconsistencies along the way.

Additionally, Excel's ability to pull data from websites using web scraping techniques can provide valuable insights into market trends or competitor listings:

1. Return to the "Data" tab and select "Get Data," then choose "From Web."

2. Enter the URL of a site containing useful property information.

3. Excel will analyze the webpage structure and let you select specific tables or lists for import.

This approach can be especially beneficial when gathering comparable listings or analyzing local market conditions dynamically without needing manual updates.

To maximize effectiveness when integrating external sources, always ensure that you're validating and refreshing your data regularly. This practice helps maintain accuracy and reliability across your analyses:

- Set up automatic refresh settings by right-clicking on any imported table or connection.

- Select "Table" followed by "External Data Properties" where you can define how frequently you'd like Excel to pull fresh data—whether it's every time the file opens or at set intervals during active sessions.

In the end, mastering external data integration empowers real estate professionals to create compelling narratives supported by robust datasets—keeping them competitive in an ever-evolving landscape where information is crucial. Each connection established and dataset consolidated in one place transforms not just numbers but also enhances informed decision-making that stands out in presentations and strategy sessions alike.

CHAPTER 8:
MANAGING REAL
ESTATE CRM
WITH EXCEL

Designing a CRM Template

Designing an effective CRM template in Excel goes beyond mere aesthetics; it involves crafting a powerful tool that boosts your efficiency and effectiveness as a real estate agent. A well-structured CRM template enables you to manage relationships, track interactions, and analyze data in ways that can significantly impact your success. By concentrating on essential components and practical functionalities, you can create a template tailored to the unique demands of your real estate practice.

To set up this structure, open Excel and label your columns accordingly:

1. In cell A1, enter "Client Name.

2. In cell B1, input "Contact Number.

3. In cell C1, add "Email Address," followed by "Property

Preference" in D1.

4. Continue adding relevant columns based on your unique needs—consider including "Last Contact Date," "Next Follow-Up," or "Notes.

Once you've defined the necessary fields, focus on formatting for enhanced readability and usability. Utilize Excel's formatting tools to make your template user-friendly. For example, applying bold fonts to header rows distinguishes them from data entries. Additionally, using cell borders and alternating row colors improves visual clarity, making it easier to navigate through your information at a glance.

Next, think about incorporating data validation techniques to ensure accuracy in your entries. This can be achieved by restricting inputs in certain columns to predefined options or formats—such as ensuring phone numbers follow a specific format or creating dropdown lists for common property types (e.g., "Single Family Home," "Condo," "Land"). To implement this:

1. Select the column where you want to apply validation.

2. Navigate to the "Data" tab on the Ribbon and click "Data Validation."

3. Choose "List" from the options under "Allow," then input your predefined options separated by commas.

By establishing these validations early on, you reduce entry errors and maintain data consistency—an essential factor for generating reliable reports later.

Another useful feature is conditional formatting, which allows you to visually identify important information quickly. Take this example, if follow-up dates are approaching or have passed without action, you can set up conditional formatting to highlight these cells in red:

1. Select the relevant column containing follow-up dates.

2. Go to "Conditional Formatting" in the Ribbon.

3. Choose "Highlight Cells Rules," then "Less Than," and enter =TODAY() to flag overdue follow-ups.

This visual cue helps you prioritize client communications effectively, ensuring no lead slips through the cracks.

As you continue developing your CRM template, consider integrating hyperlinks for quick access to property listings or client websites within your document. You can easily hyperlink text within any cell by selecting it, right-clicking, and choosing "Hyperlink." This functionality allows instant access to additional information without cluttering your sheet with extra columns.

Tracking interactions is another vital aspect of a CRM system. Create a separate sheet within your workbook dedicated solely to logging calls or meetings with clients. Each entry should include columns for the date of interaction, method (phone/email/meeting), summary notes, and any action items arising from those discussions.

1. Label this new sheet as "Interaction Log.

2. Implement similar formatting strategies as before for consistency.

3. Use Excel's filtering capabilities on this sheet so you can quickly sort through interactions based on dates or clients.

Leveraging Excel's analytical tools enables you not only to manage client relationships but also to assess their value over time—informing business decisions based on concrete data rather than intuition alone.

Finally, regular updates are essential for maintaining an effective CRM system. Set aside time weekly or bi-weekly to review and refine your data entries, ensuring completeness and accuracy while reflecting any changes in client preferences or statuses.

Creating a comprehensive CRM template specifically tailored for real estate requires thoughtful consideration of both design and functionality; it must evolve alongside your business practices. By implementing these strategies—from foundational organization to advanced data techniques—you empower yourself not only to manage relationships more efficiently but also to enhance the quality of service provided to every client who engages with you. With each thoughtfully filled and formatted cell, you're laying the groundwork for deeper connections and smarter decision-making that contribute directly to greater success in your real estate endeavors.

Tracking Leads and Client Interactions

Effectively tracking leads and client interactions is crucial for real estate agents who want to stay competitive. Your CRM template serves not only as a database but also as a dynamic hub that promotes communication, strengthens client relationships, and ultimately drives sales. By systematically organizing and updating your tracking mechanisms, you can ensure that no detail slips through the cracks and that every potential opportunity is fully leveraged.

Begin by creating a dedicated worksheet in your Excel workbook for tracking leads. This worksheet should feature columns for essential data points such as lead name, source, status, priority level, and notes regarding the lead's preferences or concerns. This structured approach allows you to monitor each lead's position in the sales funnel, providing clarity on which relationships require nurturing or follow-up.

To set up this tracking sheet:

1. In cell A1, enter "Lead Name.

2. In cell B1, input "Lead Source" (e.g., Referral, Website).

3. Add "Status" in cell C1 (e.g., New, Follow-Up, Converted).

4. Include "Priority Level" in D1 to indicate urgency —consider using a dropdown list with options like High, Medium, or Low.

5. Finally, add a column labeled "Notes" to capture specific details relevant to each lead.

With the basic structure established, it's essential to leverage Excel's built-in functions to analyze your data effectively. Take this example, you can use the COUNTIF function to quickly determine how many leads fall into each status or priority category.

In your Status column (C), you might use the formula =COUNTIF(C2:C100,"New") to count all leads marked as "New," adjusting the range based on your expected number of entries.

By embedding this formula in your summary dashboard— perhaps on a separate sheet—you'll gain immediate visibility into how many leads are awaiting contact versus those ready for conversion discussions.

Regularly updating your lead tracking sheet after each client interaction is equally important. Whenever you communicate with a lead via email or phone call, log that interaction right away in your worksheet. To facilitate this process, add columns for Date of Interaction and Method of Communication (Phone/Email/In-Person). Keeping these records current provides valuable insights into engagement levels and informs your outreach strategies moving forward.

A systematic approach could look like this:

1. In cell E1, write "Date of Interaction.

2. In cell F1, enter "Method of Communication.

3. Ensure consistency in formatting by standardizing date entries—consider using "MM/DD/YYYY" to avoid confusion.

For a more sophisticated tracking mechanism, consider using Excel's conditional formatting features to flag leads that haven't been contacted within a specified timeframe. For example, you can set rules to highlight cells in the Date of Interaction column where the date exceeds 14 days.

When leads go too long without contact—a critical red flag—you'll receive an immediate visual cue prompting timely follow-ups.

Integration plays a key role in analyzing client interactions over time. You might create pivot tables summarizing engagement patterns based on source or status while keeping detailed logs for individual conversations. This method allows you to see which outreach methods yield high conversion rates while providing deeper insights into client preferences gleaned from notes taken during interactions.

Don't underestimate the impact of personalizing communications based on previous interactions recorded in your template; personalized outreach often fosters stronger client relationships. Take this example, if a client expressed interest in specific property features during initial discussions, ensure that information is easily accessible for future conversations.

As your network grows larger and more complex—and it will!—your tracking capabilities should evolve accordingly within Excel. Regularly reviewing both your lead sheet and interaction logs will help ensure everything remains relevant while providing opportunities for adjustments based on market trends or shifts in client expectations.

Through diligent management of leads and strategic documentation of interactions using Excel's powerful tools

—you're not just managing prospects; you're cultivating lasting partnerships built on trust and responsiveness. Each successful connection paves the way for increased referrals and repeat business—the cornerstones of sustainable growth in this ever-evolving industry landscape.

Scheduling Follow-ups and Meetings

In the fast-paced world of real estate, effectively scheduling follow-ups and meetings is crucial. Every interaction with a client or lead presents an opportunity to build trust, clarify expectations, and ultimately close deals. A well-organized schedule not only enhances your professionalism but also demonstrates your commitment to client satisfaction. Excel offers powerful tools to streamline this process, ensuring that no important follow-up slips through the cracks.

Start by creating a dedicated worksheet for scheduling follow-ups and meetings. This sheet will act as your central hub for managing appointments and facilitating timely communication with clients. Include essential columns such as the client's name, meeting date, time, status, and any relevant notes regarding the meeting's purpose or agenda.

Setting up your scheduling sheet is straightforward:

1. Label cell A1 as "Client Name.

2. In cell B1, enter "Meeting Date.

3. In cell C1, input "Meeting Time.

4. Use cell D1 for "Status" (e.g., Scheduled, Completed, Canceled).

5. Finally, dedicate cell E1 to "Notes" for capturing details about each meeting.

With this framework established, begin populating the sheet with upcoming meetings and follow-ups. Make it a habit to log these details immediately after setting an appointment to maintain accuracy and avoid confusion later on.

For example, if you schedule a follow-up call with a prospective buyer interested in a property they viewed last week, enter their name in column A, the planned call date in column B, and the time in column C. You can mark the meeting status as "Scheduled" in column D while using column E to jot down specific topics you want to discuss—such as their questions about financing options or updates on similar properties.

To further enhance your scheduling capabilities, consider utilizing Excel's conditional formatting feature to color-code your meetings based on their status. This visual aid allows you to quickly scan your schedule for pending follow-ups or completed meetings at a glance. Take this example, you could set rules to highlight entries marked "Scheduled" in yellow and those marked "Completed" in green. This simple distinction provides an immediate overview of your current engagements without extensive review.

Flexibility is vital when working with client schedules, as circumstances often change in real estate. Ensure that your scheduling worksheet allows for quick edits so you can easily adjust dates and times if a meeting needs to be rescheduled or canceled due to unforeseen circumstances—such as a last-minute property showing—without losing track of previous interactions.

Incorporating reminders into your workflow will also significantly enhance your scheduling effectiveness. While Excel doesn't have built-in alert functionalities like dedicated calendar applications, you can create reminders using tools like Outlook or Google Calendar linked to your Excel data. By setting reminders based on the dates entered in your worksheet, you'll receive notifications prompting timely follow-ups right at crucial moments.

Take this example, if you've scheduled a follow-up call for March 15th at 2 PM regarding that prospective buyer's financing questions, set an alert one day prior so you're reminded to prepare any necessary documentation or insights beforehand.

Regularly reviewing this sheet—perhaps weekly—will keep all appointments fresh in your mind while allowing room for adjustments as new leads emerge or existing relationships evolve. This proactive approach ensures you remain responsive and engaged with every client interaction.

And, don't overlook the power of analysis once you've gathered enough data on past meetings and follow-ups. You can use Excel's functions such as COUNTIF or AVERAGEIF to analyze how many leads convert after certain types of meetings or how long it typically takes from first contact until closing based on different engagement methods.

For example:

- To find out how many leads were successfully converted after an initial consultation meeting versus those who required multiple touchpoints before deciding—use COUNTIF with criteria set against statuses logged in column D.

- Or calculate average times between meetings and conversions by employing AVERAGEIF against dates logged—providing valuable insight into optimizing future interactions based on empirical data trends rather than assumptions alone.

In summary, mastering scheduling through Excel equips you with organized records while transforming each interaction into a strategic move toward nurturing client relationships more effectively over time. By leveraging these structured approaches alongside insightful analysis tools within Excel, you're not merely tracking tasks; you're strategically positioning yourself as an indispensable partner throughout each client's journey toward homeownership or investment success.

Automating Contact Information Entry

Automating contact information entry can significantly enhance your productivity as a real estate agent. In a field where time is crucial and accuracy is essential, implementing an automated system to manage client details can save you countless hours and minimize the risk of errors. Excel offers powerful tools for seamless data entry and organization, making it an excellent choice for this purpose.

Start by creating a dedicated worksheet specifically for client contact information. This sheet should include relevant columns that allow you to efficiently capture essential details. A recommended structure might consist of fields such as "First Name," "Last Name," "Email Address," "Phone Number," "Property Interests," and "Notes."

To set up your contact information worksheet, follow these steps:

1. In cell A1, label it "First Name.

2. In cell B1, enter "Last Name.

3. Designate cell C1 for "Email Address.

4. Use cell D1 for "Phone Number.

5. Label cell E1 as "Property Interests" to track the types of properties your clients are interested in.

6. Finally, allocate cell F1 for "Notes" to capture any additional pertinent details.

Once your worksheet is structured, you can begin populating it with client data. To streamline data entry further, consider utilizing Excel's data validation feature to create drop-down lists for fields like "Property Interests." This not only speeds up the process but also ensures consistency in how information is recorded.

Take this example, if several clients are interested in single-family homes versus condos, create a drop-down list in column E with these options. When adding a new client, you can simply select their property interest from the list instead of typing it out each time.

Another effective way to automate contact entry is by using Excel's built-in forms feature or creating user forms with VBA (Visual Basic for Applications). This allows you to design a simple form that prompts you for necessary details whenever you need to add a new contact. The data entered into this form will automatically populate your contact information sheet, reducing manual entry and minimizing typographical errors.

To create a basic user form in Excel:

1. Press Alt + F11 to open the Visual Basic Editor.

2. Insert a new UserForm by right-clicking on any item in the Project Explorer window and selecting "Insert" > "UserForm.

3. Add text boxes for each field (such as First Name and Last Name) along with command buttons (like Submit).

4. Write code that takes the input from these text boxes and places it into your worksheet.

This approach simplifies the process and promotes better data management habits, ensuring each addition is uniform and systematic.

Maintaining accuracy over time is another critical aspect of any automated system. Implementing conditional formatting can quickly highlight missing or incorrect entries within your contact list. For example, if an email address lacks an "@" symbol or if a phone number doesn't match the expected format, conditional formatting can shade those cells red until corrected.

And, consider linking this worksheet with external sources

such as web forms or CRM systems through APIs or connectors available in Excel's Power Query feature. This way, any time a potential lead fills out their information online—say through your website—it can automatically flow into your Excel workbook without requiring manual intervention on your part.

Regularly reviewing your contact database ensures that outdated information is updated promptly; set aside time weekly to verify entries against actual interactions or other communication logs you maintain elsewhere.

Once you've compiled enough client data, leveraging analytical functions within Excel can provide valuable insights into trends related to property interests or common inquiries among leads—information that can inform your marketing strategies moving forward.

Take this example, using COUNTIF functions will allow you to analyze how many clients are interested in specific types of properties based on their recorded interests. This knowledge can help tailor future outreach efforts effectively.

For example:

- If you're tracking interests in column E labeled "Property Interests," you could use the formula =COUNTIF(E:E,"Single-Family Home") to determine how many clients have expressed interest in single-family homes specifically.

By automating contact information entry through these methods in Excel, you not only enhance efficiency but also position yourself to engage more meaningfully with clients over time—transforming raw data into actionable insights that drive success in real estate transactions.

As this framework becomes second nature, you'll find yourself spending less time on administrative tasks and more time nurturing relationships that propel your career forward

—ensuring each interaction contributes to building trust and fostering long-term connections with clients eager for guidance on their real estate journeys.

Analyzing Client Data

Analyzing client data is a crucial step in refining your real estate strategies. With the vast amount of information generated from leads and clients, effective data analysis transforms raw numbers into actionable insights. The goal is not only to collect data but to understand and leverage it to inform your decisions, enhance marketing strategies, and improve client relationships.

Begin by organizing your client information in Excel. A well-structured spreadsheet provides the foundation for effective analysis. Building on your contact information worksheet from the previous section, consider adding columns that facilitate deeper insights. Take this example, including fields like "Last Contact Date," "Source of Lead," and "Client Status" can offer vital context for each entry.

Once you have these elements in place, you can start analyzing trends within your client base. Tracking how clients found you—whether through referrals, online ads, or open houses —can reveal which marketing channels are most effective. To analyze this data effectively:

1. Create a column labeled "Source of Lead" to categorize how each client discovered your services.

2. Add another column titled "Last Contact Date" to keep track of when you last communicated with each client.

With this structure established, you can use Excel's COUNTIF function to quantify the effectiveness of your outreach efforts. For example, if you want to determine how many clients originated from online ads, apply the formula:

=COUNTIF(G:G,"Online Ad")

This formula counts every instance of "Online Ad" in column G (your Source of Lead column), giving you immediate insight into successful campaigns.

Examining time intervals can also uncover patterns in client engagement. By calculating the average number of days between contacts, you can assess whether you're effectively nurturing leads or allowing them to slip through the cracks. To do this:

1. In a new column titled "Days Since Last Contact," input a formula that subtracts the current date from the date in "Last Contact Date."

2. Use: =TODAY()-H2 (assuming H2 contains your last contact date).

This method helps ensure timely follow-ups and strengthens relationships with potential clients.

Visualizing your data significantly enhances comprehension. Charts and graphs can illustrate trends over time or provide breakdowns by categories such as property interests or demographic data. Take this example, creating a pie chart that represents the percentage of clients interested in different property types allows you to easily identify where to concentrate your marketing efforts.

To create a chart:

1. Select the relevant data range.

2. Navigate to the Insert tab on the Ribbon and choose a chart type that meets your analysis needs—be it a pie chart for categorical distribution or a line graph for tracking interest over time.

These visuals convey findings more effectively than rows of numbers alone.

Another valuable feature in Excel is PivotTables, which enable dynamic data analysis without the need for complicated formulas. You can summarize client statuses or interests with just a few clicks. To create a PivotTable:

1. Select your entire dataset.

2. Go to Insert > PivotTable.

3. Choose where to place the table and click OK.

4. Drag fields like "Property Interests" into rows and "Count of Clients" into values.

This gives you a quick overview of how many clients are interested in various property types, making it easier to tailor your outreach efforts.

For example, if your data indicates that younger clients prefer condos while older clients lean towards single-family homes, adjusting your marketing messages accordingly can lead to better engagement rates.

Lastly, it's essential to regularly update and evaluate your data collection processes. Periodically assess whether new fields need to be added based on changing market conditions or shifts in client demographics—and ensure all team members are trained on entering and analyzing this information consistently.

By dedicating time to understanding and analyzing client data using Excel's capabilities, you're not merely managing names and numbers; you're developing strategic insights that will guide how you engage with both current and prospective clients. This analytical rigor ultimately translates into tangible results in real estate transactions.

Armed with these analytical techniques, you'll navigate complex datasets with ease, transforming insights into proactive strategies that drive success and bolster your reputation as a knowledgeable real estate professional committed to effectively meeting client needs.

Managing Email and Phone Logs

Managing email and phone logs is crucial for effective communication in real estate. Building strong relationships with clients requires careful tracking of interactions to ensure timely follow-ups and personalized service. By setting up an organized system in Excel, you can streamline your communication process and enhance your responsiveness to client needs.

Begin by creating a comprehensive log that captures essential details for each interaction. Include columns for the client's name, date of communication, contact method (such as email or phone), a summary of the conversation, and any required follow-up actions. This structured approach allows you to quickly reference key information and maintain clarity on ongoing discussions.

Take this example, you might format your log with column A for the client's name, column B for the date of communication, column C for the contact method, column D for a conversation summary, and column E for follow-up actions. This setup keeps all relevant details in one accessible place.

Consistency is important when entering data. For example, if you label contact methods in column C as "Email," "Phone Call," or "In-Person Meeting," it's best to use these terms uniformly. This practice not only enhances clarity but also simplifies future analysis.

To improve your logging system further, consider using conditional formatting to highlight upcoming follow-up dates. By entering follow-up dates in column E and applying formatting rules to change cell colors as deadlines approach, you create visual reminders that help ensure no client interaction goes unnoticed. To set this up:

1. Select the range in your follow-up column.

2. Navigate to Home > Conditional Formatting > New

Rule.

3. Choose "Format cells that contain" and set it to highlight when the date approaches today.

This small adjustment transforms your log from a simple document into an active management tool.

Over time, tracking interactions can reveal patterns in client preferences. For example, if you discover that certain clients favor phone calls over emails, adjusting your approach can lead to improved engagement. You can use Excel's COUNTIF function to analyze this behavior by counting interactions through each contact method with a formula like:

=COUNTIF(C:C,"Phone Call")

This formula provides an immediate count of all phone call interactions recorded in column C.

Consider also creating a summary sheet within your workbook that consolidates key metrics from your logs. This sheet could include total interactions per client, average response times, or frequent inquiries received. Utilizing functions like AVERAGE or SUM will enable you to gain quick insights into your performance and understand client preferences better.

Excel's filtering capabilities can also help you focus on specific time frames or types of interactions. Take this example, if you're preparing for an upcoming open house event and want to reach out to clients who previously expressed interest in similar properties, applying filters allows you to isolate those entries effortlessly.

As you accumulate data over time, regularly reviewing and refining your logging process is essential. Set aside time weekly or monthly to clean up outdated entries or merge duplicates, ensuring accuracy and relevance in your records.

An anecdote comes to mind: one real estate agent I

worked with transformed their conversion rates significantly after implementing a structured logging system for their communications. Overwhelmed by scattered notes and missed follow-ups before using Excel's capabilities, they found themselves more organized and able to provide timely updates and tailored responses that resonated with their clients' needs.

In the end, managing email and phone logs effectively positions you as a responsive professional in real estate. When clients feel valued through prompt communication and personalized attention, it fosters trust—an invaluable currency in this industry. By developing a systematic approach with Excel for tracking these interactions, you're not just logging information; you're enhancing relationships that can lead to successful transactions down the line.

With each entry into your communication log, remember that you are shaping the narrative of your client relationships —one defined by attention to detail and a commitment to exceptional service.

Integrating with Other CRM Tools

Integrating with other CRM tools is vital in the real estate sector, where efficiency and seamless communication can determine success. Excel serves as a valuable ally, acting as a bridge between various CRM systems to enhance your workflow. By streamlining processes and consolidating data, you can improve client interactions and optimize your marketing efforts.

To start, identify the key CRM tools you currently use, such as Salesforce, HubSpot, or Zoho CRM. Each of these platforms offers distinct features tailored to different aspects of customer relationship management. However, maintaining a cohesive workflow often necessitates transferring data between systems while preserving critical information. Excel offers an effective solution for importing, exporting, or merging data from these platforms.

For example, you can use Excel to import contact lists from your primary CRM tool. Most CRMs allow you to export contacts as CSV files. After exporting the file, you can open it in Excel to edit or refine the data before importing it back into your main system. This process might include removing duplicates or updating outdated information to ensure your records remain current.

Establishing a standard format for your data is crucial when integrating with other CRM systems. Ensure that the fields in your Excel spreadsheet align with those in your CRM tool. Take this example, if your CRM uses "First Name" and "Last Name" instead of simply "Name," maintaining consistency is essential during data transfers to prevent mismatches. You could create an Excel sheet with headers like "Client ID," "First Name," "Last Name," "Email," and "Phone Number." Adhering to this structure facilitates smooth transitions and minimizes errors.

Automation can significantly enhance the management of ongoing integration tasks. Excel's built-in features, such as Power Query, enable you to connect directly to certain CRMs for real-time data updates. Power Query allows you to automatically pull data from various sources into a single worksheet, ensuring that any changes made in your primary CRM are reflected in your Excel workbook without manual input.

And, regular updates between systems can improve communication with clients. Take this example, if you track client interactions in Excel while using another platform for lead generation, integrating these systems ensures that every contact activity updates seamlessly across all tools. This way, when you follow up with clients or send newsletters, you rely on the most current information available.

You might also consider automating reports that merge insights from both Excel and your CRM system. By using pivot tables within Excel, you can summarize important metrics—such as conversion rates or follow-up effectiveness —and visualize them through charts. This enhances the presentation quality when discussing results with colleagues or stakeholders.

For a practical example, imagine you want to analyze which marketing campaigns generate the highest number of leads from your CRM data stored in Excel. You could create a pivot table that organizes leads by campaign source while filtering out irrelevant entries based on criteria like geographic location or client type.

Another effective strategy involves using APIs (Application Programming Interfaces) provided by many CRMs for deeper integration with Excel workflows. If you're comfortable with coding—or willing to learn—you can develop scripts that automate repetitive tasks such as sending emails based on updated client information in your spreadsheet.

A real estate agent I know shared how they connected their email marketing tool directly with their database via an API script written in Python combined with Excel functions to manage their leads effectively. The outcome? Their response times improved significantly because they could personalize outreach based on historical interaction data compiled from multiple platforms without manual extraction each time.

Although integrating various tools into one ecosystem may initially seem daunting, establishing these connections fosters efficiency and enhances collaboration among teams involved in closing deals. When all parties work from consistent datasets—whether sales agents following up on inquiries or marketing teams crafting targeted campaigns—you create an environment conducive to success.

To wrap things up, integrating Excel with other CRM tools not only facilitates better data management but also transforms how you interact with clients by streamlining processes and enabling informed decisions based on comprehensive insights drawn from all available resources. By investing time into this integration process now, you're setting yourself up for future success—simplifying operations while ultimately strengthening the client relationships that are crucial for excellence in real estate.

Dashboard Creation for CRM Analysis

Creating dashboards for CRM analysis is a powerful way to transform raw data into actionable insights, enabling real estate agents to make informed decisions swiftly. A well-constructed dashboard consolidates various metrics and key performance indicators (KPIs) into a single, visually appealing interface. This holistic view allows agents to monitor their performance at a glance and identify trends that could shape their strategies.

To begin, identify the key metrics that are most relevant to your real estate operations. These may include lead conversion rates, average response times, and total sales figures over specific periods. Once you have pinpointed these essential metrics, you can start designing your dashboard in Excel.

Utilize Excel's capabilities by creating a dedicated worksheet for your dashboard. Lay out the identified metrics in separate cells; for example, if you're tracking lead conversion rates, allocate one cell for the total number of leads and another for the number of converted leads. From there, use formulas to automatically calculate the conversion rate—simply enter = (Converted Leads / Total Leads) * 100. This formula provides an immediate visual representation of your conversion effectiveness.

Excel truly shines when it comes to visual representation. After populating your dashboard with key figures, enhance its impact by incorporating charts. Take this example, you might create a line chart that illustrates your lead conversion rates over time. To insert a chart, highlight your data range, navigate to the "Insert" tab, select "Chart," and choose the type that best suits your information—whether it's a line, bar, or pie chart.

Another powerful tool within Excel is conditional formatting, which adds visual cues related to performance metrics directly on your dashboard. For example, if your conversion rate dips below a predetermined threshold—say 25%—you can set up conditional formatting rules to color the cell red. This immediate feedback prompts timely action and decision-making.

As you build your dashboard, consider how often it will need updating. If you're working with live data from your CRM system, take advantage of Power Query to connect directly to your data source. This integration allows you to refresh data in real-time with just a click. To set this up, navigate to the "Data" tab in Excel, select "Get Data," followed by "From Other Sources," then choose your CRM tool and follow the prompts for seamless linking.

Incorporating slicers can further elevate interactivity within your dashboard. Slicers act as visual filters that enable users to narrow down data based on selected criteria easily. Take this example, when analyzing sales by region or agent performance over different timeframes, slicers allow for instant filtering—enhancing usability for team members who may not be as familiar with Excel.

To illustrate the impact of effective dashboards on decision-making in real estate: consider an agent who leverages their dashboard not only for performance tracking but also for forecasting future sales trends based on historical data. By displaying monthly sales figures alongside predictive analytics derived from previous years' trends, agents can strategize their marketing efforts more effectively—targeting high-potential areas or adjusting campaigns as needed.

Once you've constructed your dashboard and linked it with live data sources or manual inputs as necessary, remember to share this vital tool with your team or stakeholders. You can publish it via Excel Online or share it as an interactive PDF for those who need easy access without editing capabilities.

Keep in mind that creating a dashboard is not a one-time task; it requires regular review and updates based on evolving business goals or new metrics arising from market changes. Collect feedback from users about what insights they find most valuable and make adjustments accordingly—ensuring the dashboard remains relevant and useful over time.

In the end, an effective dashboard simplifies complex datasets into understandable visuals that drive better decision-making in real estate operations. By harnessing Excel's robust features —from formulas and conditional formatting to charts and Power Query—you are well-equipped to build a comprehensive CRM analysis tool that enhances operational efficiency and informs strategic planning in your real estate practice. Your commitment to mastering these techniques positions you as not just a participant in the industry but as an influential leader capable of leveraging data for exceptional results.

CHAPTER 9: USING MACROS FOR REAL ESTATE EFFICIENCY

Introduction to Macros in Excel

In the world of Excel, macros offer a transformative capability that can significantly streamline your workflow. Essentially, a macro is a recorded series of actions or commands that you can execute with a single click. This powerful feature allows you to automate repetitive tasks, enhancing productivity. For real estate agents, mastering macros can save hours spent on manual data entry, report generation, and formatting—freeing up more time for client interactions and strategic planning.

To begin using macros in Excel, the first step is to enable the Developer tab, which contains all macro-related features. You can do this by navigating to the "File" menu, selecting "Options," and then choosing "Customize Ribbon." In the right panel, check the box for "Developer" and click "OK." With the Developer tab now visible in your ribbon, you gain access to essential tools for recording and managing macros.

Recording your first macro is a straightforward process. Click on "Record Macro," and you will be prompted to name it—choose something descriptive like "FormatReports" for easy identification later. You also have the option to assign a shortcut key to make executing the macro even more efficient. After setting this up, every action you perform in Excel will be recorded until you click "Stop Recording." Take this example, if you often format property data by applying specific styles or formulas to cells, carry out those actions now; they will be saved as part of your macro.

Imagine you've recorded a macro to format a table of property listings. Whenever you input new data—such as new sales or rental properties—you can simply run the macro instead of adjusting fonts, colors, and borders manually each time. To execute your macro, return to the Developer tab, select "Macros," choose "FormatReports," and click "Run." The result is immediate: your data appears polished and ready for presentation without tedious formatting steps.

Editing macros is another essential aspect of mastering this powerful feature. By clicking on "Macros" in the Developer tab, you can view a list of all recorded macros. Selecting one and choosing "Edit" opens the Visual Basic for Applications (VBA) editor, where you can view and modify the underlying code. While this may seem daunting at first glance, VBA offers significant customization opportunities. For example, if you need to adjust which cells are formatted or add additional calculations, doing so within the VBA editor enhances your automation capabilities.

While macros are incredibly useful for speeding up repetitive tasks, they do come with considerations regarding security and usability. Since macros can potentially harbor harmful code from untrustworthy sources, it's crucial to enable them only from reliable origins. And, while running macros requires minimal interaction once set up correctly, providing training or documentation for team members who might use these tools ensures everyone remains informed and efficient in their execution.

Consider a scenario where your real estate agency regularly prepares monthly sales reports across various property types —residential, commercial, and industrial. Instead of manually compiling these reports each month—a process that could take hours—you can create a macro that consolidates relevant data from multiple sheets into a single summary report. This automation not only saves time but also minimizes human error in data handling.

To further enhance your Excel functionality through macros, explore using loops and conditions within your VBA code. These concepts allow you to apply actions across multiple datasets or implement logic-based decisions during execution —for instance, changing cell colors based on whether property prices exceed certain thresholds or automating email notifications when sales figures hit specific targets.

Your journey with macros doesn't end at the basics; as you become more comfortable with this toolset, delve into advanced techniques such as creating user forms or incorporating error handling into your code. These enhancements can lead to robust solutions tailored specifically for real estate workflows—like input forms for new property listings that automatically populate databases while ensuring consistency in data entry.

In the end, mastering macros equips real estate agents with an arsenal of tools that empower them to work smarter rather than harder. Automating routine tasks frees up valuable time for more strategic endeavors—such as client outreach or market analysis—transforming how you operate within the industry. By fully embracing this capability within Excel's ecosystem, you're not just improving efficiency; you're elevating your entire professional approach towards becoming a leader in real estate analytics and operations management.

Recording Your First Macro

Recording your first macro in Excel is a significant milestone that can greatly enhance your efficiency by automating tasks that might otherwise seem tedious and time-consuming. The process is straightforward, making it accessible even for those who are just beginning to explore Excel's advanced features. By leveraging macros, you can streamline repetitive actions and improve your overall workflow.

To get started, first ensure the Developer tab is visible in your Excel ribbon. If it's not, simply go to the "File" menu, select "Options," then "Customize Ribbon," and check the box next to "Developer." This tab contains all the essential tools for creating and managing macros, putting everything you need right at your fingertips.

Once you have the Developer tab enabled, begin by clicking on "Record Macro." A dialog box will prompt you to name your macro; choose a descriptive name, such as "MonthlyReportFormatter," so you can easily remember its purpose. You can also assign a shortcut key for quicker access —using Ctrl + Shift + R, for example, allows you to execute the macro with minimal effort in the future. After clicking "OK," every action you take will be recorded until you click "Stop Recording."

Let's look at a practical example. Suppose you're compiling data from recent property listings into a formatted report. Your usual process involves adjusting fonts, colors, and applying specific formulas. With the macro recording feature activated, proceed through these familiar steps: formatting cells for prices, highlighting new listings, or inserting headers. Each of these actions will be captured as part of your macro.

After finishing these tasks and clicking "Stop Recording," your macro is now ready to replicate those formatting steps effortlessly. When new data arrives— like an influx of properties—you can simply run the "MonthlyReportFormatter" macro with a click or keystroke, instantly applying your preferred styles without having to repeat each individual task.

Editing macros can further enhance their utility. Return to the Developer tab and click on "Macros." Here, you'll find a list of all recorded macros; select one and hit "Edit" to enter the Visual Basic for Applications (VBA) editor. While it may seem daunting at first glance, this interface offers remarkable customization options. Take this example, if certain reports require additional calculations, editing in VBA provides the flexibility you need.

Imagine needing to adjust which columns receive specific formatting based on property price categories—for example, changing the font color to red for properties exceeding (1 million while keeping others in black. With a basic understanding of VBA, making these adjustments becomes quite manageable.

It's also important to consider security when using macros. Since they can automate various commands—including potentially harmful ones if sourced improperly—it's crucial to enable macros only from trusted sources. Educating your colleagues about safe practices will help ensure responsible use of this powerful tool.

Now envision a scenario where you regularly compile sales reports across various property types—like residential versus commercial—and need to summarize them monthly. Instead of struggling with manual entry or consolidation each time —a process that could take hours—creating a dedicated macro could aggregate data from several worksheets into one comprehensive report. This automation minimizes not only the time spent but also reduces the chances of human error during data entry.

As you become more comfortable with macros, you'll discover advanced techniques that can further enhance your productivity; for instance, integrating loops or conditional logic within your VBA scripts could facilitate bulk operations across datasets or trigger automatic alerts when certain performance metrics are met—such as notifying agents via email when sales exceed targets.

Your journey doesn't end with basic recording; improving your proficiency by exploring user forms or implementing error handling in macros can elevate your automation capabilities even further. This could lead to tailored solutions that specifically address real estate tasks—such as input forms designed for property listings that ensure uniformity in data collection across team members.

In the end, mastering the recording and effective utilization of macros empowers real estate professionals like yourself to work more efficiently and redirect your efforts toward strategic initiatives—such as nurturing client relationships or conducting detailed market analyses. By embracing these functionalities within Excel, you can transform daily operations and position yourself as an innovative leader who effectively leverages technology in real estate analytics and management practices.

Editing Macros in VBA

Editing macros in Visual Basic for Applications (VBA) allows you to enhance and customize the functionality of your automated tasks in Excel. After recording a macro, the next step is to tailor it to meet your specific needs or correct any errors that may have occurred during the recording process. This flexibility is one of the key strengths of using macros in Excel.

To begin editing a macro, navigate back to the Developer tab where you recorded it. Click on "Macros" to view a list of all your recorded macros. Select the macro you wish to edit and click on "Edit." This will open the VBA editor—a separate window where you can view the code that corresponds to your recorded actions. Although this interface may seem daunting at first, its intuitive structure becomes clearer with practice.

Familiarizing yourself with the basic components of VBA code is essential. The syntax is relatively straightforward; each recorded action translates into a line of code. Take this example, a simple formatting action like making a cell bold appears as follows:

```vba
Range("A1").Font.Bold = True
```

This line specifies that cell A1's font should be bold. You can modify this line or add new commands as needed. For example, if you also want to change the text color, you can expand the code:

```vba
Range("A1").Font.Bold = True

Range("A1").Font.Color = RGB(255, 0, 0) ' This changes text color to red
```

The ability to edit macros proves especially valuable when adapting them for various situations. Take this example, if you have a macro that formats sales reports but now need to include additional metrics such as commission percentages, you can insert lines of code that dynamically compute these new values based on data inputs:

```vba
Dim commission As Double

commission = Range("B2").Value * 0.05 ' Assuming B2 contains the sale amount

Range("C2").Value = commission ' Outputs commission in column C
```

` ` `

With this small adjustment, running your macro will not only format the report but also automatically calculate and display commissions.

Security considerations are crucial when working with VBA macros, particularly in shared environments. Always ensure that macros come from trusted sources and educate your team about the risks associated with running unknown scripts. This precaution helps minimize vulnerabilities and maintain data integrity.

Consider how this capability to edit and customize macros can streamline your workflow further. For example, if different clients prefer varying formatting styles for reports—some favor bold headers while others prefer colorful backgrounds —you can create a single macro that prompts users for their preferences through input boxes:

```vba
Dim userChoice As String

userChoice = InputBox("Enter your preferred style: Bold or Colorful")

If userChoice = "Bold" Then

' Apply bold formatting code here

ElseIf userChoice = "Colorful" Then

' Apply colorful formatting code here

End If
```

This kind of conditional logic transforms a basic macro into an interactive tool that meets individual needs without duplicating effort.

As you explore deeper into VBA editing, consider incorporating loops and arrays for more complex operations. Take this example, if you're compiling data from multiple worksheets into a single summary report, using a loop can efficiently iterate through each sheet:

```vba
Dim ws As Worksheet

For Each ws In ThisWorkbook.Worksheets

' Code to aggregate data from each worksheet goes here.

Next ws
```

This approach not only saves time but also enhances accuracy by ensuring all relevant data is processed consistently.

The world of VBA is expansive and full of potential for enhancing productivity in real estate tasks. You might also explore error handling techniques; adding mechanisms that catch errors during execution can help troubleshoot issues effectively without disrupting your workflow.

In the end, mastering the editing of macros in VBA positions you at the forefront of efficiency within Excel. Tailoring automation tools specifically for real estate operations allows you to focus on high-value tasks like client engagement and strategic planning rather than getting bogged down by routine data management. As these skills develop, you'll not only gain time-saving tools but also cultivate a robust understanding of how technology can elevate your real estate practice into something truly exceptional.

Automating Repetitive Tasks

Repetitive tasks can drain your productivity and diminish your enthusiasm for working with data. Fortunately, Excel provides powerful features that enable you to automate these mundane activities, freeing up your time to focus on what truly matters: building client relationships and closing deals.

One of the most effective ways to automate tasks in Excel is through the use of macros. Macros are sequences of instructions that can be recorded and executed with a single command, allowing you to perform complex tasks effortlessly. For example, if you regularly format data for reports—adjusting column widths, applying specific font styles, or highlighting key figures—you can record these actions as a macro. Once created, you can apply these changes across various worksheets or workbooks with just a click.

To create your first macro in Excel, start by enabling the Developer tab on the ribbon. Here's how: go to File > Options > Customize Ribbon, then check the box for Developer. With the Developer tab now available, follow these steps:

1. Click on Record Macro in the Developer tab.

2. Assign a name to your macro—be sure to avoid spaces and special characters.

3. Choose where to store your macro; usually, "This Workbook" is sufficient.

4. Optionally, assign a shortcut key for quicker access.

5. Click OK and perform the actions you want to automate.

6. Once finished, return to the Developer tab and click Stop Recording.

To run your macro later, simply navigate back to the Developer tab, select Macros, choose your recorded macro from the list, and click Run.

In addition to macros, consider utilizing Excel's built-in features like AutoFill and Flash Fill to expedite data entry processes. AutoFill allows you to drag fill handles across cells based on patterns in your data—whether it's dates or sequential numbers—saving precious time on repetitive tasks.

Flash Fill works similarly but is even more dynamic. It recognizes patterns in adjacent cells as you type. For example, if you have a list of client names stored in one column that need formatting (like changing "John Doe" to "Doe, John"), you simply begin typing "Doe" next to "John Doe." As soon as Excel identifies the pattern (in this case, reversing the names), it will suggest filling down automatically.

Take this example:

- Original: John Doe

- Desired: Doe, John

You would start typing "Doe" next to "John Doe," and after typing just a few examples of similar transformations, Excel can complete the rest of the list using its predictive capabilities.

Additionally, creating templates specifically tailored for frequently performed tasks—like property comparison sheets or expense reports—can significantly enhance your workflow. Templates provide pre-set formats where you only need to input specific data each time.

To create an efficient template:

1. Design your spreadsheet layout with all necessary formulas already embedded.

2. Format headers and categories clearly for ease of use.

3. Save it as an Excel Template file (.xltx) so every new document opens with this setup intact.

Using templates not only ensures consistency across reports but also reduces errors associated with manual formatting each time.

As we explore automation further in Excel, integrating VBA (Visual Basic for Applications) opens up even more possibilities. With VBA coding skills—easily learned over time —you can write scripts that handle more complex functions beyond basic macros, such as creating automated market analysis reports or client tracking systems tailored specifically for real estate needs.

Embracing automation through macros, built-in features like AutoFill and Flash Fill, and custom templates fosters efficiency while giving you valuable time back from tedious operations. This allows you to spend each moment at your desk strengthening client relationships or strategizing your next big deal rather than getting bogged down in repetitive chores.

As you incorporate these automated strategies into your daily Excel operations, you'll likely find that they not only enhance your productivity but also improve your satisfaction in managing real estate transactions effectively. In the end, this evolution will elevate your professional profile as someone adept at leveraging technology for business success.

Utilizing Macros for Reporting

Utilizing macros in Excel for reporting can significantly enhance the way you compile and present information. By automating repetitive tasks, macros become a powerful ally, making data management both efficient and streamlined. When you record a series of actions that you frequently perform—such as formatting reports or generating summaries—you create a macro that captures these steps, allowing you to execute them with a single command.

To maximize the benefits of macros in your reporting, start by identifying the common tasks you regularly undertake. Take this example, if you often generate reports on property sales, think about automating the formatting of your data. This could involve highlighting cells based on specific values, like using conditional formatting to emphasize sales that exceed a certain threshold, or adjusting column widths for better readability. By recording these formatting actions into a macro, you ensure that each time you prepare the report, your custom format is applied instantly.

Creating your first reporting macro is a straightforward process. Begin by enabling the Developer tab in Excel and launching the macro recording feature. Click on Record Macro, give it an intuitive name—such as "FormatSalesReport"—and choose "This Workbook" as the storage location. Optionally, set a keyboard shortcut for quick access. Perform each step— whether applying specific styles or filtering data—and Excel will capture your actions. Once you've completed the steps, stop the recording, and your macro will be ready for use whenever needed.

To run your newly created macro:

1. Navigate to the Developer tab.

2. Select Macros.

3. Highlight your macro and click Run.

It's like having a personal assistant who remembers your preferred layout every time.

In addition to simple macros, consider integrating them with Excel's built-in features for even greater efficiency in reporting. The SUBTOTAL function is particularly useful when working with filtered datasets. It allows you to perform calculations such as SUM or AVERAGE while ignoring hidden rows. For example, if you've filtered properties by location and want to calculate the average sale price of the visible properties, using SUBTOTAL ensures accuracy without manual recalculations each time filters change.

Adding charts to your automated reporting process can further enhance clarity and visual appeal. Once you've established a macro that formats your data correctly, you can create another macro to generate key charts automatically— such as bar graphs showing sales trends over time or pie charts breaking down sales by property type. These visuals are invaluable when presenting information to clients or stakeholders who prefer quick insights over raw numbers.

Dynamic reporting goes beyond just generating data; it also involves enhancing user interaction. For example, consider employing slicers—intuitive buttons for filtering data dynamically within PivotTables or regular tables—alongside macros that refresh or update these elements automatically when your datasets change.

Imagine setting up a comprehensive report for potential clients that showcases various properties based on their budget ranges. By linking slicers to your data table, clients can interactively filter properties without manually sifting through numerous rows. Pairing this functionality with macros ensures that any changes made via slicers automatically refresh related charts or summaries in real-time.

While automation through macros is incredibly valuable, maintaining clean code within them is equally important. This practice helps avoid errors and complications down the line if modifications are needed. Take this example, commenting on sections of code clarifies their purpose, simplifying debugging when adjustments are necessary.

Embracing macros not only boosts efficiency but also empowers you to provide timely insights tailored specifically to real estate clients' needs—ensuring they receive comprehensive reports quickly. As these practices become second nature, you'll likely see an increase in both productivity and the quality of the reports you generate.

In summary, effectively leveraging macros transforms mundane reporting tasks into seamless operations where technology enhances your capabilities—not merely as a tool but as an integral part of your workflow strategy for real estate success. Your ability to produce polished and insightful reports swiftly will impress clients and position you as an authority in the industry, adept at blending real estate expertise with technological proficiency.

Debugging Common Macro Errors

Debugging common macro errors is a vital skill for anyone aiming to fully leverage Excel automation. While macros can greatly enhance your workflow, encountering issues during their execution is common. Developing the ability to identify and resolve these errors will not only save you time but also boost your confidence in using Excel more effectively.

To begin, it's important to familiarize yourself with the various types of errors that can occur when running macros. One frequent problem is syntax errors—mistakes in the code that hinder proper execution. For example, if a line incorrectly references a range, such as "A1:A10" instead of "A1:A100," Excel will generate an error. A quick review of your macro's code can help you spot these mistakes. Using the Visual Basic for Applications (VBA) editor, you can step through each line by pressing F8, allowing you to identify exactly where the failure occurs and why.

Run-time errors represent another common source of problems. These occur when the macro attempts to execute an invalid action. Take this example, if your macro tries to access a worksheet that has been deleted or renamed, Excel will be unable to locate it and will produce an error message. In these cases, verifying that the worksheet names in your code match those in your workbook can often resolve the issue.

Logic errors are more subtle and usually stem from incorrect assumptions about how data should be processed within your macro. For example, if you expect a range to contain only numerical values but it also includes text entries, calculations may yield unexpected results or even fail. To reduce this risk, consider incorporating error handling in your VBA code with "On Error" statements. This approach enables you to manage potential errors gracefully, allowing for troubleshooting without crashing the entire macro.

Here's a simple error-handling structure you might find useful:

```vba
Sub ExampleMacro()

On Error GoTo ErrorHandler


' Your code here


Exit Sub


ErrorHandler:

MsgBox "An error occurred: " & Err.Description

End Sub
```

By integrating this snippet into your macros, you'll receive alerts when errors occur, providing a message box with details about the issue rather than letting the macro fail silently.

Thoroughly testing your macros before relying on them is essential. One effective strategy involves creating test scenarios with sample data that mimics real-life situations while protecting your actual data integrity. This controlled environment helps catch potential issues early and ensures that modifications behave as intended.

Take this example, if you're developing a macro that formats and summarizes sales data for multiple properties at once, consider testing it on a small set of fictitious property sales data first—perhaps including edge cases like zero sales or duplicate entries. This way, you can observe its behavior under various conditions without risking important records.

Documentation is also crucial in the debugging process. Keeping track of changes made within your macros allows you to revert if something goes wrong and analyze why specific modifications may have caused issues later on. Adding comments throughout your VBA code can clarify complex sections and remind you of their intended purposes during future reviews.

For example, if you've created a macro that processes sales data but are unsure why it occasionally skips entries, commenting on each logical block can help pinpoint where things may be going awry during debugging sessions.

Additionally, utilizing Excel's built-in debugging tools can significantly expedite problem identification. The Immediate Window in the VBA editor lets you evaluate expressions and variables at runtime, offering insights into what's happening behind the scenes as your macros execute.

When faced with persistent issues that seem insurmountable, seeking support from online forums or user groups dedicated to Excel programming can provide valuable perspectives. Engaging with others who have encountered similar challenges often leads to new solutions or best practices that may not be immediately apparent.

To wrap things up, mastering debugging techniques not only boosts individual productivity but also ensures reliable execution of automated processes within Excel. By dedicating time to understanding common macro errors and implementing best practices for coding and testing, you'll empower yourself to create robust tools tailored specifically for real estate reporting needs. In the end, this will lead to a smoother workflow where automation enhances accuracy and effectiveness in delivering quality insights consistently for your clients.

Best Practices for Macro Security

Navigating the world of macros in Excel opens up a realm of possibilities, but it also necessitates an understanding of security best practices to protect your valuable data. As you automate processes and streamline tasks, safeguarding your macros against vulnerabilities becomes essential. Integrating robust security measures not only protects your work from potential threats but also builds trust among users who depend on these automated solutions.

A key component of macro security is familiarity with Excel's built-in security settings. When you create or run macros, Excel typically issues warnings if it detects macros in a workbook. Adjusting these settings to suit your needs is crucial for balancing functionality with security. To do this, navigate to the "Trust Center" within Excel's options menu. Here, you can tailor how macros are managed: choose to enable all macros, disable them entirely, or allow only those that are digitally signed.

For enhanced protection, consider digitally signing your macros. This process involves acquiring a digital certificate that authenticates your identity as the macro creator. By signing your code, you assure users that it originates from a trusted source. To sign your macro, obtain a digital certificate and then access the VBA editor to apply it to your code. Once signed, anyone opening the workbook will see that it has been verified, significantly reducing the risk of executing harmful code.

Additionally, it's crucial to save your workbooks in secure locations. Utilizing cloud storage solutions like OneDrive or SharePoint offers added safety through automatic backups and version history—especially important when handling sensitive data such as client information or financial records. In cases of data corruption or loss, having multiple backups allows for smooth restoration without major disruptions.

To further minimize risks associated with user inputs, ensure that your VBA code is structured with input validation checks. These checks help avoid errors caused by unexpected data types or formats. For example, if a macro expects a date input but receives text instead, implementing validation will enable the macro to handle discrepancies effectively.

Here's a simple implementation of input validation:

```vba
Sub ValidateInput()

Dim inputDate As Variant

inputDate = InputBox("Please enter a date:")


If Not IsDate(inputDate) Then

MsgBox "Invalid date entered. Please try again.

Exit Sub

End If


' Proceed with further processing using valid input

End Sub
```

In this scenario, if a user inputs something other than a valid date format, the macro provides immediate feedback and prevents incorrect processing.

User education is another critical element of macro security. Ensure that all users running these macros understand best practices for managing files that contain them. Encourage them to refrain from enabling macros in files received from unknown sources or suspicious emails, as these are common entry points for malware.

Regularly reviewing and updating your macros is also essential. As Excel continues to evolve with new features and enhancements, revisiting older code helps ensure it remains efficient and secure against emerging threats. This proactive approach mitigates risks associated with outdated practices or deprecated functions.

Lastly, fostering a culture of awareness around data protection goes beyond just macro security; it encompasses all aspects of using Excel effectively. Promote discussions within your team or organization about data integrity and security. Sharing insights about recent software security breaches can keep everyone informed about potential threats and encourage adherence to best practices.

By establishing strong macro security protocols alongside effective coding practices and user education initiatives, you enhance both the functionality and reliability of your Excel solutions. This comprehensive approach empowers you and your team to leverage automation confidently while upholding rigorous standards for data protection—a critical factor in successfully navigating today's data-driven landscape.

Advanced Macro Techniques

As you explore advanced macro techniques, optimizing your workflows and boosting efficiency becomes essential. By mastering these methods, you'll find it easier to manage complex tasks, ultimately streamlining your real estate operations. A standout feature of macros is their ability to automate repetitive tasks that often consume valuable time and resources.

Take this example, imagine you regularly send property listings to clients. Rather than manually creating emails each time, you can develop a macro that gathers data from your listings and sends personalized emails directly from Excel. This not only saves time but also reduces the likelihood of errors that come with manual entries.

To illustrate, let's create a macro that automates the process of sending emails based on property data stored in an Excel worksheet. Suppose you have a table containing client names, email addresses, and property details. The following VBA code snippet demonstrates how to construct such a macro:

```vba
Sub SendPropertyEmails()

Dim OutlookApp As Object

Dim OutlookMail As Object

Dim ws As Worksheet

Dim lastRow As Long

Dim i As Integer


Set ws = ThisWorkbook.Sheets("Listings")

lastRow = ws.Cells(ws.Rows.Count, "A").End(xlUp).Row

Set OutlookApp = CreateObject("Outlook.Application")


For i = 2 To lastRow ' Assuming the first row contains headers

Set OutlookMail = OutlookApp.CreateItem(0)

With OutlookMail

.To = ws.Cells(i, 2).Value ' Email address in column B

.Subject = "New Property Listing: " & ws.Cells(i, 1).Value ' Property title in column A

.Body = "Dear " & ws.Cells(i, 3).Value & "," & vbCrLf & vbCrLf & _

We are excited to share our latest listing: " & ws.Cells(i, 1).Value
```

& "." & vbCrLf & _

Details: " & ws.Cells(i, 4).Value & "." & vbCrLf & vbCrLf & _

Best regards," & vbCrLf & "Your Real Estate Team

.Display ' Use .Send to send immediately without displaying

End With

Next i

Set OutlookMail = Nothing

Set OutlookApp = Nothing

End Sub

` ` `

In this code, we loop through each row in the "Listings" worksheet, creating an email for each entry. The Display method allows you to review the email before sending; simply replace it with Send to automate the process entirely.

Another essential aspect of enhancing your macros is incorporating error handling. This practice ensures your macros can manage unexpected situations gracefully, preventing crashes or misleading results. Implementing error handling in VBA is both straightforward and beneficial.

For example:

` ` `vba

Sub SafeEmailSending()

On Error GoTo ErrorHandler

' Email sending code here...

Exit Sub

ErrorHandler:

MsgBox "An error occurred: " & Err.Description

End Sub

``` 

By adding an error handler like this, you ensure that if something goes wrong—whether it's a connection issue with Outlook or a missing email address—your macro won't abruptly stop. Instead, it will provide a descriptive message that aids in troubleshooting.

Advanced macros can also leverage user-defined functions (UDFs), allowing you to create custom calculations tailored specifically to your needs. For example, if you frequently compute a unique commission structure based on various parameters, a UDF can simplify this task. Here's an example of a UDF that calculates commission based on sale price and rate:

```vba
Function CalculateCommission(salePrice As Double, rate As Double) As Double

CalculateCommission = salePrice * (rate / 100)

End Function
```

You can use this function directly within Excel cells just like any built-in function. Combining user-defined functions with standard formulas enhances your analytical capabilities significantly.

Additionally, consider integrating macros with form controls
```

in Excel for a more interactive user experience. Adding buttons that trigger specific macros can streamline user interactions considerably. You can easily insert buttons from the Developer tab and link them directly to your macros. This approach makes it accessible for users who may not be familiar with running scripts directly in the Visual Basic for Applications (VBA) editor.

Creating an engaging interface not only boosts productivity but also minimizes friction when training team members on new tools or processes.

Also, documentation is crucial when developing advanced macros. Including clear comments within your code provides guidance for future reference or for other users who may work with your macros later on. By documenting what each section of code does, you ensure that even complex automation remains comprehensible.

To wrap things up, mastering advanced macro techniques not only enhances productivity but also enables you to build scalable solutions tailored for real estate operations. By wisely leveraging automation and incorporating robust practices around error handling and user engagement, you position yourself for long-term success in utilizing Excel as an invaluable tool in your real estate career. Embrace these advanced strategies and witness how they transform the efficiency of your daily tasks while elevating your analytical capabilities in the dynamic real estate market.

CHAPTER 10:
BUILDING A REAL
ESTATE DASHBOARD

*Purpose of Dashboards
in Real Estate*

U nderstanding the purpose of dashboards in real estate is essential for leveraging data effectively. A well-designed dashboard acts as a central hub for visualizing critical metrics and insights, allowing real estate professionals to make informed decisions swiftly. Imagine having all the essential performance indicators at your fingertips, transforming raw data into actionable intelligence that can guide your next move.

Dashboards simplify complex datasets, presenting them in visually digestible formats. In an industry where time is crucial, the ability to view key metrics—such as sales trends, property performance, and client interactions—all in one place is invaluable. This visual representation helps you identify trends and anomalies that might be overlooked in traditional reports. Take this example, tracking sales performance across various regions can highlight thriving areas and those needing additional marketing efforts or strategic adjustments.

Picture a scenario where you manage multiple listings. With a dashboard, you could visualize the average days on market for properties by neighborhood alongside their sale prices. This dual insight enables quick conclusions about pricing strategies or marketing needs based on comparative analytics. Tools like Excel allow you to create charts that dynamically reflect this data, offering real-time updates as new information becomes available.

One of the standout features of dashboards is their ability to integrate various data sources into a single view. Whether pulling sales figures from your CRM or listing data from property management software, consolidating everything into one dashboard significantly enhances workflow efficiency. For example, if you're using Excel alongside tools like Google Analytics to track website traffic or social media engagement, linking these insights provides a comprehensive view of how marketing efforts translate into actual leads and sales.

Creating an effective dashboard starts with identifying the metrics that matter most to your business goals. Begin by asking critical questions: What are my key performance indicators (KPIs)? Are there specific trends I need to monitor? By clarifying these answers upfront, you can tailor your dashboard's layout and functionality accordingly. Take this example, if customer satisfaction is vital for your agency's reputation, prominently including client feedback scores will keep this metric top of mind.

When designing your Excel dashboard, choosing the right visualizations for each metric is crucial. Bar graphs are effective for comparing values over time—like monthly sales figures—while line charts excel at displaying trends over longer periods. For quick snapshots of individual property performances or comparisons among several listings, pie or donut charts can visually represent portions of a whole. The goal is clarity; users should grasp insights instantly without sifting through excessive detail.

To enhance interactivity further, consider implementing slicers within your Excel dashboard. This feature allows users to filter data dynamically without altering the underlying datasets directly. For example, if you're tracking sales across multiple regions but want to focus solely on one area for analysis, slicers provide that flexibility seamlessly.

Keeping dashboards updated with current data is another vital aspect. Automating the refresh process—where possible —ensures that decision-makers always work with the latest information without needing manual intervention each time they check their dashboards.

Effective communication also plays a crucial role when sharing insights with stakeholders or team members. A well-structured dashboard not only reflects data accurately but also tells a story through its design and layout. It should align with strategic objectives while remaining user-friendly enough for anyone to navigate regardless of their technical expertise.

To wrap things up, mastering the art of creating effective dashboards transforms how real estate agents analyze and present data. By synthesizing various sources into cohesive visuals that highlight key metrics relevant to business goals —and utilizing features like dynamic charts and interactive slicers—you empower yourself and your team to act decisively based on insights rather than guesswork. Embracing this approach enhances operational efficiency and positions you as a data-savvy professional capable of making informed decisions in today's fast-paced real estate environment.

Designing Effective Dashboards

Designing an effective dashboard in Excel goes beyond simply inserting charts and tables; it requires a thoughtful approach to your data's narrative. Start by viewing your dashboard as a storytelling tool, where each element contributes to a cohesive message that guides viewers through the data, enabling them to quickly glean insights. This perspective transforms a mere collection of numbers into a compelling story, helping stakeholders understand performance at a glance.

Begin by identifying the specific questions your dashboard needs to address. Are you tracking property sales, client interactions, or market trends? For example, if your goal is to monitor the performance of different neighborhoods, focus on key metrics such as average days on the market and sale prices in those areas. A clear understanding of your objectives allows you to streamline your dashboard effectively, reducing clutter while maximizing impact.

Once you've pinpointed your key metrics, think about the most effective ways to present them visually. Not all data points hold the same significance; some require immediate attention while others serve as background context. For urgent insights—like shifts in market prices—a color-coded gauge or sparkline can capture attention instantly. In contrast, historical trends might be best represented with line charts, which clearly illustrate changes over time.

Incorporating interactivity can further enhance user experience and engagement with your dashboard. Excel's slicers are an excellent tool for this purpose, allowing users to dynamically filter data sets without navigating complex menus or altering the main dataset. Take this example, if you're analyzing sales data by quarter and region, adding slicers enables users to isolate specific data points with a simple click, facilitating quick comparisons without overwhelming them with extraneous information.

Automation is another critical aspect of effective dashboard design. Regularly updated data ensures that decision-makers have access to current figures rather than outdated statistics.

You can achieve this by setting up automated refreshes in Excel; linking your dashboard directly to live data sources ensures users always interact with the latest information available.

Additionally, pay careful attention to the layout of visual elements on your dashboard. A thoughtful arrangement enhances readability and naturally prioritizes important information. Group related metrics together and use white space strategically to avoid overwhelming viewers. Consider positioning the most critical KPIs at the top or center of your layout, as these areas typically draw the most attention.

Clarity is essential not only in design but also in labeling and titling each section of your dashboard. Every visual should feature clear titles and legends that explain what viewers are observing without ambiguity. This straightforward approach minimizes misunderstandings and allows users—regardless of their technical expertise—to engage confidently with your dashboard.

Soliciting feedback from end-users during the design process is also wise. Those who will utilize the dashboard daily may offer valuable insights into what works best for their needs or preferences, which you might overlook as a designer. Engaging potential users can help refine features before finalizing the layout; making adjustments based on real-world usability creates dashboards that resonate more profoundly with their intended audience.

Finally, keep in mind that effective dashboards evolve over time as business needs change and new technologies emerge. Remain open to revisiting and revising your designs based on feedback or shifts in strategy within your organization. An adaptable mindset not only keeps your dashboards relevant but also demonstrates your commitment to excellence in data presentation.

By thoughtfully considering these factors—purposeful

storytelling, visual clarity, interactivity, automation, user feedback, and adaptability—you will create dashboards that empower real estate professionals to make informed decisions swiftly and confidently amidst the fast-paced demands of their industry. Mastering these elements enhances individual productivity and positions you as an innovative thinker capable of leveraging data-driven insights effectively within any organization.

Key Metrics for Real Estate Agents

Sales performance metrics are particularly foundational. For example, tracking the average sale price per square foot can uncover pricing trends in specific neighborhoods. To implement this in Excel, you can create a table with columns for property addresses, sale prices, and square footage. By applying the formula =Sale_Price/Square_Footage, you can easily derive the price per square foot—a powerful metric that is comprehensible to both clients and colleagues.

Another vital metric to monitor is the days on the market, which offers insight into how quickly properties are being sold across different markets or price brackets. By gathering data on listing dates and sale dates, you can calculate the average number of days properties remain unsold with the formula =AVERAGE(Sale_Date - Listing_Date). Visualizing this information through charts helps illustrate whether your properties are selling faster or slower than market averages, providing valuable context for your strategy.

Equally important are client-related metrics that can refine your approach to follow-ups and relationship management. Consider maintaining a log of client interactions—such as calls, emails, and meetings—and categorizing these touchpoints. By summarizing this data in Excel, perhaps using pivot tables, you can swiftly identify clients who may need more attention or those poised to make a buying decision.

Market trends also play a crucial role in your analysis.

Monitoring inventory levels—specifically how many homes are available at any given time—can indicate shifts in demand or supply constraints. A simple line chart illustrating changes in inventory over several months allows you to visualize whether you're in a buyer's or seller's market. This visual aid is especially impactful during client presentations, enabling you to justify pricing strategies or suggest optimal times for buyers to enter the market.

It's essential to keep an eye on conversion rates from leads to sales as well. Understanding how efficiently you're transforming inquiries into transactions can highlight opportunities for improvement within your sales process. To track conversion rates effectively, maintain a record of generated leads alongside successful sales. The formula =(Total_Sales/Total_Leads)*100 provides a clear percentage of your effectiveness, while pivot tables can facilitate deeper analysis by breaking down conversions by source or campaign.

Additionally, evaluating marketing effectiveness through return on investment (ROI) from various campaigns is invaluable. By comparing expenses with revenue generated from those campaigns, you can determine which marketing strategies yield the best results and which may require re-evaluation. The straightforward formula for calculating ROI is =(Revenue - Cost)/Cost, expressed as a percentage. This analysis empowers you to make informed decisions about resource allocation moving forward.

Tracking referral sources is also advantageous; understanding where your business originates allows you to nurture relationships with top-performing sources while appropriately managing less effective channels. Create a spreadsheet to capture information about each referral's origin and associated outcomes; regular reviews of this data will guide your networking and marketing strategies.

Finally, never underestimate the value of customer

satisfaction metrics like the Net Promoter Score (NPS). Gathering feedback from clients after transactions enables you to assess their satisfaction levels and willingness to recommend your services. Calculating an NPS score based on client responses provides insight into overall service quality and highlights areas for enhancement.

By concentrating on these key metrics—sales performance, client interactions, market trends, conversion rates, marketing ROI, referral sources, and customer satisfaction—you establish a robust framework that not only supports daily operations but also lays the groundwork for long-term success in real estate. Tracking and analyzing these figures within Excel significantly enhances your strategic capabilities while fostering growth in your practice. Each metric offers insights that contribute not only to individual transactions but also to overarching business strategies aimed at driving profitability and reputation in an increasingly competitive marketplace.

Integrating Live Data Feeds

Integrating live data feeds into your Excel spreadsheets can revolutionize the way you analyze and visualize real estate information. With access to real-time data, you can make informed decisions that reflect the latest market conditions, trends, and client preferences—an invaluable capability in a fast-paced field like real estate, where market dynamics can change rapidly.

Picture this: tracking property prices, sales data, or interest rates as they fluctuate throughout the day. For example, by connecting to a real estate API that provides live listings, you can automatically populate your Excel sheets with the most current information. Setting this up usually requires some programming knowledge or tools designed for API integration. Fortunately, using Power Query in Excel simplifies the process significantly.

To illustrate this, let's consider integrating Zillow's API to access property listing data. After registering for an API key from Zillow, open Excel and head to the Data tab. From there, select "Get Data," then "From Other Sources," and choose "From Web." Enter the API URL provided by Zillow along with your key parameters, and Power Query will fetch the data directly into your workbook.

Once the data is imported, you can manipulate and analyze it just like any other information in Excel. Take this example, if you're interested in tracking average home prices across different neighborhoods, you can use PivotTables to group data by area and calculate the average sale price. Simply drag and drop fields like "Neighborhood" into Rows and "Sale Price" into Values, setting it to compute the average.

In addition to property listings, incorporating live economic indicators can further enhance your analysis. Economic factors such as mortgage rates or unemployment statistics significantly influence market behavior. You might connect to sources like FRED (Federal Reserve Economic Data) for these indicators. Again using Power Query, enter FRED's API endpoint that corresponds to the specific economic indicators you want to monitor.

Take this example, if you wish to track interest rate changes over time, creating a chart that displays these rates alongside your sales data could reveal insightful correlations between economic conditions and housing demand. After importing the interest rate data through Power Query, you can use a line graph to visually represent these trends against home sales.

Collaboration is another area where live data feeds excel. If you're working on a team project, having a shared workbook with automatically updated information keeps everyone aligned with current metrics without requiring constant manual updates. By integrating platforms like Microsoft Teams with your Excel environment, team members can comment on changes in real time while accessing live updates directly within their shared documents.

And, integrating automation through macros can enhance efficiency when working with live data feeds. Once you've established connections for regular updates of property listings or market indicators via APIs or Power Query processes, consider creating a macro that refreshes all queries at set intervals—perhaps every hour—to ensure you're always viewing the most recent figures available.

A practical example involves an agent who specializes in luxury properties. By integrating live feeds from multiple listing services (MLS) into their custom Excel dashboard, they maintained up-to-the-minute awareness of competitive listings and price changes in their target markets. This capability not only allowed them to advise clients more effectively but also positioned them strategically against competitors.

Embracing these practices places you at the forefront of real estate technology—an increasingly vital advantage as clients expect professionals to leverage cutting-edge tools effectively. As you become proficient in integrating live feeds into your workflows via Excel, you'll uncover new insights hidden within every dataset—insights that can empower your strategies and enhance decision-making processes across all areas of your business operations.

In the end, integrating live data feeds transforms static spreadsheets into dynamic analytical tools capable of driving strategic growth in your real estate practice. This integration not only improves operational efficiency but also lays the groundwork for more predictive analyses as market conditions continuously evolve around us.

Dashboard Interactivity with Slicers

Creating interactive dashboards in Excel enhances not only your data visualization but also your ability to make quick, informed decisions. One particularly powerful tool in this regard is the slicer, which enables users to filter data visually and intuitively. This engaging feature allows you and your team to dynamically analyze real estate data, ensuring that the insights you derive are always relevant and timely.

Imagine a dashboard that consolidates property listings, sales figures, and client information into one cohesive view. As you explore this data, the ability to filter through various parameters—such as property type, price range, or geographic location—can significantly reshape your understanding of market trends. This interactivity fosters a deeper comprehension of your data; for example, if you are tracking sales performance across different neighborhoods, a slicer lets you isolate sales figures for a specific area with just a click.

To implement slicers in your Excel dashboard, start by ensuring your data is structured as a table. You can do this by selecting your dataset and navigating to the "Insert" tab, then choosing "Table." Once your data is formatted as a table, adding slicers is straightforward. Click anywhere within the table, go to the "Table Design" tab (or "Table Tools"), and select "Insert Slicer." From there, choose the columns you'd like to filter on—such as "Property Type," "Sale Price," or "Status.

After inserting your slicers, they will appear as distinct visual elements on your worksheet. These slicers enable real-time filtering of data; for instance, if you want to view only luxury properties priced above)1 million among active listings, simply click the relevant option in the slicer. Instantly, all connected charts and tables will update to reflect this selection.

The versatility of slicers extends beyond basic filtering; they can be linked to multiple PivotTables or charts simultaneously. That means if you have various visualizations representing different aspects of your real estate metrics—like sales over time or inventory levels—selecting an option in one slicer will adjust all linked elements accordingly. This interconnectedness creates a cohesive narrative within your dashboard.

Consider a practical scenario where an agent prepares for a quarterly review meeting with their team. They've developed an interactive dashboard displaying year-to-date sales across several property categories: single-family homes, condos, and commercial properties. By incorporating slicers for each category and price range, they allow team members to effortlessly explore performance during discussions. This not only saves time but also facilitates targeted conversations based on live data insights.

Customization further enhances the effectiveness of your slicers. You can modify their appearance—changing colors or sizes—to align with your overall dashboard theme or improve visibility for presentation purposes. Additionally, positioning slicers logically within your layout can enhance user experience; placing them near relevant charts allows for intuitive navigation.

Another valuable feature is the ability to use multiple slicers simultaneously for refined analysis. For example, if you're interested in properties sold within a specific timeframe while filtering by agent performance or listing price tiers, layering multiple slicers enables you to drill down into precise insights. Each layer of filtering leads to more targeted conclusions that can influence strategic decisions—whether adjusting marketing efforts or reallocating resources among agents based on performance metrics.

One common challenge when using slicers is managing large datasets effectively. As you incorporate more filters into your dashboard design, consider their impact on clarity and usability. Keeping it simple is essential; avoid overwhelming users with too many options at once. Focus on critical metrics relevant to immediate business objectives while allowing room for deeper analysis when needed.

To further illustrate these concepts, imagine an agency utilizing their interactive dashboard during open houses or client meetings. Agents can present real-time market data by manipulating slicers based on client interests—for instance, displaying recently sold properties in desired neighborhoods while highlighting specific amenities or pricing trends in those areas.

Harnessing the power of slicers transforms standard Excel dashboards into immersive tools that actively engage users in their data exploration journey. This interactivity not only strengthens analytical capabilities but also promotes collaboration among teams who can confidently discuss insights backed by live updates rather than static numbers.

Incorporating these practices into your Excel dashboards equips you with invaluable tools for making swift and informed decisions—a crucial skill set in today's fast-paced real estate environment where every moment counts and opportunities arise unexpectedly. As you master these interactive features within Excel, you'll be better prepared not just to react but also to anticipate shifts in market dynamics —all while providing exceptional value to clients through insightful guidance based on real-time analysis.

Using KPIs and Target Indicators

Measuring performance through Key Performance Indicators (KPIs) and target indicators is crucial for real estate professionals aiming to gain a competitive edge. KPIs provide quantifiable metrics that guide decision-making, helping you concentrate on the areas that drive your business's success. These indicators transcend mere numbers; they embody critical elements of your strategy, enabling you to track progress, identify opportunities, and effectively tackle challenges.

To utilize KPIs effectively in Excel, begin by defining what success means for your real estate business. This might involve metrics such as the number of properties sold per month, average days on the market, lead conversion rates, or customer satisfaction scores. By establishing clear goals, you can select indicators that align with your objectives and yield meaningful insights.

Once you've identified your KPIs, the next step is to set up a dashboard in Excel that visually represents these indicators. Excel's charting capabilities allow for immediate insights into your performance data. Take this example, if one of your KPIs is the monthly number of sales closed, creating a line graph can help visualize trends over time. Start by organizing your sales data into a table format, then select the relevant data points and navigate to the "Insert" tab to choose a line chart. This visualization reveals patterns and fluctuations in sales activity, providing key information for forecasting future performance.

You can also streamline KPI calculations using formulas in Excel. For example, to analyze your lead conversion rate, divide the number of leads converted by the total number of leads generated. In Excel, this formula might look like:

= COUNTIF(B:B,"Closed") / COUNT(B:B)

In this formula, "B" represents the column containing your lead statuses. This simple calculation gives you a quick snapshot of how efficiently leads are being converted into clients.

To keep these insights dynamic and relevant, incorporate real-time data updates into your dashboard. If you're using an external CRM or property management tool, many systems offer seamless integration with Excel through data import functions or APIs. Regularly updating your KPIs not only enhances accuracy but also allows for timely adjustments based on current performance.

In addition to basic tracking, pairing targets with your

KPIs introduces accountability and motivation. Establish benchmarks for each KPI; for instance, if closing 10 sales per month is ideal based on past performance, set this as your target. You can visualize these targets on your dashboard using conditional formatting—turning cells green when targets are met and red when they fall short. This method offers an at-a-glance understanding of where efforts are succeeding or require adjustment.

An essential aspect of utilizing KPIs is the continuous review and refinement of these metrics in response to changing market conditions or personal business strategies. Periodically reassess whether your chosen indicators remain relevant as market dynamics evolve. For example, during periods of rapid growth or shifts in consumer behavior due to economic factors, you may need to adjust which KPIs you prioritize.

Consider a scenario where you manage a portfolio of rental properties. While occupancy rates are strong at 95%, you notice that rental price growth has stagnated over recent months. By analyzing rent pricing against competitors (a separate KPI), you discover that your prices aren't keeping pace with market trends revealed through comprehensive research. Armed with this insight, you can adjust pricing strategies accordingly—illustrating how KPIs inform actionable business decisions.

Another compelling example is tracking customer satisfaction through surveys conducted after transactions close. The feedback gathered offers critical insights into client experiences that can shape future service offerings and enhance overall client relations. By correlating high satisfaction scores with repeat business metrics (another KPI), you gather evidence supporting further investments in customer relationship management initiatives.

Collaboration within teams using shared dashboards can significantly amplify insights gained from KPIs as well. Utilize

Excel's sharing features to allow team members to contribute data updates or comments directly on the shared file. This collaborative environment fosters collective ownership of performance metrics while enhancing engagement among team members regarding their roles in achieving targets.

Effectively leveraging KPIs requires both strategic setup and an ongoing commitment to analysis and action based on those insights. The clarity gained from structured data transforms how you approach challenges and opportunities within your real estate practice.

As you refine these skills in utilizing KPIs and targets through Excel, you'll cultivate a data-driven culture within your organization that promotes accountability while maximizing potential growth opportunities—an indispensable asset in today's competitive real estate landscape. The true power lies not only in understanding past performance but also in strategically preparing for what's next based on informed decisions drawn from robust performance indicators.

Publishing and Sharing Dashboards

Creating an impactful dashboard in Excel involves more than just effective data visualization; it requires thoughtful consideration of how you publish and share these dashboards to maximize their effectiveness. By making insights accessible to team members, stakeholders, and clients, you foster collaboration and facilitate informed decision-making. This sharing process transforms raw data into a collective asset that everyone can utilize for strategic advantages.

Begin with the fundamentals: a well-structured dashboard should be both intuitive and visually engaging. After assembling your dashboard with essential KPIs and insights, explore the various publishing options available in Excel. If your primary audience is using Microsoft Teams or SharePoint, leveraging Excel's cloud capabilities enables you to publish your dashboards online directly. This approach not only guarantees real-time updates but also allows multiple users to access the same version simultaneously, minimizing errors that can arise from mismatched data.

To publish a dashboard, start by saving your workbook in OneDrive or SharePoint. Then, navigate to the "File" menu in Excel and select "Share," followed by "Publish to Web." This feature generates a link that you can distribute to your audience. By embedding this link in emails or internal communications, you provide convenient access to your dashboard while maintaining control over who can view it.

When sharing dashboards, it's essential to consider user permissions carefully. Establishing appropriate access levels is crucial; some users may need editing privileges while others only require viewing access. You can manage who can view or modify your data through the "Share" options, allowing for a tailored approach that upholds data integrity.

Once your dashboard is shared, encourage interaction with it. Excel facilitates comments and notes within shared workbooks—use these features to solicit feedback from team members regarding the insights presented. Engaging colleagues in discussions about performance metrics nurtures a culture of collaboration and continuous improvement, whether it's analyzing underperforming KPIs or sharing insights on market trends that influence strategy.

Real-time updates are vital for effective decision-making. For example, if you're tracking property sales data, ensuring that your dashboard reflects the most current figures empowers stakeholders to act swiftly on emerging trends or anomalies. By connecting to live data sources via Power Query or external APIs, your dashboard can refresh automatically with each new input, enhancing accuracy and keeping everyone aligned on performance.

Visual clarity is another critical aspect of publishing dashboards. Utilize Excel's extensive formatting tools to present information in an easily digestible manner. Highlight important figures using conditional formatting—immediate color changes can quickly alert viewers to areas needing attention. Ensure that graphical elements such as charts and gauges are clear and uncluttered, focusing on key insights rather than overwhelming users with excessive information.

Additionally, consider how you can visually narrate the story behind the numbers. Instead of relying solely on raw data points, incorporate visualizations that illustrate performance trends over time or comparisons against targets. Take this example, including a line chart showing monthly sales alongside target benchmarks provides contextual clarity about performance, making it easier for viewers to identify successes and areas needing improvement.

Another innovative strategy is to integrate narrative elements into your dashboards through text boxes or comments that explain significant shifts in data trends—such as a sudden dip in sales due to seasonal factors or unexpected market shifts. These contextual notes enhance understanding and encourage proactive strategizing among team members.

Finally, regularly gather feedback from users about the functionality and relevance of published dashboards. Conducting quick surveys or informal check-ins can help identify which aspects are effective and which areas may need refinement. This iterative approach ensures that your dashboards remain effective tools for their intended purpose.

Publishing and sharing dashboards goes beyond simply disseminating information; it creates a channel for collaborative growth within your organization. By prioritizing accessibility, interaction, visual clarity, and ongoing feedback loops, you not only drive engagement but also cultivate a culture where data-driven decision-making flourishes.

By elevating how you publish and share these valuable tools, you amplify their impact on your business strategies and client engagements—an essential component as you navigate the evolving landscape of real estate success through mastery of Excel's capabilities.

Using Power BI with Excel

Power BI serves as a powerful ally when integrated with Excel, offering advanced data visualization and analytics capabilities that can significantly enhance your real estate practice. By connecting these two tools, you can transform raw data into dynamic, interactive reports that provide deeper insights and support informed decision-making. The synergy between Excel's data manipulation strengths and Power BI's robust visualization features allows you to maximize the potential of your data.

To begin this integration, ensure that both applications are installed on your computer. Start by preparing your data in Excel—this involves organizing your datasets into tables and ensuring the information is clean and structured. Once your data is ready, the next step is to load it into Power BI. Open Power BI Desktop, select "Get Data," and choose "Excel" to locate your workbook. This initial step establishes a direct link between the two platforms, enabling seamless updates as your data evolves.

After importing your data, you'll enter the Power Query Editor, a powerful feature that lets you perform various transformations on your data without modifying the original Excel file. For example, if you're managing property listings with columns for location, price, and square footage, you might want to filter out properties above a certain price point or those missing essential details. In Power Query, you can apply filters or modify columns before loading the final dataset into Power BI.

Once your data is loaded into Power BI, the real magic occurs in the report view. Here, you can create interactive dashboards using intuitive drag-and-drop functionalities. If you're interested in analyzing property sales trends over time, simply select your date column as a visual axis and drag in sales figures to generate a line chart. This instant visualization allows you to observe fluctuations in sales volume across different months or seasons.

To enhance user interactivity, leverage slicers—visual filters that enable users to segment data dynamically based on specific criteria such as location or price range. Take this example, if your report highlights overall sales trends but you want users to focus on a particular neighborhood or property type, adding a slicer for these categories allows them to filter the entire dashboard instantly.

Power BI also excels at integrating data from multiple sources —a significant advantage in real estate where information often resides in various locations. You can merge Excel datasets with other sources like SQL databases or web APIs. For example, if you maintain one Excel file for client interactions and another for property listings, Power BI enables you to blend these datasets into a unified view. This way, you could display client demographics alongside property performance metrics to uncover patterns that inform your marketing strategies.

Once you've created a comprehensive report, effective sharing is crucial for collaboration within your team or with clients. In Power BI Desktop, simply click "Publish" to share your report directly to the Power BI service. This process makes your reports accessible via web or mobile devices—ensuring stakeholders can view them anytime and anywhere.

Another key feature of Power BI is its ability to refresh data automatically from Excel files saved in OneDrive or SharePoint. For example, if you've set up automatic updates for property listings in Excel, these changes will be reflected in real-time on your Power BI dashboard without requiring manual intervention. This guarantees that all users are working with the most current information available—an essential factor when making time-sensitive decisions in real estate.

Visual aesthetics are equally important; take advantage of Power BI's extensive customization options to enhance clarity and engagement. Adjust color schemes to align with branding guidelines or utilize custom visuals that resonate with your audience's preferences—whether they are potential homebuyers looking for stylish designs or investors seeking straightforward financial reports.

As you develop reports in Power BI based on Excel data, remember to incorporate narratives around the visuals. Adding textual insights alongside graphs provides valuable context—for example, explaining why certain areas are trending upwards due to recent developments or shifts in market demand.

The combined use of Excel and Power BI not only enriches how you visualize and share real estate data but also amplifies strategic planning capabilities across various operational aspects—from client engagement tactics to performance evaluations of agents or properties.

Harnessing this powerful duo equips you with innovative tools that enhance both analytical rigor and presentation effectiveness—ultimately driving better outcomes in an industry where informed decisions can make all the difference between success and stagnation. As technology continues to evolve within real estate analytics, mastering these integrations becomes essential for standing out in a competitive landscape.

CHAPTER 11: REAL ESTATE PROJECT MANAGEMENT WITH EXCEL

Creating Project Plans

Creating project plans in Excel is an essential skill for real estate professionals looking to enhance their workflow and ensure timely task execution. A well-structured project plan goes beyond merely outlining goals and timelines; it also identifies necessary resources, assigns responsibilities, and anticipates potential risks. This clarity empowers agents to manage multiple listings, transactions, and client interactions with ease.

To start developing a solid project plan, first define the project's scope. Consider what you aim to achieve—are you launching a new marketing campaign for a property or preparing for an open house? Specify your objectives, such as "Increase leads by 30% within three months" or "Host an open house on March 15th." Clearly articulated objectives lay the groundwork for all subsequent steps.

Next, break down these goals into actionable tasks. Take this example, if your aim is to host an open house, your task list might include scheduling the event, preparing marketing materials, arranging refreshments, and sending invitations. Assign due dates to each task to ensure accountability. A straightforward table in Excel can help you organize this information with columns labeled "Task," "Owner," "Due Date," and "Status."

To visually track progress, consider using Excel's conditional formatting features. Color-code tasks according to their status —green for completed tasks, yellow for those in progress, and red for overdue items. This visual representation not only enhances organization but also provides quick insights into what requires immediate attention.

Once you've organized your tasks, it's vital to assign responsibilities clearly. Designate who is accountable for each task—whether it's you or a team member. This collaborative approach fosters teamwork and ensures alignment with the project's goals.

Establishing timelines is equally important, and this is where Excel's built-in features can be particularly useful. You can create Gantt charts to visually represent your project timeline. To set one up in Excel, list your tasks vertically on the left side of your sheet and place corresponding start and end dates horizontally across the top. Use bar charts to illustrate task durations; this visual layout allows you to identify overlaps at a glance and allocate resources effectively.

To further improve communication about your project plan, integrate regular check-in meetings into your schedule. Use Excel to document agendas and meeting minutes directly within your project workbook. This practice keeps everyone informed and serves as a valuable reference point for future discussions.

As you implement the project plan, make it a habit to regularly update its status in Excel. This not only helps track progress against deadlines but also highlights any challenges that may arise during execution. If a task falls behind schedule or requires additional resources, document these changes directly on your spreadsheet so that adjustments can be made promptly.

Finally, after completing each project phase or reaching significant milestones, conduct a retrospective analysis using Excel to assess what worked well and what could be improved. Create a separate worksheet to capture lessons learned alongside suggestions for future projects. This reflective process ensures continuous improvement in planning practices while keeping all team members informed about best practices moving forward.

By following this structured approach to creating project plans in Excel, real estate professionals can navigate complexities more effectively while maintaining high levels of organization —ultimately leading to greater success in achieving their objectives and delivering exceptional client service.

Task Assignment and Timeline Tracking

Effective task assignment and timeline tracking are essential for real estate professionals seeking to enhance their workflow. After establishing the foundation of a project plan, the next step is to clearly define, assign, and monitor tasks within a structured timeline. This approach not only fosters collaboration among team members but also keeps all stakeholders focused on achieving shared goals.

Begin by developing a comprehensive task list based on your project objectives. Take this example, if you're launching a new marketing initiative for a property, identify specific tasks such as designing promotional materials, coordinating social media outreach, and scheduling client follow-ups. Clearly articulating each task and breaking it down into smaller, manageable actions—like "create flyer design," "set up Facebook ad," and "contact previous clients"—clarifies expectations and simplifies progress tracking.

Assigning ownership of each task is crucial for promoting accountability. Use an Excel column labeled "Assigned To" to designate responsibility for each action item. This practice streamlines communication and ensures everyone understands their roles within the broader project context. For example, if John is in charge of social media outreach and Lisa is managing print advertisements, clearly marking these responsibilities fosters a sense of ownership and pride in completing tasks.

To enhance transparency in tracking progress, introduce a "Status" column in your spreadsheet that indicates whether tasks are "Not Started," "In Progress," or "Completed." Regularly updating this status during team meetings or check-ins allows everyone to stay informed about current efforts and overall progress.

Excel's built-in features can further simplify timeline tracking. Utilizing formulas like TODAY() or NETWORKDAYS() enables automatic calculation of deadlines based on start dates while excluding weekends or holidays. For example, if a task starts on March 1st and needs to be completed within ten business days, you can set your formula to update the due date automatically based on those criteria.

Visual aids such as Gantt charts can elevate your timeline tracking process. To create one in Excel, list all tasks vertically in one column and place dates horizontally across the top row. Highlight task durations with color-coded bars that span the corresponding dates, instantly revealing overlaps or bottlenecks in your schedule.

Regular communication through scheduled check-ins is vital for maintaining momentum and addressing potential roadblocks promptly. During these meetings, review the status of assigned tasks directly from your Excel sheet, documenting key points and decisions in a section labeled "Meeting Notes." This practice not only keeps a historical record but also provides insights into effective strategies for future projects.

As deadlines approach or milestones are reached, utilize Excel's comment feature for quick notes or reminders related to specific tasks. This functionality ensures that vital information stays attached directly to relevant tasks rather than being scattered across different documents.

Once projects conclude or reach significant phases, conduct a thorough review using Excel's capabilities to facilitate retrospective discussions among team members. Create a new worksheet titled "Lessons Learned" where participants can capture both successes and challenges encountered throughout the process. Analyzing what worked well—and what didn't—enables teams to refine their methods moving forward.

In summary, effective task assignment coupled with robust timeline tracking creates an environment where real estate professionals can operate at peak efficiency while maintaining clarity on individual contributions toward collective goals. With Excel as your ally in managing these processes systematically, you'll be better equipped to tackle complex real estate projects, deliver exceptional client service, and ultimately enhance your professional standing in a competitive market.

Resource Allocation and Budgeting

Resource allocation and budgeting in real estate can often feel like navigating a labyrinth. However, by adopting a systematic approach, you can simplify these processes and ensure that your projects are completed on time and within budget. The key to success lies in balancing resource management with budget adherence, as both factors significantly influence the overall outcome of your project.

Start by identifying all the resources necessary for your

project. This includes not only financial resources but also human capital, materials, and technology. Take this example, if you're organizing a property showcase, you'll need to consider venue costs, marketing materials, staff assignments, and technology such as virtual tour software. A useful first step is to create an Excel spreadsheet to clearly visualize your resource requirements.

Next, develop a budget spreadsheet to monitor projected expenses against actual costs. Set up columns for "Budgeted Amount," "Actual Amount," and "Variance." For example, if you allocate (2,000 for advertising but end up spending)2,500, the variance will highlight areas of overspending. Analyzing these variances is vital; it offers insights into spending patterns that may necessitate adjustments in future projects.

To improve budgeting accuracy, take advantage of Excel's formulas for automatic calculations. A simple formula like =SUM(B2:B10) can quickly sum up all budgeted amounts for easy reference. If you want to create dynamic projections based on historical data, using the AVERAGE function can help establish realistic cost expectations derived from previous projects. This data-driven approach empowers decision-making with concrete evidence rather than mere estimates.

After establishing your budget, focus on resource allocation—strategically deploying your assets for maximum effectiveness. Utilize Excel's features such as data validation to create drop-down lists that categorize resources by type or availability status. Take this example, if certain contractors are only available on specific dates, having a list of their availability can streamline scheduling and minimize conflicts.

Incorporating conditional formatting into your resource allocation sheet allows you to visually identify areas that may require attention. For example, if a line item exceeds 80% of its budgeted amount while there are still weeks left until project completion, conditional formatting can highlight this automatically—enabling proactive management of potential budget overruns.

Regularly reviewing both resource usage and budget status throughout the project lifecycle is also essential. Schedule weekly check-ins to compare planned versus actual allocations using pivot tables in Excel. This approach facilitates quick assessments of how resources are being utilized relative to expectations. If you observe consistent underutilization of certain resources or persistent overspending in others, you can make timely adjustments.

For visual representation of resource allocation versus budget performance, consider creating charts directly within Excel. A clustered column chart comparing "Budgeted Amount" against "Actual Amount" provides immediate insight into your financial standing at a glance. Visual data representation can enhance discussions during team meetings about future financial strategies.

Once projects conclude or specific phases are completed, leverage Excel's analytical capabilities for post-project evaluations. Create dedicated sheets to analyze the effectiveness of resource allocations and adherence to budgets. Reflect on what worked well and what didn't; capturing these lessons within Excel fosters transparency and lays the groundwork for continuous improvement.

In summary, mastering resource allocation and budgeting through Excel transforms what could be a chaotic process into a structured framework that enhances accountability and clarity among team members. By meticulously documenting expenditures and monitoring resources—and adapting strategies based on real-time insights—you position yourself as a knowledgeable leader capable of steering projects efficiently in the dynamic landscape of real estate management.

Using Gantt Charts for Scheduling

Scheduling in real estate often resembles a high-stakes puzzle, where each piece must fit perfectly to ensure that projects run smoothly. Gantt charts serve as an invaluable tool in this context, allowing professionals to visualize project timelines and coordinate tasks efficiently. By translating complex schedules into a clear graphical format, Gantt charts enable real estate teams to plan and manage their workflows with precision.

To create a Gantt chart in Excel, begin by establishing a structured table. Your initial columns should include Task Name, Start Date, End Date, Duration, and Assigned To. Take this example:

Task Name	Start Date	End Date	Duration	Assigned To
Market Analysis	01/01/2024	01/15/2024	15	John
Property Show Prep	01/16/2024	01/30/2024	14	Sarah
Final Walkthrough	02/01/2024	02/05/2024	5	Team

Once this foundational data is set up, you can leverage Excel's bar chart feature to transform your project timeline into a Gantt chart. Highlight the duration of each task by creating a stacked bar chart; use the Start Date as the base for your bars and then add the Duration series on top.

After selecting your data range and inserting a stacked bar chart, your tasks will be represented as horizontal bars aligned with dates on the timeline. To enhance clarity, consider formatting the bars with different colors for various phases or task types—such as marketing versus property management—so stakeholders can quickly grasp progress at a glance.

A practical tip is to use Excel formulas to automatically calculate duration based on start and end dates. By entering the formula =DATEDIF(B2,C2,"d") into the Duration column (assuming B represents Start Date and C represents End Date), you can accurately reflect how many days each task will take without manual calculations.

Managing dependencies between tasks is crucial for preventing delays from one phase affecting another. Identify critical paths—the sequence of essential tasks that dictate project completion—using features like cell linking in Excel. For example, if Property Show Prep cannot commence until Market Analysis is complete, you can link the end date of Market Analysis to the start date of Property Show Prep to automate scheduling adjustments.

Regular updates are essential for keeping your Gantt chart relevant and actionable. As tasks progress or delays occur, adjust dates directly within your spreadsheet; Excel will automatically reflect these changes visually on your chart. A good practice is to schedule weekly reviews to assess progress against planned timelines and communicate updates to stakeholders accordingly.

Gantt charts also facilitate collaboration within teams. By sharing an updated version through Excel Online or similar platforms, team members can access real-time data from anywhere. Consider setting permissions that allow team members to edit specific sections while keeping core scheduling intact—this approach helps maintain control over project integrity while fostering teamwork.

To enhance communication regarding schedules further, integrate comments or notes into specific cells within your Gantt chart. This feature allows team members to leave feedback or updates directly related to particular tasks without cluttering the overall view of your timeline.

To wrap things up, utilizing Gantt charts in Excel significantly simplifies the scheduling complexities inherent in real estate projects. By visually representing timelines, automating calculations, effectively managing dependencies, and promoting collaboration among team members, you enhance project transparency and accountability. This meticulous organization empowers real estate professionals to keep their projects on track while confidently navigating the fast-paced demands of their industry.

Tracking Project Milestones

Tracking project milestones is essential for successful real estate management. It ensures that each phase of a project is completed on time and helps identify potential bottlenecks before they escalate into larger issues. Excel is particularly well-suited for this purpose, offering tools that facilitate easy tracking, updating, and sharing of critical milestones.

To begin effectively tracking milestones in Excel, start by creating a clear and organized spreadsheet. Set up columns for Task Name, Start Date, End Date, Milestone Status, Responsible Person, and Comments. This structured approach provides comprehensive visibility over project timelines and accountability.

| Task Name | Start Date | End Date | Milestone Status | Responsible Person | Comments |

| Market Analysis | 01/01/2024 | 01/15/2024 | Completed | John | On schedule |

| Property Show Prep | 01/16/2024 | 01/30/2024 | In Progress | Sarah | Awaiting materials |

| Final Walkthrough | 02/01/2024 | 02/05/2024 | Not Started | Team | Scheduled |

To enhance the visual aspect of your tracking sheet, incorporate conditional formatting. By using color codes for different milestone statuses—such as green for completed tasks, yellow for those in progress, and red for overdue tasks —you can quickly assess where attention is needed. To apply conditional formatting in Excel, select the Milestone Status column, navigate to the Home tab, click on Conditional Formatting, and create rules based on text values.

Excel also allows you to use formulas for automated status updates. Take this example, you could implement an IF statement to automatically mark tasks as "Overdue" if today's date surpasses the End Date. The formula =IF(TODAY()>C2,"Overdue","On Track") provides real-time feedback about each task's status.

Establishing reminders is another vital feature that helps you stay on top of milestones. You can utilize Excel's built-in notification features or integrate with Outlook to set calendar reminders as key dates approach. This integration ensures that important deadlines are not overlooked amid daily activities.

Collaboration becomes seamless when milestones are tracked within shared workbooks. Using Excel Online or shared files through cloud services allows team members to access updates in real time. Encourage all stakeholders to input their progress directly into the sheet; this practice fosters a sense of ownership over tasks and enhances team accountability.

Another powerful tool in Excel is the use of data validation lists for managing responsible persons effectively. By creating a drop-down list of team members in the Responsible Person column, you minimize errors associated with manual entry while ensuring clarity regarding accountability for each milestone.

Regular review sessions should be scheduled to discuss progress and challenges related to milestone tracking. These meetings serve as checkpoints to align team efforts and recalibrate timelines if necessary. During these sessions, leverage your tracking sheet as a visual aid—highlight completed milestones while focusing on those requiring immediate action.

Documenting comments related to each milestone can be invaluable for future reference. Use the Comments column not only for current updates but also to record insights gained during each project phase. This historical data can be instrumental when evaluating effective strategies or identifying areas for improvement in future projects.

In summary, tracking project milestones through Excel equips real estate professionals with a robust framework for efficient timeline management. The combination of structured data entry, visual aids like conditional formatting, automated notifications through formulas, and collaborative efforts creates an environment where every team member is engaged in achieving project goals. By embracing these techniques, you ensure that your projects progress smoothly while minimizing risks associated with delays or miscommunication.

In the end, meticulous milestone tracking enhances operational efficiency and empowers you as a real estate professional to fulfill commitments made to clients and stakeholders alike—an essential component in building trust and fostering long-term relationships within the industry.

Risk Assessment and Management

Risk assessment and management in real estate is not merely a precaution; it is an essential strategy for ensuring the long-term success of your projects and investments. With ever-changing market conditions, regulatory shifts, and unforeseen events, identifying potential risks early can mean the difference between thriving and merely surviving. Excel provides powerful tools that can streamline this process, enabling you to analyze risks, develop effective mitigation strategies, and monitor their impact over time.

Begin by creating a comprehensive risk register in Excel. This document should include columns for Risk Description, Probability of Occurrence, Impact Assessment, Risk Level (High, Medium, Low), Mitigation Strategies, Responsible Party, and Status. Organizing this information offers clear visibility into existing risks and outlines how they will be managed.

| Risk Description | Probability | Impact | Risk Level | Mitigation Strategy | Responsible Party | Status |

| Market downturn | High | High | Critical | Diversify portfolio |

John | Active |

| Regulatory changes | Medium | High | Significant| Stay updated on legislation | Sarah | Monitoring |

| Natural disasters | Low | High | Moderate | Ensure proper insurance | Team | Review |

Evaluate each risk based on its likelihood of occurrence and potential impact. Take this example, you might rate the probability of a market downturn as high due to current economic trends while considering its impact as critical because it could significantly affect property values. This dual assessment enables effective prioritization of risks.

To enhance the visual appeal of your risk register, leverage Excel's conditional formatting features. Use color coding to indicate risk levels: red for critical risks requiring immediate attention, yellow for significant risks needing ongoing monitoring, and green for low-level risks that are under control. This visual representation allows you to quickly grasp the overall risk landscape at a glance.

To keep your risk management strategy adaptable, incorporate formulas that calculate the overall risk level based on individual assessments. For example, implementing a simple scoring system can help quantify risks. By assigning numerical values to probability (1-5) and impact (1-5), you can create an overall risk score with a formula like =B2*C2. This score will then determine whether a specific risk falls into high or low categories based on predefined thresholds.

Once potential risks are identified, developing targeted mitigation strategies is crucial. Each strategy should be specific, actionable, and assigned to a responsible party who will oversee its implementation. For example, if regulatory changes pose a significant risk due to pending legislation affecting property taxes or zoning laws, designate someone on your team to regularly monitor legislative updates and ensure compliance.

Regular updates to your risk register are vital for effective management. Schedule periodic reviews—perhaps quarterly or following significant project milestones—to assess new risks that may have emerged or evaluate the effectiveness of existing mitigation strategies. During these reviews, encourage team members to share their insights; they often have unique perspectives on potential risks based on their roles within the project.

Enhancing your risk management process can also be achieved through Excel's collaboration features. By sharing your risk register via Excel Online or cloud-based platforms like OneDrive or SharePoint, team members can update their progress in real time. This approach fosters transparency within the team and ensures that everyone remains informed about the current status of each identified risk.

In addition to proactive monitoring of identified risks, consider using scenario analysis as a supplementary tool. Create separate worksheets in your Excel workbook dedicated to different "what-if" scenarios—such as drastic market declines or sudden regulatory shifts—and assess how they might impact your projects financially or operationally. Analyzing these scenarios prepares you for swift decision-making when challenges arise.

Documenting lessons learned throughout each project's lifecycle related to risk management is invaluable for continuous improvement. Allocate a section within your workbook solely for reflections on what worked well in managing risks and where improvements could be made in future projects. This repository will serve as an essential reference point when planning future endeavors or onboarding new team members.

Risk assessment and management in real estate through Excel is an ongoing process that demands attention but offers significant rewards by safeguarding investments against uncertainties. By adopting structured approaches like maintaining a detailed risk register combined with regular reviews and proactive measures tailored through collaborative efforts within Excel's framework, you'll navigate potential pitfalls more effectively than ever before.

In the end, mastering these techniques strengthens not only your projects but also solidifies your reputation as a reliable real estate professional who anticipates challenges before they escalate—building trust with clients while ensuring long-term success in an ever-evolving marketplace.

Performance Metrics and Reports

Performance metrics and reports are essential tools for any successful real estate agent. They provide the means to measure effectiveness, track progress, and make informed decisions that propel your business forward. Excel stands out as a powerful ally in this process, enabling you to gather data, analyze it, and generate reports that can significantly influence your strategies and interactions with clients.

To begin, identify key performance indicators (KPIs) that align with your business objectives. In real estate, common KPIs might include the number of properties sold, average days on market, sales price to list price ratio, and customer satisfaction scores. Each of these metrics offers insight into different facets of your performance. For example, monitoring the average days on market can help you evaluate how effectively you are pricing properties.

Once you have established relevant KPIs, create a dedicated Excel workbook for tracking these metrics. Designate a worksheet for each KPI where you can log data over time. Take this example, if you're tracking the number of properties sold each month, you might structure your worksheet as follows:

| Month | Properties Sold | Target | Variance |

| January | 10 | 12 | -2 |

| February | 8 | 12 | -4 |

| March | 15 | 12 | +3 |

In this example, the Variance column allows for a quick assessment of how well you're meeting your targets. You can use formulas to automate calculations; for instance, in cell D2 (the first variance cell), you would enter =B2-C2 to automatically calculate the difference between sold properties and targets.

Visual representation is crucial for making data easy to understand at a glance. Take advantage of Excel's charting features to create line graphs or bar charts that highlight trends over time. For example, plotting "Properties Sold" against "Target" provides a clear visualization of your performance relative to expectations, making it easier to communicate results during team meetings or presentations.

Regular updates to your performance metrics are necessary to maintain accuracy and relevance. Schedule monthly reviews to input new data and analyze trends. During these sessions, reflect on any significant changes—such as an uptick in sales during a specific season—that could inform future strategies.

Additionally, incorporating conditional formatting into your spreadsheets enhances clarity. For example, apply color coding to the Variance column: green for positive variances, indicating you are meeting or exceeding goals, and red for negative variances, signaling underperformance. This immediate visual feedback helps prioritize areas that require attention.

Since reporting is vital for effective stakeholder communication, consider creating summary reports at regular intervals—whether weekly or monthly—that encapsulate key insights from your KPIs. In a separate worksheet titled "Monthly Summary," compile highlights such as total properties sold, average days on market, and notable client feedback:

| Metric | Value |

| Total Properties Sold | 33 |

| Average Days on Market | 28 |

| Customer Satisfaction Score | 92% |

You can enhance this summary with visual elements such as pie charts illustrating customer satisfaction or bar graphs comparing monthly sales performance over time. These summaries serve not only as internal reports but also as valuable tools when meeting with clients or stakeholders seeking a quick overview of your accomplishments.

To further elevate your reporting process, consider utilizing Excel's advanced features like PivotTables for dynamic analysis of large datasets. If you manage multiple listings across various neighborhoods or property types, PivotTables allow you to quickly summarize sales data based on different criteria, such as location or property size, without manually filtering through extensive lists.

Take this example, if you want to analyze performance by neighborhood, set up a PivotTable that enables you to drag and drop fields like "Neighborhood," "Properties Sold," and "Average Sale Price." This flexibility allows for rapid data dissection from various angles—providing deeper insights into which areas yield better returns or require more marketing efforts.

Finally, documenting lessons learned from each reporting cycle is crucial for refining your strategies over time. Dedicate a section within your workbook to notes about what worked well and areas needing improvement based on insights gathered from your metrics analysis. Reflecting on these observations fosters continuous growth and adaptability in your approach.

In summary, the performance metrics and reports generated

through Excel are more than mere numbers; they tell the story of your business trajectory. By committing to systematic tracking and analysis using these tools, you sharpen your operational strategy while enhancing client relationships through transparency and accountability in reporting results. This ability to present solid data reinforces trust and positions you as a knowledgeable professional ready to navigate the complexities of the real estate market effectively.

CHAPTER 12: STRATEGY OPTIMIZATION USING EXCEL

SWOT Analysis for Decision Making

U nderstanding SWOT analysis is essential for real estate agents seeking to make informed decisions that can profoundly influence their careers. The SWOT framework—representing Strengths, Weaknesses, Opportunities, and Threats—offers a structured approach to evaluate both internal and external factors affecting your business environment. By systematically analyzing these components, you can develop strategies that capitalize on your strengths while addressing areas for improvement.

Start by identifying your unique strengths as a real estate agent. These may include your extensive market knowledge, strong negotiation skills, or a well-established network of clients and industry contacts. Documenting these attributes clarifies what distinguishes you from competitors. Take this example, if you have a proven track record of closing deals in a particular neighborhood, this strength can be prominently featured in your marketing efforts.

Equally important is recognizing your weaknesses—areas where you might lack expertise or resources. Perhaps you find digital marketing challenging or struggle to stay updated on market trends. Acknowledging these shortcomings isn't a form of self-criticism; rather, it offers clarity on where improvement is needed. This awareness enables you to seek training or mentorship to enhance your skills in these specific areas.

Opportunities represent the most exciting aspect of the SWOT analysis, as they highlight potential avenues for growth. In the real estate sector, opportunities may arise from emerging neighborhoods, new developments, or shifts in buyer demographics. For example, if urban areas are increasingly attracting young professionals seeking affordable housing options, adapting your strategies to target this demographic can be advantageous. Staying informed through local market reports can help you identify such trends early on.

However, threats should not be underestimated; they encompass external challenges that could impede your success. Factors like economic downturns, heightened competition from new agents, or regulatory changes can all pose risks to your business model. Conducting thorough research allows you to anticipate these threats and develop contingency plans to mitigate their impact.

After completing your SWOT analysis, compile your findings into an Excel worksheet for easy reference and future planning. Create four distinct sections—one for each element of SWOT—and fill them out accordingly:

| Strengths | Weaknesses |

| Strong negotiation skills | Limited experience in digital marketing |

| Established client base | Difficulty keeping up with market trends |

| Opportunities | Threats |

| Growth in affordable housing markets | Increased competition |

| Development projects in the local area | Economic downturn affecting sales |

This structured overview not only clarifies your position but also serves as a visual reminder of areas that require focus or enhancement.

Using this analysis strategically can guide several key decisions: how to market yourself effectively by highlighting strengths while addressing weaknesses; which opportunities to pursue based on current market trends; and how to prepare for potential threats that could disrupt your business flow.

Take this example, if your analysis shows that your strength lies in negotiation but you have weaknesses in digital marketing, consider investing time in online courses that focus on social media advertising techniques tailored for real estate agents. This approach not only addresses a weakness but can also transform it into an opportunity by increasing your visibility among potential clients.

And, it's beneficial to revisit this SWOT analysis regularly—perhaps quarterly—to ensure its relevance amidst the ever-changing real estate landscape. As markets evolve and personal growth occurs, so too will the insights gained from this exercise.

Integrating data-driven approaches into your decision-making enhances the effectiveness of your strategies and builds resilience against market volatility. Real estate is notoriously unpredictable; being proactive through structured evaluations like SWOT equips you with actionable insights that shape both immediate tactics and long-term goals.

To wrap things up, conducting a thorough SWOT analysis serves as both a reflective practice and a strategic tool that empowers real estate agents to navigate their careers effectively within the complexities of the marketplace. Each element of the SWOT framework informs critical aspects of decision-making and operational strategy—from refining personal branding efforts to identifying growth opportunities —all essential for achieving sustained success in this dynamic industry.

Financial Scenarios and What-If Analysis

Financial scenarios and what-if analysis are essential tools for making informed decisions in the real estate landscape. They empower agents to evaluate various potential outcomes based on changing variables, enhancing strategic planning and risk management.

To begin, financial scenarios help visualize different outcomes based on specific assumptions. For example, you might project property sales under various market conditions—such as stable, increasing, or decreasing property values. By creating separate models for each scenario, you can assess how shifts in the market might impact your revenue, expenses, and ultimately, your profit margins.

To effectively implement this analysis in Excel, start by establishing a simple financial model. Create a worksheet that includes key inputs like sale prices, the number of units sold, and associated expenses for each property transaction. Formulas can then be used to calculate expected profits based on these inputs. Here's a basic setup:

1. Input Section: Define your variables:
2. Sale Price per Unit: (300,000
3. Number of Units Sold: 5
4. Total Expenses (Marketing + Closing Costs):)50,000

5. **Profit Calculation Formula:

6. Total Revenue = Sale Price per Unit * Number of Units Sold

7. Profit = Total Revenue - Total Expenses

This structure allows you to easily adjust figures to see how different sale prices or costs influence overall profitability.

Next, consider utilizing Excel's built-in tools like Data Tables or Scenario Manager for what-if analysis. These features enable quick generation of results based on changing input values without the need to manually adjust each parameter.

Take this example, using the Data Table feature:

1. Create a column with potential sale prices (e.g., (250,000;)300,000; (350,000).

2. Set up a formula next to this column that calculates profit based on the sale price.

3. Highlight both columns and navigate to Data > What-If Analysis > Data Table.

4. In the dialog box that appears, select the appropriate row or column input cell corresponding to your sale price.

This approach generates a table displaying potential profits at each sale price point—helping you identify break-even points and strategies for profit maximization.

You might also explore scenarios involving variable interest rates that could impact mortgage payments for buyers. By creating a model with different interest rates, you can illustrate how these changes affect buyer affordability and potentially influence your sales volume.

In addition to these basic tools, incorporating advanced functions like NPV (Net Present Value) and IRR (Internal Rate of Return) into your analyses offers deeper insights into investment properties. For example, if you have a property with projected cash flows over several years, applying these functions will help determine its present value considering various discount rates:

- NPV Function:

``` excel
=NPV(discount_rate, cash_flow_range)
```

- IRR Function:

``` excel
=IRR(cash_flow_range)
```

These financial calculations not only assist in assessing current investments but also facilitate accurate forecasting of future performance.

What-if analyses extend beyond numbers; they encourage strategic thinking about potential future developments in the real estate market. Take this example, if new regulations are implemented or economic conditions shift due to external factors like interest rate hikes or changes in consumer behavior, having pre-established scenarios allows for rapid responses backed by data rather than relying solely on intuition.

Regularly revisiting these financial scenarios is crucial for staying relevant in an ever-evolving market landscape. As new data emerges—such as changes in local zoning laws or emerging housing trends—updating your models accordingly ensures accuracy and positions you as an adaptive real estate professional who leverages insights for informed decision-making.

In the end, mastering financial scenarios and what-if

analysis enhances your ability to navigate uncertainty while strengthening your credibility with clients and stakeholders alike. Presenting data-driven insights about property investments or market trends backed by thorough analyses establishes you as a knowledgeable authority capable of guiding clients confidently through their real estate journeys.

Portfolio Balancing and Diversification

For balancing a real estate portfolio and achieving diversification, the principles are akin to those of sound investing in any financial market. The primary objective is to minimize risk while maximizing returns through a strategic allocation of resources across various asset classes. In the realm of real estate, this means managing a portfolio of properties, each with its own distinct characteristics and potential for returns.

A crucial first step is understanding the different types of properties you can include in your portfolio. Consider categories such as residential, commercial, industrial, and mixed-use developments. Each category behaves differently under various economic conditions. For example, during an economic downturn, residential properties may hold their value better than commercial spaces due to the consistent demand for housing. Conversely, in a thriving economy, commercial properties could outperform residential ones as businesses expand.

To effectively balance your portfolio in Excel, begin by organizing your assets into distinct categories within a spreadsheet. Create columns to list property types, locations, purchase prices, current valuations, and annual income generated from each asset. A basic layout might look like this:

| Property Type | Location | Purchase Price | Current Value | Annual Income |

| Residential | Downtown |)400,000 | (450,000 |)30,000 |

| Commercial | Suburbia | (600,000 |)700,000 | (50,000 |

| Industrial | Riverside |)500,000 | (550,000 |)45,000 |

Once your portfolio data is clearly laid out, you can leverage Excel's features to analyze performance effectively. Take this example, the SUM function can aggregate the annual incomes from each property type:

```excel
=SUM(E2:E4)
```

This formula allows you to calculate the total annual income from all properties simultaneously.

Next, focus on diversification—specifically determining how much capital to allocate to each property type based on their respective risks and potential returns. A common strategy is the 60/40 rule: allocating 60% to stable investments like residential properties and 40% to higher-risk options such as commercial properties that offer greater returns.

To simulate how different allocations might impact overall portfolio performance in Excel:

1. Create a new section labeled "Proposed Allocations," where you can experiment with varying percentages across property types.

2. Calculate projected income based on these allocations using simple formulas that reference your original data.

For example:

- If you allocate 60% to residential and anticipate an income yield of 7%, you can calculate projected income like this:

```excel
```

=0.6 * (Total Annual Income) * (Yield Percentage)
` ` `

This projection provides insight into whether such an allocation could yield satisfactory returns compared to alternatives.

Another powerful tool within Excel is scenario analysis, which enables you to visualize how changes affect your portfolio's performance under different conditions—an essential feature when considering diversifying into new markets or types of real estate investments.

Suppose you're contemplating entering a new geographic market or investing in a different property type. You can use Data Tables or Scenario Manager for this purpose:

1. Create a model that outlines expected costs associated with entering a new market (such as renovations or market entry fees).

2. Set up scenarios reflecting various income potentials based on market performance—like low-demand versus high-demand situations.

3. Utilize the Scenario Manager feature (Data > What-If Analysis > Scenario Manager) to input different values for sales prices or rental incomes associated with these scenarios.

Once you've set up your scenarios and conducted analyses, evaluate which combinations offer the best risk-reward ratio while ensuring your portfolio remains balanced against unforeseen shifts in market dynamics.

Diversification also involves staying informed about trends that impact various sectors within real estate—from technological advancements affecting commercial leases to demographic shifts influencing housing demands.

Regularly reviewing and updating your portfolio strategy

ensures alignment with current market realities rather than relying solely on historical data. This practice not only enhances resilience but also positions you as a forward-thinking agent capable of navigating complexities adeptly.

By balancing risk across multiple asset classes and utilizing tools like Excel for analysis and projections, you're not merely managing a real estate portfolio; you're crafting a strategic approach toward building wealth over time—one informed decision at a time. This proactive stance fosters confidence among clients who view you not just as an agent but as a trusted advisor guiding them through intricate investment landscapes with clarity and insight.

Trend Analysis and Forecasting

Understanding market trends and forecasting future movements are crucial elements of strategic decision-making in real estate. Analyzing historical data to project future performance can set successful agents apart from their less effective counterparts. Excel is a powerful tool in this analytical process, allowing agents to visualize patterns, derive insights, and make informed predictions based on available data.

To begin trend analysis, it's essential to gather accurate historical data. Start by compiling relevant information on property prices, sales volumes, rental rates, and market demographics over a defined period. For example, consider collecting monthly data for the past five years regarding residential properties in your area. This dataset might include metrics such as average sale prices, inventory levels, and days on the market. Structuring this information in an Excel worksheet will facilitate effective analysis.

With your data organized, you can utilize Excel's built-in features to identify trends. A straightforward approach is to create line graphs or charts that visually represent the data. Take this example, plotting average sale prices over time can quickly reveal whether property values are trending upward or downward:

1. Highlight the relevant data range.

2. Navigate to the "Insert" tab.

3. Select "Line Chart" and choose your preferred style.

This visual representation allows for an immediate assessment of trends; an upward slope indicates rising prices, while a downward slope may suggest declining market conditions. Incorporating moving averages can help smooth out fluctuations, providing a clearer view of long-term trends.

Beyond basic visualization, Excel enables users to conduct more complex analyses using regression functions. By applying linear regression analysis, you can quantify the relationships between variables—for instance, how changes in interest rates might influence housing prices. The LINEST function is particularly useful in this context:

```excel
=LINEST(Y-values, X-values)
```

This function generates a slope coefficient that indicates how much Y (e.g., home price) is expected to increase or decrease as X (e.g., interest rates) changes.

Forecasting future property values involves estimating trends based on past performance. A straightforward method for this is Excel's FORECAST function:

```excel
=FORECAST(new_x_value,                     known_y_values, known_x_values)
```

For example, if you anticipate an increase in interest rates next year (new_x_value), you can use historical sale prices (known_y_values) and corresponding interest rates (known_x_values) to estimate how this change might impact future home prices.

Scenario analysis is also vital for evaluating various outcomes based on different assumptions about future conditions. Take this example, if you're considering investing in a neighborhood undergoing revitalization, you might analyze several scenarios—such as the potential effects of new schools being built or local businesses thriving.

To implement scenario analysis effectively in Excel:

1. Use Data Tables to vary two key inputs simultaneously—like anticipated rental rates and property appreciation.

2. Set these inputs in rows and columns within your worksheet.

3. Create formulas that calculate resulting metrics such as total revenue or net cash flow based on these inputs.

By adjusting assumptions in real-time within these tables, you gain immediate insights into how different scenarios could affect your investment strategies.

Paying attention to market-specific indicators is also crucial for improving forecasting accuracy. Keep an eye on leading indicators like building permits issued or employment rates within your target area; these factors can signal shifts in demand well before they become evident in pricing trends.

As you enhance your ability to analyze trends and conduct forecasts using Excel's robust functionalities, it's important not to rely solely on quantitative data. Integrating qualitative insights—such as community sentiment or industry news—can significantly influence buyer behavior.

In the end, mastering trend analysis and forecasting

empowers real estate professionals with the foresight needed to navigate market dynamics effectively. By leveraging Excel's capabilities for detailed data examination alongside intuitive insights into market movements, you position yourself as an astute agent who is not only prepared to respond but also to anticipate shifts within the industry landscape. This guarantees that your clients receive exceptional guidance amid changing circumstances.

Cultivating this analytical expertise creates a substantial competitive edge; clients will recognize your knowledge and confidence during negotiations and when advising them on potential investments. This solidifies your role not just as their agent but as their trusted advisor who understands the complexities of an ever-evolving marketplace.

Market Comparative Analysis

Market comparative analysis is a fundamental tool for making informed decisions in real estate. By evaluating how properties compare in terms of features, pricing, and market conditions, agents can strategically position themselves and their listings. Utilizing Excel can greatly enhance this process, turning raw data into actionable insights.

To begin your comparative analysis, start by gathering relevant data on comparable properties in your area. Concentrate on key metrics such as square footage, the number of bedrooms and bathrooms, the age of the property, and recent sale prices. For example, when assessing residential homes in a specific neighborhood, aim to collect information on at least five recently sold properties that share similar characteristics with the property you are analyzing. Organizing this data in an Excel spreadsheet will provide clarity and ease of use.

Once your data is organized, you can leverage Excel's capabilities to create a comparative pricing matrix. This matrix enables you to compare properties side by side effectively. To construct it:

1. Create columns for each property feature (e.g., address, square footage, sale price).

2. Input the corresponding values for each property.

3. Use conditional formatting to highlight discrepancies or standout features—consider color-coding homes that are significantly above or below average pricing based on square footage.

This visual representation offers immediate insights into how your target property stands relative to others. Take this example, if you notice that homes with similar square footage are priced lower than your listing, it may prompt a reevaluation of your pricing strategy.

To enhance your analysis further, consider using Excel's AVERAGE and MEDIAN functions to calculate average prices per square foot within your dataset. These metrics can be instrumental in determining a competitive price point for your listing:

```excel
=AVERAGE(range_of_prices)
=MEDIAN(range_of_prices)
```

For example, if you input sale prices into cells B2 through B6 and wish to calculate the average price per square foot based on their respective sizes in column C:

```excel
=AVERAGE(B2:B6)/AVERAGE(C2:C6)
```

This calculation provides a clearer understanding of market dynamics and can guide your pricing decisions effectively.

Incorporating graphical representations also enhances your analysis. Creating a scatter plot in Excel allows you to visualize relationships between variables like price per square foot and days on market. To do this:

1. Highlight the relevant data range.

2. Navigate to the "Insert" tab.

3. Select "Scatter" from the Charts section.

A scatter plot can reveal trends that may not be immediately apparent through numerical data alone—such as whether higher-priced homes tend to sell faster or remain on the market longer.

Conducting a SWOT analysis (Strengths, Weaknesses, Opportunities, Threats) for the properties under review is also crucial. While not an Excel function itself, organizing these insights within an Excel worksheet can clarify strategic considerations during negotiations. By creating separate sections for each element of the SWOT analysis within your spreadsheet, you visually map out how a particular property aligns with market trends and buyer expectations.

Additionally, it's important to stay informed about external factors affecting the market landscape. Local developments or changes in zoning laws can significantly influence property values. By monitoring such changes through news articles or local government announcements and integrating this information into Excel alongside your comparative analysis data, you'll gain a comprehensive view of what drives real estate dynamics in your area.

Effective comparative analysis relies not only on quantitative data but also on qualitative factors—such as neighborhood reputation or community amenities—that should not be overlooked. Include these aspects as notes within your Excel file or as separate columns in your comparative matrix for quick reference.

Mastering market comparative analysis equips real estate agents with vital insights that lead to more strategic decision-making and negotiation tactics. By combining quantitative data analyzed through Excel with qualitative assessments, agents enhance client relationships and solidify their position as knowledgeable authorities in the field. This dual understanding empowers agents to present compelling arguments when advocating for their clients' interests while ensuring they remain competitive in an ever-evolving market landscape.

As you refine your analytical skills using these methods in Excel, remember that being proactive about understanding market comparisons fosters trust and confidence among clients—an invaluable asset in any real estate career.

Creating Playbooks for Real Estate Deals

Creating playbooks for real estate deals is an essential practice that streamlines operations and enhances an agent's ability to respond effectively to diverse market situations. A well-structured playbook serves as a valuable resource, encapsulating strategies, processes, and best practices tailored to various types of transactions. The primary objective is to ensure consistency, efficiency, and professionalism in every deal.

To begin developing your playbook, identify the core components it should include. A comprehensive playbook typically features sections such as property acquisition strategies, client engagement protocols, marketing plans, and negotiation tactics. Each section should offer enough detail to guide you through the complexities of real estate transactions while remaining flexible enough to adapt to unique scenarios.

Let's start with the property acquisition strategies section. This part should outline your criteria for evaluating potential properties. Consider creating an Excel spreadsheet that lists key factors like location, price range, property type, and condition. A scoring system can be helpful here; assign weights to each criterion based on its importance to your overall investment goals. For example:

```excel
=IF(AND(Location="Desirable", Condition="Good"), 1, 0) +
IF(Price <= Budget, 1, 0) * Weight_of_Price
```

This formula enables you to assess properties objectively based on your predetermined criteria. Utilizing Excel's SORT and FILTER functions allows you to quickly focus on the most promising leads from your list.

| Channel | Campaign Type | Start Date | End Date | Responsible Agent |

| Facebook Ads | Targeted Ads | 01/05/2023 | 01/12/2023 | Agent Name |

| Open House | Event | 01/15/2023 | 01/15/2023 | Agent Name |

This table format provides clarity regarding tasks and deadlines while making it easy to track progress.

When addressing negotiation tactics in your playbook, include strategies tailored for various scenarios—whether you're representing buyers or sellers. Analyzing historical data from previous deals using Excel can reveal effective negotiation techniques. By examining past transactions, you can identify which approaches yielded the best outcomes and use this insight to inform future negotiations.

Take this example, consider recording data in an Excel sheet that details previous negotiations:

| Property Address | Buyer/Seller | Original Price | Final Price | Negotiation Tactics Used |

| 123 Main St | Seller | (300,000 |)285,000 | Offered quick closing |

| 456 Oak Ave | Buyer | (250,000 |)240,000 | Highlighted cash buyer status |

Regularly reviewing this data allows you to adjust your approach based on proven effectiveness in similar contexts.

And, it's vital to keep your playbook updated as market conditions evolve or as you acquire new strategies through experience or training. Set reminders using Excel's calendar function for periodic reviews—quarterly or bi-annually—to evaluate whether your existing tactics remain relevant or if adjustments are needed.

Integrating qualitative elements into your playbook can also add depth. Including testimonials from past clients about their experiences during specific transactions or presenting case studies of successful deals executed using these methods can provide motivation and context that enrich the data-driven aspects of your playbook.

In the end, creating a robust playbook for real estate deals empowers agents to act decisively and strategically in various situations while maintaining high standards of service throughout every transaction. It becomes a living document that adapts alongside you—a tool designed not just for immediate use but also for ongoing professional development and success in a competitive landscape.

Competitor Analysis

Conducting a thorough competitor analysis is essential for any real estate agent looking to establish a successful niche in the market. Gaining insights into your competitors—their strengths, weaknesses, and strategies—can significantly inform your own business approach. Rather than viewing competition as a threat, think of it as an opportunity for learning and adaptation.

Start by identifying your direct competitors: the agents or agencies operating in your geographical area who target similar client demographics. A simple Excel worksheet can help you organize this information effectively. Create columns for competitor names, locations, market segments (e.g., residential or commercial), and their unique selling propositions (USPs). For example, if you identify three agents specializing in luxury properties, document their names along with what distinguishes them, such as exceptional marketing strategies or specialized knowledge.

After establishing this foundational framework, delve deeper into each competitor's online presence. Explore their websites and social media profiles to understand how they present themselves to potential clients. Pay attention to the type of content they share: Are they highlighting client testimonials? Providing market updates? Or offering educational resources? This information can reveal insights into their marketing strategies and engagement tactics. Take this example, if one competitor frequently posts success stories from satisfied clients, it might indicate a robust referral network or a strong emphasis on client satisfaction.

Next, assess their pricing strategies. Compare their commission rates with yours and consider any incentives they may offer, such as reduced fees for first-time buyers or bundled service packages. Add this information to your Excel sheet under a new column titled "Pricing Strategies." Understanding your position relative to competitors will guide your pricing decisions and help identify areas for adjustment. If most competitors maintain similar rates but one has begun undercutting prices while preserving service quality, it could signal a noteworthy market shift.

Monitoring competitors' marketing efforts is another critical aspect of your analysis. Use Excel to track the various marketing channels these agents employ—such as email campaigns, social media ads, local print media placements, or community events. Create columns for each channel and note specific campaigns you observe. For example, if a competitor heavily invests in Facebook advertising but receives low engagement compared to organic posts on Instagram, it may suggest that potential clients in your area favor visual content over text-heavy ads.

In addition to quantitative data analysis, qualitative assessments are equally important. Review customer feedback on platforms like Google or Yelp, focusing not only on ratings but also on the content of reviews. What do clients appreciate most about these competitors? Are there recurring complaints? Compile this feedback into a separate section of your Excel sheet labeled "Client Feedback." By identifying common themes in customer experiences—whether it's responsiveness or expertise—you can glean valuable insights into areas where you can improve.

Finally, synthesize the collected data into actionable insights. Use conditional formatting within Excel to highlight trends where competitors excel and areas where they fall short. Take this example, if several agents struggle with timely communication yet are praised for their market knowledge, you should strive to enhance your responsiveness while maintaining expert-level insight into property markets.

Competitor analysis is more than just data collection; it's about interpreting that data strategically to elevate your service offerings above the competition's noise. By effectively leveraging Excel as both an analytical tool and a strategic planning framework, you position yourself not just as another option in the marketplace but as an informed choice grounded in data-driven decisions.

Engaging constructively with competitors fosters personal growth and can lead to significant improvements in your agency's performance metrics. As you develop a deeper understanding of the competitive landscape through ongoing analysis and strategic adaptations based on concrete findings from this exercise, you're likely to see increased client satisfaction and referrals—all stemming from informed decision-making rooted in rigorous research.

CHAPTER 13: HANDLING PROPERTY TRANSACTIONS WITH EXCEL

Documenting Transactions and Contracts

D ocumenting transactions and contracts is a vital aspect of real estate operations. While the multitude of details involved can seem overwhelming, a systematic approach can streamline your workflow and elevate your professionalism. Excel serves as an excellent platform for organizing these essential documents, helping you maintain accuracy and compliance throughout each transaction.

Begin by creating a comprehensive template in Excel to capture all transaction details. This template should feature key columns such as Transaction ID, Client Name, Property

Address, Contract Date, Closing Date, Sale Price, Commission Rate, and Notes. By establishing this structure from the outset, you set yourself up for success and ensure that no important information falls through the cracks.

Take this example, when managing a residential property sale, start by entering the Transaction ID as a unique identifier in the first column. Follow this with the client's name and property address. The Contract Date should reflect when both parties signed the agreement, while the Closing Date indicates when the transaction is officially complete. Clearly documenting these dates enables you to track timelines effectively and hold yourself accountable to clients.

To further enhance your documentation process, consider utilizing Excel's data validation feature. For example, in the Commission Rate column, you can restrict entries to specific values—such as 2%, 3%, or 5%—to prevent discrepancies down the line. This not only streamlines data entry but also ensures consistency across multiple transactions.

As you input details for each transaction, use additional columns for notes regarding specific conditions or client preferences. If a buyer requests certain renovations before closing, documenting this information fosters clear communication and sets realistic expectations.

Once your initial data is populated, leverage Excel's powerful filtering capabilities to segment transactions based on various criteria. You might filter by date range to identify upcoming closings or categorize them by client type—such as first-time buyers versus seasoned investors. This organizational strategy aids in strategic planning and prioritizing tasks based on urgency.

Integrating hyperlinks to electronic copies of contracts within your Excel sheet can further enhance accessibility. By inserting hyperlinks in a dedicated column that directs you to cloud storage where all contracts are securely stored, you save time and improve document accessibility during meetings or client interactions.

Consider expanding your documentation efforts beyond sales transactions to include rental agreements and property management contracts within the same workbook using separate sheets. This consolidated approach provides a comprehensive overview of your business while maintaining detailed records relevant to each category.

The significance of documenting transactions goes beyond simple record-keeping; it is essential for legal compliance as well. Accurate documentation safeguards both you and your clients in case disputes arise later on. For example, if a commission dispute surfaces months after closing, having clear records will substantiate agreed-upon terms.

To ensure compliance and accuracy in your documentation practices, establish a routine for regular record reviews. Monthly audits of your transaction logs can help identify any missing information or inconsistencies before they escalate into problems. During these audits, cross-reference with other data sources like bank statements or client communications to validate entries.

By utilizing Excel's built-in functionalities, you not only enhance your efficiency but also present a more professional approach to handling documentation in real estate transactions. Over time, as you refine these processes and incorporate best practices into your daily operations, you'll likely notice improvements in both client satisfaction and overall productivity.

In the end, mastering transaction documentation in Excel positions you as an organized professional who values accuracy—a trait highly regarded by clients in the real estate industry. By adopting these practices now and continuously refining them as needed, you're paving the way for long-term success while fostering trust with every client interaction through meticulous attention to detail.

Cost and Fee Calculation

Calculating costs and fees in real estate transactions is an essential skill that can greatly influence both your profitability and client satisfaction. With a solid understanding of these calculations, you can provide clients with precise estimates, helping them grasp the financial implications of their decisions. Excel serves as an invaluable tool in this process, enabling straightforward computations and simplifying complex scenarios.

Start by creating a dedicated Excel spreadsheet tailored for cost and fee calculations. This spreadsheet should include key sections such as Property Price, Closing Costs, Agent Commission, and Additional Fees. By organizing your workbook this way, you streamline data entry and ensure all relevant information is captured in one central location.

Take this example, if you're handling a residential sale priced at (300,000, enter this figure in the Property Price cell. Next, identify the typical closing costs associated with the sale, which generally range from 2% to 5% of the property price. To automate this calculation in Excel, input a simple formula in the Closing Costs cell: =B2*0.03 (where B2 refers to the Property Price). This will yield an estimated closing cost of)9,000 based on a 3% rate.

The agent commission is another vital component of your calculations. Typically expressed as a percentage of the property sale price, it's crucial to communicate this clearly to clients upfront. You can create a column for Commission Percentage and enter a value—say 3%. To calculate the actual commission fee automatically, input the formula =B2*C2 in the Agent Commission cell. For a (300,000 sale at a 3% commission rate, this will result in another)9,000.

In addition to these core elements, consider including other potential fees in your spreadsheet—such as inspection fees, appraisal fees, or title insurance costs. Create separate columns for each fee type and enter estimated amounts based on your experience or standard industry practices.

For example, if you expect an inspection fee of (500 and appraisal costs around)300, simply add these amounts in their designated columns. The advantage of using Excel is its ability to summarize these values effortlessly; utilize the SUM function to calculate total costs with ease. Input this formula in a Total Fees cell: =SUM(D2:F2) (assuming D2 through F2 contain your individual fees). This allows you to quickly present clients with a comprehensive breakdown of all expenses associated with their transaction.

Real estate transactions often involve various scenarios that may require rapid recalculations. Excel's dynamic capability to adjust values when inputs change is particularly beneficial. Take this example, if there's a change in the agent commission structure or if closing costs increase unexpectedly due to new regulations, simply update those cells; Excel will automatically recalculate totals based on your revised figures.

To enhance clarity in your calculations further, consider using conditional formatting. For example, set rules that highlight total costs exceeding a specific threshold—this provides visual cues that help you quickly identify potentially problematic transactions.

To streamline communication with clients regarding these calculations even more effectively, think about generating professional reports directly from your Excel workbook. By neatly formatting your spreadsheet—adding headers for each section and utilizing bold fonts—you create documents that are easy to share via email or print for meetings.

Integrating comments within your Excel workbook can also clarify any assumptions made during calculations. Take this example, if certain costs are estimated based on previous transactions or industry standards, insert notes alongside those cells so clients understand how those figures were derived. This transparency fosters trust and ensures everyone is aligned regarding financial expectations.

In the end, mastering cost and fee calculations through Excel not only boosts your efficiency but also enhances your professional credibility within the real estate market. Clients value agents who can provide clear financial insights alongside property expertise. As you refine these skills and adopt systematic approaches to calculations, you position yourself as a knowledgeable ally in their real estate journey —someone who truly understands how every dollar impacts their investment decisions.

By focusing on accuracy and clarity throughout this process, you foster trust and establish yourself as an essential resource for clients navigating complex transactions in today's fast-paced real estate environment.

Tracking Offers and Counteroffers

Tracking offers and counteroffers is a vital part of real estate transactions, influencing both negotiations and client satisfaction. An organized approach to managing this information can streamline your workflow and foster transparency with clients, keeping them informed and engaged throughout the buying or selling process.

To start, create a dedicated Excel workbook for tracking offers and counteroffers. Your spreadsheet should feature columns for Property Address, Buyer Name, Offer Amount, Counteroffer Amount, Status, and Date Received. This structured format allows you to maintain a clear overview of each transaction's progress.

Take this example, if you receive an initial offer for a property listed at (350,000, you would log the details in your spreadsheet. Under the appropriate buyer's name and address, input)340,000 in the Offer Amount column. To ensure consistency and avoid confusion later, establish a standardized date format—such as MM/DD/YYYY—for all entries.

As negotiations unfold, tracking counteroffers becomes essential. When you present a counteroffer of (345,000 back to the buyer, simply update their row by entering this figure in the Counteroffer Amount column. Consolidating all relevant information in one place enables you to see how negotiations progress over time.

To further streamline your tracking system, utilize Excel's data validation feature. For example, create a drop-down list in the Status column with options like "Pending," "Accepted," "Rejected," or "Withdrawn." This allows you to quickly update each offer's status while maintaining consistent terminology throughout your records.

Adding extra columns for comments or notes can also enhance your analysis of trends or patterns in offers and counteroffers. Document reasons behind specific offers or details about client expectations that may influence negotiations. Take this example, if a buyer expresses urgency due to personal circumstances, make a note in their row; this context can be invaluable for future interactions.

Excel's filtering capabilities are particularly useful for reviewing specific offers without having to sift through extensive data manually. By applying filters—such as sorting by date received or status—you can easily identify pending offers that need follow-up or require further action.

Implementing conditional formatting can help highlight important information at a glance. For example, if an offer exceeds the asking price or falls significantly below expectations, you can set rules to automatically color-code these entries—red for low offers and green for those above asking price—allowing you to prioritize which deals require immediate attention.

As counteroffers are made and negotiations evolve, remember

to frequently update your spreadsheet. This dynamic approach enables you to respond promptly to both clients and other agents involved in the transaction. The flexibility of Excel allows you to adjust numbers rapidly; changing an offer amount automatically recalculates totals related to commissions or net proceeds right before your eyes.

Clients may also want to visualize how different offers affect their financial outcomes during negotiations. To facilitate this understanding directly from your tracking sheet, consider creating additional columns that calculate potential net proceeds based on each offer or counteroffer presented. By using formulas like =B2-C2 (where B2 is the Offer Amount and C2 represents estimated closing costs), you provide a clear picture of what clients might expect financially if they accept any given offer.

Finally, when finalizing deals or summarizing negotiations for clients, think about exporting these tracking sheets into professional reports or presentations. A well-organized summary not only emphasizes numbers but also showcases your thoroughness and attention to detail—qualities that clients highly value when navigating complex transactions.

By mastering the tracking of offers and counteroffers through Excel's various functionalities—such as data validation lists for consistent statuses; conditional formatting for visual cues; and structured documentation—you not only improve your efficiency but also elevate your role as a trusted advisor throughout the negotiation process. Clients appreciate agents who proactively manage communications with clarity while providing insights that effectively guide their decisions.

Managing Closing Procedures

Managing closing procedures is a critical phase in any real estate transaction, often determining the ultimate success of a deal. A well-structured approach can significantly enhance client satisfaction and streamline your operations. By utilizing

Excel, you can create an organized system that tracks all closing-related tasks, documents, and timelines effectively.

Start by developing a dedicated closing checklist within your Excel workbook. This checklist should outline every necessary step from the moment an offer is accepted until the keys are handed over to the new owner. Key columns to include are Task Description, Assigned To, Due Date, Status, and Notes; these will help you keep track of each component of the closing process.

Take this example, when you receive acceptance on an offer for a property, log this milestone in your checklist. Detail tasks such as securing financing, scheduling inspections, and preparing closing documents. Assign specific responsibilities to team members or partners—like lenders or inspectors—to ensure accountability throughout your network. Under Task Description, you might list "Schedule Home Inspection," with a Due Date set for one week after acceptance.

As you navigate the closing process, updating the Status column becomes essential. Utilize options like "Not Started," "In Progress," "Completed," and "Delayed" to provide clarity on where each task stands. This transparency enables both you and your clients to have a clear view of progress at any time. If an inspection is postponed due to weather conditions, you can quickly update its status and add notes to explain the situation.

Excel's conditional formatting feature can greatly enhance your workflow. For example, if a task is approaching its due date and remains marked as "Not Started," you can set a rule that highlights that row in red. This visual cue acts as an immediate reminder to follow up on pending items before they potentially delay the closing timeline.

Another vital element of managing closing procedures is tracking document submissions. Create additional columns for critical documents such as the purchase agreement, title report, disclosures, and loan documents. Next to each document name, include checkboxes that indicate whether they have been received. This lets you quick visual confirmation of all required paperwork without needing to sift through emails or files.

Consider automating reminders for important deadlines using Excel's formula capabilities. For example, if your timeline dictates that inspections should occur within ten days post-acceptance, use a formula like =IF(TODAY()>Due_Date_Cell,"Overdue","On Track") to indicate whether any tasks are falling behind schedule.

To further streamline access to important documents, embed hyperlinks within your spreadsheet linking directly to electronic versions stored on cloud services like OneDrive or Google Drive. Take this example, linking directly to the signed purchase agreement enables immediate retrieval without searching through multiple folders—a significant time-saver when deadlines are looming.

Clear and concise communication is also vital during this phase. Use your spreadsheet as a platform to document conversations with clients or other parties involved in the transaction. A dedicated notes column can capture key details about discussions related to potential issues with title searches or changes in financing plans.

Incorporating a timeline visualization within Excel can enhance clients' understanding of when each task requires attention while keeping everyone aligned throughout the process. You might use Gantt charts or simple bar graphs to visually represent progress against deadlines; this provides clients with a snapshot view of how close they are to finalizing their purchase.

Finally, ensure that all information gathered throughout the closing process is easily exportable into professional reports or presentations once the deal closes. Summarizing all activities

—along with outcomes such as final sale price or concessions made—demonstrates thoroughness and professionalism while enhancing client trust in your capabilities as an agent.

By establishing an organized structure for managing closing procedures through Excel's various functionalities—checklists for tasks; conditional formatting for deadlines; document tracking systems; automated reminders—you not only improve your efficiency but also bolster your clients' confidence in their real estate journey. This proactive management fosters stronger relationships and positions you as a reliable guide through one of life's most significant transactions.

Commission Calculations and Tracking

Calculating and tracking commissions is a vital component of real estate transactions, significantly impacting your income and overall business success. By adopting a structured approach to this process, you can ensure accuracy while enhancing your financial management and reporting capabilities. Utilizing Excel can simplify what might otherwise be a complicated calculation into a streamlined and efficient system.

Start by creating a dedicated spreadsheet for commission calculations within your Excel workbook. This sheet should include key columns that capture essential details: Property Address, Sale Price, Commission Rate, Total Commission, Agent Share, and Notes. Each column plays an important role in determining how much you or your agency will earn from each transaction.

For example, imagine you close on a property priced at)300,000 with a commission rate of 6%. To calculate the total commission, input the sale price into one cell and the commission rate in another cell formatted as a percentage. In the Total Commission column, use the formula =Sale_Price_Cell * Commission_Rate_Cell. With these entries,

Excel will calculate the total commission as (18,000 for this transaction.

If you collaborate with multiple agents or partners on transactions, tracking agent shares can further clarify your commission calculations. Take this example, if you're splitting the total commission evenly between two agents (including yourself), you would enter =Total_Commission_Cell / 2 in the Agent Share column. This reflects that each agent receives)9,000.

Given that commissions can vary widely based on property types and negotiations, it's crucial to maintain flexibility in your spreadsheet layout. You may find it useful to create separate sheets for different transaction types—such as residential sales versus commercial leases—ensuring that relevant formulas are applied according to varying commission structures.

Another important aspect is monitoring pending transactions. Adding a column labeled "Status" can help indicate whether a deal is closed or still under negotiation. Simple designations like "Closed," "Pending," or "Lost" will clarify where each potential income source stands at any given time.

Visual aids can enhance your understanding as well; consider integrating charts or graphs to represent your commission income over time. Using Excel's charting tools allows you to quickly visualize earnings trends across months or quarters —valuable for personal reflection and strategic planning discussions with team members.

Staying organized extends beyond calculations; it also involves maintaining accurate records of communications regarding commissions. A dedicated notes section can track discussions with clients about commission rates or adjustments made during negotiations. This documentation will serve as an invaluable reference should questions arise later about how commissions were structured.

To further improve this system, automate reminders for critical payment timelines. For example, if payment is due within 30 days after closing a sale, use conditional formatting rules to highlight rows where payments are overdue so they stand out at a glance.

When it comes time to generate reports for tax purposes or performance reviews, having this structured data readily available simplifies the process immensely. With just a few clicks in Excel, you can filter out closed transactions for the year and summarize total commissions earned—a task that might otherwise take hours if done manually using traditional methods.

By incorporating these elements into your commission tracking system, you create a powerful tool that not only helps you manage earnings but also reinforces trust with clients and partners through transparency and efficiency in financial matters. Leveraging Excel's capabilities allows you to organize and calculate commissions effectively, enhancing your workflow while maximizing every earning opportunity within your real estate practice.

In the end, mastering this aspect positions you as not only skilled in closing deals but also proficient in managing the financial foundations essential for long-term success in real estate—freeing you to focus on what truly matters: building relationships and serving your clients effectively.

Maintaining Transaction Compliance

Maintaining compliance throughout real estate transactions is not merely a legal requirement; it also serves as a strategic advantage that distinguishes you in a competitive market. Navigating the complexities of compliance, from document management to adherence to local regulations, can often feel daunting. However, by leveraging Excel, you can establish a streamlined process that ensures compliance while enhancing operational efficiency.

Begin by crafting a comprehensive compliance checklist tailored to your region's specific requirements and your business model. This checklist should encompass essential documents, including purchase agreements, disclosures, inspection reports, and closing statements. To organize this effectively in Excel, create a table where each row represents a different transaction and each column corresponds to a compliance requirement. For example, include columns for "Document Type," "Received Date," "Completed," and "Notes." This layout provides clarity on pending documents and highlights outstanding items that need your attention.

Consider a scenario involving a residential sale. When you input the property details into your spreadsheet, be sure to include a checklist of all necessary documentation linked to that transaction. If an inspection report needs to be obtained by a specific date, using conditional formatting in Excel can be particularly beneficial. You might apply a rule that changes the cell color for dates that have passed today's date, providing a visual cue that keeps compliance issues front and center.

Another crucial element is ensuring the security of sensitive client information throughout the transaction process. Implementing password protection for your Excel files adds an extra layer of security. Navigate to File > Info > Protect Workbook > Encrypt with Password to restrict access to authorized personnel only, safeguarding sensitive documents and data.

As transactions progress through various stages—such as offer acceptance, inspections, and negotiations—it's essential to log any changes or updates meticulously. Including a comments section in your compliance table can effectively document important conversations or amendments regarding specific deals. Take this example, if clients request modifications to certain terms after initial agreements are signed, recording these changes in your spreadsheet promotes transparency and helps mitigate disputes later on.

Setting reminders for critical deadlines associated with each transaction's lifecycle is equally important. By utilizing Excel's built-in functions like TODAY() alongside conditional formatting rules, you can automatically flag upcoming deadlines such as contract expirations or inspection due dates. For example, entering formulas like =IF(Deadline_Cell < TODAY()+7, "Due Soon", "") in an adjacent column will proactively alert you about tasks needing immediate attention.

Regular audits of your compliance processes also enhance accountability within your organization. Schedule periodic reviews to assess completed transactions against your checklist. Using PivotTables can simplify this analysis by summarizing how many properties closed successfully versus those that faced compliance-related issues or delays.

Incorporating feedback loops into your workflow is another vital step in maintaining effective compliance. After closing transactions, gather insights from clients regarding their experiences with documentation handling and communication throughout the process. Analyzing this feedback not only helps refine your approach over time but also fosters stronger relationships built on trust and reliability.

By integrating these practices, you establish not only an efficient system for maintaining transaction compliance but also cultivate confidence among clients who value professionalism and transparency in every interaction. The outcome is an empowered real estate practice where regulatory adherence becomes second nature rather than a burdensome task.

Mastering these aspects of transaction compliance with Excel by your side sets the stage for smoother operations that ultimately benefit both you and your clients. By prioritizing accuracy and clarity, you ensure preparedness for audits while positioning yourself as a trusted professional dedicated to excellence within the real estate landscape.

Generating Transaction Reports

Generating transaction reports is a crucial element of effective real estate management. For agents, having a reliable method to compile and analyze transaction data streamlines workflows and enhances decision-making capabilities. By utilizing Excel's robust features, you can create detailed, customized reports that offer valuable insights into your transactions, helping you identify trends and refine your strategies.

Begin by setting up a dedicated worksheet for transaction reporting. Label the columns with key data points such as "Transaction ID," "Client Name," "Property Address," "Sale Price," "Closing Date," and "Commission Earned." This foundational framework allows you to input and track essential details for each transaction. Consistency in data entry is vital for maintaining integrity across your records.

Once your data is organized, take advantage of Excel's powerful filtering capabilities. If you're interested in analyzing properties sold during a specific timeframe or within a particular price range, applying filters can quickly narrow your search. Simply click on the filter icon in the header row of your table to activate this feature, then select criteria relevant to your analysis.

Next, enhance your financial assessments by utilizing Excel's SUM and AVERAGE functions to calculate total sales and average commission over designated periods. Take this example, if you're evaluating quarterly performance, you might use a formula like =SUMIF(C:C,"Q1",E:E) to sum sale prices in column E corresponding to transactions listed in column C for Q1. This lets you swift evaluations of financial performance over time.

To gain further insights at a glance, consider using visual representations of your data through charts. By highlighting relevant data points and navigating to the "Insert" tab, you can create graphs that depict trends—such as sales growth or fluctuations in commission—over time. A line chart can illustrate monthly sales trends, while a bar chart may display commission earned per client. These visual aids not only enhance your reports but also facilitate discussions with clients or stakeholders by clearly presenting performance evidence.

Additionally, pivot tables are invaluable tools for efficiently summarizing large datasets. If you have numerous transactions, creating a pivot table allows for comprehensive analysis without overwhelming detail. Simply drag the "Closing Date" field into the Rows area and "Sale Price" into the Values area; this setup automatically groups transactions by month or quarter while calculating totals for each period—providing a clear overview of sales performance across various timeframes.

To further enrich your reports, consider incorporating comments or notes directly within your Excel sheet for each transaction. This practice enables you to document specific details such as unique client requests or challenges encountered during negotiations. An additional column labeled "Comments" can serve this purpose well; for instance, if a client raised concerns about property disclosures during closing, noting it here will be beneficial for future reference.

And, automating report generation can significantly save time in your workflow. By creating macros that compile data into reports with just one click, you can eliminate repetitive tasks and reduce errors associated with manual entry. To record a macro, navigate to the "View" tab, select "Macros," then choose "Record Macro." After performing the necessary steps to generate your report manually once, stop recording; this enables you to execute the task quickly in future instances with minimal effort.

Finally, ensure all generated reports are saved securely and backed up regularly. Developing a habit of saving copies both locally and on cloud storage solutions protects valuable insights from potential data loss. Establishing a well-structured filing system for archived reports facilitates easy retrieval when analyzing long-term trends or preparing for audits.

By implementing these techniques for generating transaction reports in Excel, you'll enhance both accuracy and efficiency within your real estate practice. Not only does this empower you with critical insights into operational performance, but it also positions you as a knowledgeable professional capable of making strategic decisions based on solid data analysis. Presenting clear and concise transaction reports fosters trust with clients and paves the way for sustained success in an ever-evolving market landscape.

CHAPTER 14:
MARKETING AND
ADVERTISING
ANALYSIS

Managing Marketing Campaigns

Managing marketing campaigns in real estate requires precision, organization, and a data-driven approach. Excel can play a pivotal role in streamlining these processes, allowing you to allocate resources effectively while clearly evaluating the success of your marketing efforts. By leveraging Excel's capabilities, you can track various campaign metrics and refine your strategies to achieve optimal results.

Begin by creating a comprehensive campaign tracker. Set up columns for essential data points such as "Campaign Name," "Start Date," "End Date," "Budget," "Actual Spend," "Leads Generated," and "Conversion Rate." This organized structure provides a centralized view of all your marketing activities. For example, if you're running a digital ad campaign for a new property listing, you can record specific budget details and monitor the number of leads generated from that campaign.

Once your data is organized, take advantage of Excel's conditional formatting feature to visualize campaign performance. Take this example, you can highlight cells in the "Conversion Rate" column that fall below a certain threshold in red. This immediate visual cue allows you to quickly identify areas needing attention without wading through extensive rows of data.

Next, utilize formulas to calculate key performance indicators (KPIs). The formula for conversion rate is simple: divide the number of leads generated by the total number of contacts reached through the campaign. Take this example, input this as =G2/F2 in Excel, where G represents leads generated and F represents contacts reached. This calculation yields valuable insights into your campaign's effectiveness at converting interest into actual leads.

Consider incorporating charts to represent your campaign results visually. A bar chart comparing budget versus actual spend can quickly highlight discrepancies, guiding future budget adjustments. To create this chart, select the relevant data range and navigate to the "Insert" tab to choose the bar chart option. A well-constructed visual representation not only aids internal analysis but can also be instrumental when presenting results to stakeholders or clients.

For deeper analysis, explore using pivot tables. If you've run multiple campaigns over different time periods, a pivot table can help summarize this data effectively. By dragging "Campaign Name" into the Rows area and "Leads Generated" into the Values area, you can swiftly compare which campaigns yielded the most leads side by side.

Integrating feedback loops into your marketing strategy is equally important. After concluding each campaign, consider adding a "Notes" column to document insights gained— what worked well and what didn't. For example, if an email blast resulted in high engagement but low conversions, note potential reasons such as content relevance or timing issues. This continuous improvement cycle ensures that each campaign builds on past knowledge.

Automating repetitive tasks related to your campaigns can save significant time as well. Excel's macros feature allows you to record sequences of actions—like formatting data or generating reports—that you perform frequently. By creating a macro for generating weekly reports summarizing campaign performance metrics, you make this task effortless.

Additionally, maintaining organized documentation of past campaigns is crucial for future reference and learning. Create folders within your Excel workbook for archiving completed campaigns, ensuring that all relevant data is easily retrievable when strategizing new initiatives or analyzing long-term trends.

Finally, emphasize clear communication with your team regarding results and next steps based on your findings in Excel. Sharing insights from your campaign tracker fosters collaboration and aligns everyone on strategies moving forward.

By integrating these techniques into your marketing practices using Excel, you will optimize resource allocation and enhance overall performance tracking within your real estate business. With solid data analytics skills at your disposal, you'll drive effective decision-making that translates into greater success in securing leads and closing deals amidst market competition.

Tracking Advertising Costs and ROI

Tracking advertising costs and return on investment (ROI) is essential in real estate, as it allows you to assess the effectiveness of your marketing campaigns. Every dollar spent should be justified by the results it generates. Utilizing Excel can help you create a comprehensive system for monitoring these metrics, empowering you to make informed decisions that refine your marketing strategies.

Begin by setting up a dedicated worksheet specifically for tracking advertising costs and ROI. Key columns to include are "Campaign Name," "Ad Type," "Total Budget," "Actual Spend," "Leads Generated," "Sales Closed," and "ROI." Take this example, if you're executing an online ad campaign for a new property listing, categorize it under "Social Media" and document the budget allocated versus the actual amount spent. This structured approach lays the foundation for deeper analysis.

After entering your data, calculating ROI is straightforward. The basic formula is (Net Profit / Cost of Investment) x 100. In Excel, if your net profit from a campaign is recorded in column H and the actual spend in column D, you can easily input the formula as =H2/D2*100. This calculation provides a clear picture of how effectively each campaign converts investment into profit.

Visualizing your data can significantly enhance understanding and presentation. Create graphs that illustrate trends in spending versus returns over time. For example, line charts can show monthly advertising expenses against sales closed, allowing you to identify performance peaks and troughs. To generate a line chart, select your data range, navigate to the "Insert" tab, and choose the Line Chart option. Such visual representations can be particularly compelling when discussing results with stakeholders or team members.

In addition to basic calculations, consider using advanced functions like VLOOKUP to compare campaign performance across different periods or platforms. If you maintain separate sheets for various advertising channels—such as social media versus print—VLOOKUP allows you to pull relevant data into a summary table. For example, if social media leads are documented on another sheet labeled "Social Media Leads," you can use =VLOOKUP(A2,'SocialMediaData'!A:B,2,FALSE) to retrieve the number of leads generated from that source.

Segmenting your campaigns by type—whether digital ads, print marketing, or events—can also provide insights into which channels perform best. This segmentation enables you to make targeted adjustments; for instance, if digital ads consistently yield higher leads at lower costs compared to print ads, it would be wise to allocate more budget toward digital strategies.

Creating dashboards within Excel offers an at-a-glance view of all critical metrics related to advertising performance. By consolidating charts and key figures onto a single page using Excel's Dashboard tools, you make vital information easily accessible for quick decision-making.

Don't overlook qualitative data; tracking customer feedback from various campaigns adds context that raw numbers alone may not convey. You might establish a "Feedback" column where team members can note observations or client comments regarding each campaign's effectiveness and appeal. This qualitative insight deepens your understanding of why some campaigns succeed while others do not.

Additionally, hold regular review sessions with your team to collectively assess these metrics. During these meetings, discuss which strategies were effective and which were not based on the tracked data. This collaborative approach promotes a culture of continuous improvement and ensures alignment with current goals.

To maintain accountability and transparency regarding advertising expenditures and outcomes over time, adopt consistent naming conventions for files and folders containing campaign data. A well-organized system facilitates easy retrieval when evaluating past campaigns or planning future initiatives.

By effectively leveraging Excel to track advertising costs and ROI in your real estate marketing efforts, you equip yourself with actionable insights that drive strategic adjustments and enhance overall profitability. Analyzing both quantitative data and qualitative feedback positions you as a proactive agent capable of navigating market fluctuations while maximizing every marketing dollar spent.

Analyzing Traffic Data from Digital Platforms

To effectively analyze traffic data from digital platforms, it's essential to recognize its role in shaping marketing strategies and enhancing client engagement. In the competitive real estate industry, where consumer behavior is constantly changing, understanding the origins of potential clients can yield invaluable insights. By leveraging Excel's capabilities, you can transform raw traffic data into actionable intelligence.

Begin by collecting traffic data from various digital platforms such as social media, your website, email campaigns, and paid advertisements. Tools like Google Analytics provide comprehensive reporting features that allow you to export this data in CSV format for use in Excel. Once you have gathered your dataset, create a dedicated worksheet to organize this information. Essential columns to include are "Source," "Medium," "Total Visitors," "Bounce Rate," "Leads Generated," and "Conversion Rate." This structured setup enables you to quickly interpret large volumes of data.

For example, if your traffic report indicates that Facebook ads generated 500 visitors with a bounce rate of 60%, while organic search attracted 1,000 visitors with a bounce rate of 30%, you can start evaluating the effectiveness of each channel. To calculate conversion rates directly in Excel, use the formula (Leads Generated / Total Visitors) x 100. For leads generated from Facebook recorded in cell E2 and total visitors in cell C2, the formula would be =E2/C2*100. This method not only measures performance but also aids in making informed budget allocations toward more effective channels.

Visualizing this data can significantly enhance comprehension. Creating bar charts to compare the performance of different traffic sources allows you to easily identify which channels are driving leads most effectively. To create a bar chart in Excel, simply select your source and lead data, navigate to the "Insert" tab, and choose "Bar Chart." By visualizing traffic sources alongside conversion rates, you provide a clear picture for stakeholders and facilitate team discussions.

To dive deeper into analytics, consider utilizing Excel's PivotTables. This feature simplifies the summarization of large datasets. Take this example, if you want to compare the performance of different mediums—such as social media versus email marketing—across various campaigns over time, PivotTables enable quick aggregation without complex formulas. Just select your dataset and choose "Insert PivotTable," then drag and drop relevant fields into rows and values for instant results.

Beyond quantitative metrics, qualitative aspects are also crucial for analysis. Adding columns for "Customer Feedback" or "Client Comments" can provide context that numbers alone may miss. This is particularly important when analyzing social media campaigns where engagement often includes comments or messages from potential buyers.

Regular review meetings with your team focused on this traffic analysis will foster a collaborative atmosphere aimed at refining strategies based on solid evidence. During these sessions, explore trends over time—are certain campaigns performing better during specific months? Is there a correlation between seasonal changes and lead generation? Such discussions promote an environment where continuous improvement becomes second nature.

Lastly, ensure that all files containing traffic data are systematically organized with consistent naming conventions for easy access later on. A structured approach maintains clarity and allows for quick reference to past campaigns when strategizing future initiatives.

By effectively utilizing Excel's tools to analyze traffic data from digital platforms, real estate professionals position themselves at the forefront of market dynamics. This systematic analysis empowers agents not only to track metrics but also to respond proactively to trends that can significantly impact their business outcomes—maximizing their marketing investments with precision and insight along the way.

Social Media Campaign Analysis

Analyzing social media campaigns requires a strategic approach that blends data interpretation with actionable insights. The dynamic and interactive nature of social media makes it crucial to understand how campaigns perform, as this can significantly shape your overall marketing strategy. For real estate agents, tracking metrics is essential, but leveraging these insights to enhance client engagement and brand visibility is equally important.

Begin by defining the key performance indicators (KPIs) for your campaigns. Common KPIs include reach, engagement rate, click-through rate, and lead conversion rate. These metrics offer a snapshot of how well your content resonates with your audience. Take this example, if you run a Facebook campaign promoting a new property listing, it's important to analyze the number of users who interacted with the post compared to the total number who viewed it.

After identifying relevant KPIs, gather data from the social media platforms you use—such as Facebook, Instagram, and LinkedIn. Export this data to Excel for more in-depth analysis. Essential columns in your dataset may include "Campaign Name," "Platform," "Impressions," "Engagements," "Clicks," and "Leads Generated." This structured organization facilitates pinpointing which campaigns drive results effectively.

To calculate the engagement rate for each campaign in Excel, apply the formula (Engagements / Impressions) x 100.

For example, if you recorded 200 engagements from 2,000 impressions in cells B2 and C2 respectively, you can find the engagement percentage by inputting =B2/C2*100 into another cell. This straightforward calculation reveals how effectively your content captures attention and encourages interaction.

Visualizing campaign performance can yield deeper insights into trends and areas needing improvement. Excel's chart features can assist here; consider creating line graphs to display engagement rates over time or pie charts to illustrate the distribution of leads across various platforms. Take this example, to create a line graph showing changes in engagement over weeks or months, select your date range alongside engagement figures, navigate to the "Insert" tab, and choose "Line Chart." These visual representations make it easier to identify patterns and spikes in activity.

Additionally, implementing A/B testing within your campaigns can help assess which messaging or imagery resonates better with your audience. By running two variations of an ad simultaneously—one with a specific image and another with a different tagline—you can collect data on which version performs better. Document these results in Excel alongside other campaign metrics for a comprehensive analysis.

Integrating qualitative feedback with quantitative metrics is another critical aspect of campaign analysis. Create a column titled "Customer Sentiment" to record insights from comments or direct messages received during the campaign period. This qualitative data provides context to numerical results; for example, high engagement coupled with low conversions may indicate that while users are intrigued by your content, they aren't finding what they expect upon clicking through.

Regularly reviewing this analysis with your team encourages collaboration and innovation. Discussing what worked well—and what didn't—enables continuous refinement of strategies based on evidence rather than guesswork. Foster brainstorming sessions where team members can suggest adjustments or new ideas informed by recent findings.

Finally, keeping your files organized is essential for ongoing success. Use clear naming conventions when saving files related to different campaigns and maintain an archive that allows easy access to historical data for reference during future planning sessions.

By mastering social media campaign analysis through Excel's robust features, real estate professionals can enhance their marketing efforts while gaining a deeper understanding of audience behavior and preferences. This empowers agents to develop more tailored strategies that resonate with potential clients, ultimately leading to higher engagement rates and increased conversions in an ever-evolving digital landscape.

Market Segmentation and Targeting

Understanding market segmentation and targeting is crucial for real estate agents looking to elevate their marketing strategies and effectively engage with their ideal audience. By categorizing potential clients into distinct groups based on specific criteria, agents can tailor their messaging and services to meet the unique needs of each segment. This targeted approach not only boosts engagement but also enhances conversion rates, as communication becomes more relevant and resonant.

To start, identify key demographic factors that define your target audience. Consider aspects such as age, income, family status, and geographic location. For example, first-time homebuyers typically have different concerns and aspirations compared to seasoned investors or retirees seeking to downsize. By gathering this information, you can develop a clearer understanding of whom you are marketing to and what appeals to them.

Using Excel can significantly streamline the process of organizing this data. Create a spreadsheet that lists potential clients alongside their demographic information. Include columns labeled "Name," "Age," "Income," "Location," and "Property Type Interested In." This structured format allows for easy sorting and filtering based on specific criteria. If your focus is on young families, for instance, you can filter the data by age range and preferred property type to prioritize the most relevant leads.

Next, take the time to analyze your existing client data to determine which segments are the most profitable. By calculating the average transaction value across different demographics, you can identify where to concentrate your marketing efforts. If you find that clients aged 30-40 typically purchase homes within a specific price range, direct your marketing strategies toward this group with tailored advertisements that resonate with their lifestyle needs.

With these segments identified, consider developing personalized marketing campaigns for each group. Craft targeted messaging that addresses specific pain points or aspirations unique to each segment. A campaign aimed at millennials might highlight modern amenities and smart-home features, while one directed at retirees could emphasize community services and low-maintenance living options.

Excel can also be utilized to track campaign performance across different segments. Create pivot tables to summarize results based on demographic categories; for example, a pivot table can show how many leads converted into sales from each group, allowing you to evaluate which marketing strategies are most effective. To create a pivot table, simply select your dataset, navigate to the "Insert" tab, choose "PivotTable," and drag relevant fields into the rows and values areas.

In addition to tracking performance, employing Excel charts can help visualize your findings related to market segmentation. A bar chart could effectively illustrate the number of leads generated per demographic category over time, enabling you to quickly identify trends or shifts in interest among various client groups.

Also, incorporating psychographics—an understanding of attitudes, interests, and lifestyles—adds depth to your segmentation strategy. Conducting surveys or gathering feedback through social media can provide insights into what drives potential buyers. You may discover that certain groups prioritize eco-friendly homes or proximity to schools more than others.

Finally, it's essential to continually refine your segmentation approach based on ongoing feedback and performance metrics. Regularly update your client database in Excel to reflect changes in demographic information or introduce new segments as market conditions shift. By maintaining a dynamic approach to market segmentation and targeting —leveraging Excel's analytical capabilities—you position yourself to adapt swiftly to changes in the real estate landscape.

By mastering market segmentation and targeting through precise data analysis in Excel, real estate agents can greatly enhance their marketing effectiveness. This strategic focus not only helps build stronger connections with potential clients but also fosters long-term relationships that contribute to sustainable business growth.

Designing Surveys and Customer Feedback Forms

Surveys and customer feedback forms are essential tools for real estate agents seeking to enhance their services and better understand client needs. In the fast-paced realm of real estate, where relationships and reputation are paramount, gaining insights directly from clients can set successful agents apart from the competition. To design effective surveys, it's crucial to clarify your objectives and follow best practices that promote engagement.

Begin by defining the specific goals of your survey. What insights are you hoping to gain? Are you interested in feedback on a recent property showing, or do you want to assess overall client satisfaction with your services? Establishing clear objectives will help you formulate relevant and actionable questions. Take this example, if your aim is to improve communication, you might ask clients how frequently they prefer updates during the buying or selling process.

With your goals established, focus on crafting questions that encourage meaningful responses. Closed-ended questions—those requiring a simple "yes" or "no," or ratings on a scale—are useful for quantifying data and identifying trends. For example, you might ask, "On a scale from 1 to 5, how satisfied are you with our communication?" Such questions facilitate easy analysis and comparison across responses.

However, it's important not to overlook open-ended questions that allow clients to express their thoughts in greater detail. These questions can yield nuanced insights that numerical ratings might miss. Take this example, asking, "What aspect of our service did you find most valuable?" invites specific feedback that can be invaluable for refining your approach.

To simplify the process of gathering feedback, consider using online survey tools like Google Forms or SurveyMonkey. These platforms offer user-friendly templates that streamline design while providing essential features such as response tracking and data export options. Using a structured platform not only enhances professionalism but also makes collecting and analyzing feedback more efficient.

Another key consideration is ensuring your surveys are concise. Clients often have busy schedules, so aim for brevity while still addressing important topics. A lengthy survey may lead to respondents dropping out midway through, so prioritize questions based on their relevance and significance to your objectives.

To increase response rates, pay attention to how and when you distribute your survey. Timing is critical; for example, sending a follow-up survey shortly after closing a deal can capture fresh impressions while they are still vivid in clients' minds. Additionally, consider offering an incentive for completing the survey—such as entry into a raffle or a discount on future services—to encourage participation.

After collecting responses, carefully analyze the data to identify trends and actionable insights. Look for patterns in satisfaction levels and pinpoint areas needing improvement. If multiple clients raise concerns about response times or accessibility of information, these insights can guide strategic changes in your operations.

Implementing changes based on client feedback not only enhances your service but also demonstrates to clients that their opinions matter—a vital factor in building lasting relationships in real estate. Be sure to communicate any improvements made as a result of client feedback; this transparency fosters accountability and reinforces your commitment to excellence.

To wrap things up, designing effective surveys and customer feedback forms is an indispensable practice for any real estate agent eager to elevate their business. By crafting targeted questions, utilizing user-friendly platforms, distributing surveys at optimal times, and acting on the insights gathered, agents can create a cycle of continuous improvement that benefits both their practices and their clients' experiences. In the end, this dedication to understanding client needs cultivates trust and loyalty—two invaluable assets in the competitive landscape of real estate.

Evaluating Offline Marketing Efforts

Evaluating your offline marketing efforts is essential for refining your overall strategy as a real estate agent. While digital tools and analytics are indispensable, the influence of traditional marketing methods remains significant in the industry. By understanding the performance of these offline strategies, you can improve your ability to connect with potential clients and achieve successful outcomes.

To begin this evaluation, start by gathering data on your offline marketing activities. Review each method you've used—such as print advertising, open house events, direct mail campaigns, and community engagement. For example, if you've placed an advertisement in a local newspaper, track the responses generated by that ad. A straightforward spreadsheet can help you log details like the publication date, advertisement type, and the number of inquiries or leads generated over time.

Once you've collected this data, establish key performance indicators (KPIs) to assess the effectiveness of your strategies. These could include metrics such as response rates, conversion rates from leads to clients, or return on investment (ROI) for specific campaigns. Take this example, if you distributed flyers in a neighborhood and received five calls for every 100 flyers, you have a clear baseline to evaluate that method's effectiveness.

Alongside quantitative metrics, qualitative feedback is vital for a comprehensive evaluation of your offline marketing efforts. Engage with clients during interactions—whether at open houses or through follow-up calls—and ask them how they discovered your services. Maintaining a dedicated notes section in your client management system allows you to record this information consistently. Anecdotal evidence can complement your data and provide deeper insights into what resonates with potential buyers.

Consider conducting follow-up surveys tailored for recent clients to gather specific feedback on their experiences with your offline marketing efforts. Ask questions about what prompted them to reach out or their thoughts on the promotional materials they encountered. This targeted feedback can inform adjustments to aspects like design elements or messaging based on actual client input rather than assumptions.

It's also important to evaluate your participation in networking events and community involvement. While local fairs or sponsorships can foster goodwill, measuring their impact on business outcomes is crucial. Take this example, track new contacts made at an event against deals closed within a specific timeframe afterward to assess effectiveness.

Adjusting your approach based on gathered insights is key for ongoing improvement in your marketing efforts. If a particular direct mail piece isn't generating the interest you hoped for, consider tweaking the messaging or format—testing different graphics or incorporating more compelling calls-to-action could yield better results next time.

While analyzing past initiatives is important, integrating innovative approaches based on emerging trends is equally vital. For example, if younger homebuyers are increasingly moving into an area known for its family-friendly amenities, reevaluating and adjusting your marketing strategies accordingly can position you advantageously within that emerging market segment.

To conclude this evaluation process effectively and ensure improvements take shape, develop an actionable plan based on both quantitative data analysis and qualitative client feedback. Set timelines for implementing changes while allowing flexibility; trends in real estate markets can shift rapidly.

In the end, evaluating offline marketing efforts empowers you as a real estate agent to understand what has worked and continuously refine your strategies moving forward. By systematically analyzing responses and adapting based on market dynamics and client insights, you position yourself ahead of competitors who may overlook the importance of assessment in their traditional outreach tactics. This comprehensive understanding will enhance not just visibility but also foster stronger client relationships built on trust and tailored communication.

Dashboards for Integrated Marketing Insights

Integrating dashboards into your marketing analysis can transform how you interpret and leverage data in your real estate practice. These visual tools allow you to synthesize complex information, enabling you to extract actionable insights at a glance. This capability is crucial in an industry where trends evolve rapidly, making timely decisions essential.

Start by identifying the key metrics that are most relevant to your marketing efforts. Focus on lead generation rates, conversion statistics from various channels, and engagement levels across different platforms. For example, if you've launched several advertising campaigns—both online and offline—understanding which campaign generated the highest response rate can directly inform your future strategies.

With these metrics in hand, create a dashboard that consolidates this data into a cohesive visual representation. Excel provides a range of features for building effective dashboards using charts, graphs, and tables. Begin with a straightforward layout: consider using bar graphs to compare campaign performances and line charts to illustrate trends over time.

Take this example, if you conducted a direct mail campaign alongside digital ads, display both datasets side by side on your dashboard. You might include one bar graph showing leads generated from direct mail and another for those from online ads. This visual comparison allows you to quickly determine which method was more successful over a specified period.

Enhancing your dashboard's functionality with Excel's pivot tables can further streamline your analysis. Pivot tables enable you to summarize large datasets efficiently, allowing you to explore information dynamically. For example, if you want to assess the effectiveness of different mailing lists or target demographics for specific campaigns, pivot tables make it easy to filter results based on these variables.

Incorporating conditional formatting can also help highlight key performance indicators (KPIs) visually within your dashboard. You could establish thresholds for lead conversions; for instance, if conversion rates drop below 5%, the corresponding cell could automatically turn red. This immediate visual cue helps pinpoint areas that require urgent attention without the need to sift through extensive rows of data.

Consider integrating live data feeds when applicable. If you're using platforms like Google Analytics or social media management tools that offer real-time insights into website traffic or engagement metrics, linking this data directly to your Excel dashboard can streamline your monitoring efforts. Tools like Power Query in Excel allow for seamless importing of external data and automatic updates, keeping your dashboard current without manual input.

Engaging visuals are essential; they transform raw numbers into meaningful narratives about your marketing performance. Instead of merely presenting figures related to leads generated, add context through storytelling elements within the dashboard design. Pairing visuals with concise commentary can guide viewers through the narrative behind the numbers—whether celebrating successes or identifying areas needing strategic adjustments.

Feedback is critical in refining your dashboards as well. Involve team members or trusted colleagues in reviewing the layout and functionality; their fresh perspectives may uncover insights you hadn't considered during development. It's important that everyone involved understands how to interpret the dashboard effectively—this fosters a culture of data-driven decision-making throughout your organization.

Finally, don't overlook the importance of periodic reviews of the dashboard itself. As market dynamics shift and new strategies are implemented, reassess which metrics should be emphasized or added based on emerging trends in client behavior or marketing effectiveness. Regularly updating your approach ensures that the dashboard remains relevant and continues to serve as an essential tool for integrated marketing insights.

An effectively crafted dashboard not only boasts aesthetic appeal but also facilitates swift and accurate informed decision-making processes. By harnessing these insights and adapting your strategies accordingly, you'll enhance visibility and strengthen client relationships through targeted communications grounded in real-time data analysis. This proactive approach positions you ahead of competitors who may rely solely on intuition rather than informed strategies rooted in solid data insights.

CHAPTER 15: RISK MANAGEMENT FOR REAL ESTATE AGENTS

*Identifying Risk Factors
in Real Estate*

I dentifying risk factors in real estate requires a multifaceted approach, as various elements can significantly impact your business. Given the inherent uncertainties of the real estate market, understanding these potential pitfalls is crucial for both your success and the sustainability of your operations.

Start by analyzing external economic conditions, which can profoundly influence property values and market demand. Factors such as interest rates, employment rates, and global economic shifts directly affect buyer behavior. Take this example, an increase in interest rates may deter first-time homebuyers due to higher mortgage costs, leading to a slowdown in transactions. Similarly, if unemployment rises in a region where you operate, potential buyers may hesitate, waiting for more stable financial conditions before making a purchase.

Next, consider local market trends as another critical aspect of risk assessment. Pay attention to housing inventory levels and the average number of days properties spend on the market. A rising inventory coupled with stagnant sales could signal an impending market correction, indicating that prices might drop if sellers are reluctant to adjust their expectations. On the other hand, a tight inventory may suggest rising prices, but it also risks creating an affordability crisis for buyers.

Demographic shifts are also essential in shaping real estate dynamics. Changes in population growth, age distribution, and migration patterns can reveal emerging opportunities or risks. For example, an influx of young professionals into an urban area may drive demand for rental units or starter homes. However, if economic opportunities do not keep pace with this population growth, increased vacancy rates may follow.

Additionally, regulatory changes warrant careful attention when identifying risks. Local governments may introduce new zoning laws or property taxes that can directly impact your investment strategies. Staying informed about legislative proposals and potential reforms allows you to react proactively rather than reactively to changes that could affect your bottom line.

Assessing financial health is equally important—understanding how leveraged your investments are can highlight vulnerabilities. If a significant portion of your properties is financed through debt, shifts in interest rates or disruptions in cash flow could strain your operations. Running stress tests on your portfolio under various scenarios (such as increased vacancy rates or declining rental income) will help illustrate the resilience of your investments.

Another crucial area involves examining the physical condition of properties and environmental factors that present inherent risks. Conducting thorough inspections can uncover issues like structural problems or hazardous materials (such as lead paint or mold) that may not be immediately apparent but could lead to substantial financial repercussions later on. Additionally, consider natural disaster risks based on geographic location—areas prone to flooding or earthquakes may necessitate additional insurance options or contingency plans.

In today's landscape, utilizing data analytics tools is increasingly essential for comprehensive risk assessment. By aggregating data from multiple sources—local MLS reports, economic indicators, and demographic statistics—you can gain a clearer picture of potential vulnerabilities within your real estate strategy. Tools like Excel are particularly useful; creating spreadsheets that analyze historical trends and visualize current market conditions through graphs and charts allows for quick interpretation.

Establishing a systematic approach to identifying these risk factors fosters proactive management instead of reactionary measures after issues arise. Develop checklists tailored to each property type or investment strategy; this disciplined method ensures that no critical area is overlooked during evaluations.

Engaging with professional networks can also enhance your risk identification efforts significantly. Collaborating with fellow agents or industry experts who have navigated similar challenges can provide insights into emerging threats you may not have considered.

In the end, staying ahead of risks enables you not only to safeguard your investments but also to strategically position yourself when opportunities arise amidst uncertainty. Real estate is not merely about transactions; it's about making informed decisions rooted in comprehensive analyses of all factors at play. The better prepared you are for potential setbacks today, the greater resilience you will achieve tomorrow.

Creating a Risk Assessment Framework

Developing a risk assessment framework is crucial for effectively navigating the complexities of the real estate market. This structured approach enables you to identify, analyze, and prioritize risks while implementing strategies to mitigate them. By formalizing this process, you can make informed decisions that not only safeguard your investments but also enhance your strategic positioning within the market.

Begin by establishing clear objectives for your risk assessment framework. What specific outcomes do you want to achieve? Objectives may include reducing financial exposure, improving operational efficiency, or enhancing client satisfaction. A well-defined set of goals will guide your assessment efforts and allow you to tailor your strategies accordingly.

Next, identify the various types of risks relevant to your real estate practice. These can be broadly categorized into market risks, credit risks, operational risks, legal and compliance risks, and environmental risks. Take this example, market risks may involve fluctuations in property values due to economic downturns or shifts in local demand, while operational risks could arise from inefficient processes or inadequate property management practices.

Once you've categorized these risks, delve deeper into each type by establishing specific metrics or indicators for assessment. For example, under market risks, consider tracking key performance indicators such as average days on the market or sales-to-listing ratios in your area. Monitoring these metrics over time can yield valuable insights into emerging trends and potential threats.

The next step is to gather data from various sources to inform your analysis. Utilize both quantitative data—such as financial statements and property valuations—and qualitative data—like client feedback and market sentiment reports. Tools like

Excel can be instrumental at this stage; creating a centralized database allows for streamlined data aggregation and analysis. You can employ pivot tables to synthesize information and visualize relationships among different variables.

With a comprehensive data set at your disposal, apply analytical techniques to assess potential impacts thoroughly. Scenario analysis is particularly beneficial here; evaluate best-case, worst-case, and most-likely scenarios for each identified risk factor. By modeling different outcomes based on varying assumptions—such as shifts in interest rates or changes in local employment rates—you gain insights into how these factors may affect your portfolio's performance.

Engaging stakeholders throughout this process significantly enhances the effectiveness of your risk assessment framework. Regular communication with team members, investors, and clients about potential risks identified during assessments is vital. Seeking their input on mitigating strategies can unearth perspectives that may not have been considered initially.

After analyzing the data and consulting with stakeholders, prioritize the identified risks based on their potential impact and likelihood of occurrence. Implement a simple scoring system where each risk is assigned a score based on its severity and probability; this will clarify which areas require immediate attention versus those that warrant ongoing monitoring.

Once prioritized, develop tailored mitigation strategies for each significant risk factor. These strategies might include diversifying investments across various property types or geographic locations to minimize exposure or strengthening tenant screening processes to reduce vacancy rates. Additionally, consider establishing contingency plans for high-impact scenarios like natural disasters or economic downturns.

Finally, create an ongoing review process for your risk assessment framework. The real estate landscape is continuously evolving; therefore, it's essential to revisit and revise your framework regularly based on new information or changing market conditions. Scheduling periodic assessments —such as quarterly reviews for fast-paced markets—will ensure that your strategies remain relevant and effective.

In summary, crafting a robust risk assessment framework involves clearly defining objectives while categorizing various types of risks pertinent to real estate operations. Through diligent data collection and analysis using tools like Excel, along with active stakeholder engagement throughout the process, you can not only identify but also strategically manage potential threats facing your business. This proactive approach ultimately leads to more resilient decision-making as you navigate the complex world of real estate investments.

Data Analysis for Risk Mitigation

Understanding data analysis for risk mitigation is crucial for real estate professionals looking to stay competitive in a volatile market. This process involves systematically examining data to identify potential risks and crafting actionable strategies to address them. By harnessing Excel's powerful analytical capabilities, agents can transform raw data into valuable insights that inform decision-making and improve risk management practices.

Begin by recognizing that risks in the real estate sector come in various forms. Financial risks, such as fluctuating interest rates and unpredictable property values, can significantly impact profit margins. Operational risks may arise from inefficient management practices or unexpected maintenance issues. Additionally, legal and compliance risks are critical; changes in regulations can introduce unforeseen liabilities. Understanding these risk categories provides a solid foundation for your analysis.

With a clear grasp of the types of risks involved, you can proceed to data collection. Consider both quantitative data —like historical sales figures and demographic trends—and qualitative data, such as client feedback and expert opinions. Take this example, analyzing housing price trends over the past five years through your local market's sales data will yield essential insights. Organizing this information in an Excel spreadsheet allows for efficient calculations, helping you uncover patterns or anomalies.

To visualize how different factors might influence risk, develop key performance indicators (KPIs). These metrics could include the average time properties similar to yours spend on the market or the rate of return on investment for various property types. Utilize Excel's charting tools to create graphs that clearly illustrate these KPIs. For example, plotting average sales prices against interest rates over time may reveal correlations that help predict future market movements.

A comprehensive approach involves utilizing scenario analysis within your data framework. By modeling different scenarios —such as best-case, worst-case, and most likely outcomes —you can gain deeper insights into how various variables interact under changing conditions. In Excel, tools like Data Tables or Scenario Manager facilitate this analysis. For example, if you suspect an economic downturn may reduce housing demand, create a scenario in which you lower projected sales prices and assess the impact on profitability.

Engaging stakeholders throughout this process enhances your insights significantly. Involve colleagues or clients who may offer diverse perspectives on potential risks; their input can help identify blind spots in your analysis. Consider hosting regular strategy sessions to review identified risks collectively and brainstorm mitigation tactics based on recent findings.

After analyzing the risks, prioritization becomes essential. Create a scoring system within your spreadsheet that assesses each identified risk based on two key factors: potential impact on operations and likelihood of occurrence. Assign scores from 1 to 5 (with 1 being low risk and 5 high risk) for each category. This ranking will enable you to address the highest-scoring risks first.

Once you've prioritized these threats, develop specific mitigation strategies tailored to each significant risk. This might involve diversifying investments across different property types or geographic areas to cushion against market fluctuations. Alternatively, enhancing tenant screening procedures can help minimize vacancies during downturns. Establishing protocols for regular property inspections ensures operational issues are addressed before they escalate into costly problems.

The process doesn't end with implementation; ongoing assessment is vital for effective risk management. Regularly revisiting your data analysis framework ensures it adapts to changing market conditions and emerging threats. Schedule quarterly reviews or monthly check-ins based on your market's dynamics, allowing for timely adaptations as new information arises.

In summary, employing rigorous data analysis techniques empowers real estate professionals to proactively identify risks and formulate effective mitigation strategies. By systematically categorizing risks, collecting relevant data, engaging stakeholders in discussions, prioritizing threats based on their potential impacts, and continuously reviewing strategies for efficacy, agents can navigate their careers with greater confidence within an ever-evolving landscape. Excel not only enhances this analytical process but also serves as a powerful ally in achieving sustained success in real estate investments.

Scenario Planning for Market Volatility

Scenario planning is an essential tool for real estate agents navigating the unpredictable landscape of market volatility. It provides professionals with the foresight necessary to anticipate changes, enabling them to adjust their strategies in response to evolving conditions. By harnessing Excel's powerful features, agents can develop detailed scenarios that illustrate potential market outcomes, ultimately enhancing their decision-making processes and resilience.

To effectively begin scenario planning, it's important to identify the key variables influencing your market. These might include economic indicators such as employment rates, interest rates, and housing supply metrics. For example, if you suspect that rising interest rates will reduce demand, start by gathering historical data on how past rate increases have impacted home sales in your area. Inputting this data into Excel creates a foundational dataset that will guide your scenario development.

After compiling your data, the next step is to establish a range of scenarios—best-case, worst-case, and most likely case. This structured approach allows you to visualize potential futures based on different assumptions. Utilize Excel's Scenario Manager feature to efficiently create these models. Take this example, you might outline a best-case scenario where economic growth drives increased housing demand, while a worst-case scenario could reflect a significant downturn due to high interest rates and a looming recession.

Consider modeling a hypothetical situation where interest rates rise by 1%. In your spreadsheet, develop formulas that adjust property prices and sales volumes according to this new rate. An example formula could be =IF(Interest_Rate>5%, Property_Price*0.95, Property_Price), illustrating how property values might decline as financing becomes more expensive for buyers.

Visualizing these scenarios is equally crucial. Excel's graphing capabilities enable you to plot projected sales against various economic conditions over time. Take this example, creating a line chart to display forecasted property values under each scenario can simplify complex data and facilitate strategic discussions with stakeholders.

Once you've established these scenarios, sharing insights with your team or clients is highly beneficial. Collaboration brings diverse perspectives that can significantly enrich the planning process. Consider hosting workshops where team members can analyze findings from each scenario and brainstorm strategies accordingly. Engaging clients during these sessions helps align expectations and tailor communications based on the identified risks.

It's also important to prioritize which scenarios deserve further investigation. Focus first on those deemed most likely based on current trends, but don't overlook outliers; extreme cases can provide valuable insights into market dynamics. You might create a simple scoring system within your Excel sheet, assigning points to each scenario based on criteria such as probability of occurrence and potential impact on business operations.

Once you've pinpointed critical scenarios for deeper exploration, develop targeted action plans for each. For example, if a worst-case scenario indicates a significant drop in demand during an economic downturn, consider contingency strategies such as adjusting marketing efforts or implementing flexible pricing options for properties.

As markets evolve, your scenario planning efforts should also adapt. Regularly revisit and refine your scenarios based on new data or emerging trends in the real estate sector. Setting reminders in Excel for quarterly reviews of your analysis ensures that you're always prepared for shifts that could impact your business outcomes.

In summary, leveraging scenario planning through Excel equips real estate agents with an adaptive framework for navigating market volatility. By systematically defining key variables, modeling potential outcomes using Excel's Scenario Manager, visualizing results with graphs, collaborating with stakeholders for input, prioritizing relevant scenarios for action plans, and maintaining an ongoing review process, agents enhance their strategic capabilities and position themselves for sustained success amidst marketplace uncertainty.

Insurance and Liability Management

Insurance and liability management is a vital component of a real estate agent's operations. Without a solid grasp of these areas, you not only risk financial loss but also potential reputational damage that can take years to repair. The real estate landscape is often riddled with risks, ranging from property damage and client disputes to regulatory compliance issues. To navigate these challenges effectively, using Excel as a management tool can help streamline processes, assess potential risks, and implement protective strategies.

To begin, it's important to gather all relevant insurance policies and liability coverage documents into one organized Excel workbook. Create separate sheets for various types of insurance—such as general liability, professional liability, property insurance, and specific policies related to commercial real estate transactions. This centralization allows for quick reference to coverage details whenever needed. Take this example, you might include columns for policy numbers, coverage amounts, renewal dates, and contact information for your insurance providers.

With your data organized, utilize Excel's features to track important deadlines associated with your insurance policies. Employing conditional formatting can highlight upcoming renewal dates in red when they approach within the next 30 days. This visual cue keeps you proactive regarding coverage renewals and potential lapses. For added efficiency, consider using a formula like =IF(TODAY()+30>Renewal_Date,"Renew Soon","All Good") in a dedicated column to prompt timely actions.

Risk assessment is another area where Excel proves invaluable. You can design a simple risk matrix that categorizes potential risks based on their likelihood and potential impact on your business operations. By using a scoring system from 1 to 5 for both dimensions, you can prioritize which risks need immediate attention. For example, while the risk of natural disasters like floods or earthquakes might be rated as high in certain areas, cybersecurity breaches may present a higher likelihood but potentially lower impact.

Also, creating pivot tables can help analyze historical claims data if available. By examining claims filed against properties you've managed, you can gain insights into prevalent risks in specific neighborhoods or property types. This information enables you to tailor your strategies accordingly—whether that means bolstering security measures in high-risk areas or offering clients customized insurance options based on identified trends.

Effective communication with clients about their insurance needs is equally crucial. By leveraging Excel's mail merge feature alongside Word, you can generate personalized letters outlining recommended coverage options tailored to each client's unique circumstances. Take this example, if a client is purchasing an investment property near flood-prone water bodies, they would benefit from specific flood insurance guidance included in their communication package.

It's also wise to develop training resources for new agents or team members regarding liability management practices within your company framework using Excel-based templates. An onboarding checklist ensures all agents are well-versed in essential protocols related to documentation and risk management as they engage in transactions.

As legislation concerning real estate evolves—especially regarding environmental factors and data protection—staying informed is key to effective insurance management. Establishing a section in your Excel workbook dedicated to regulatory updates offers an easily accessible reference point for compliance checks during transactions.

Finally, regularly reviewing your insurance needs in tandem with changes in your business operations will help you identify gaps in coverage or areas needing adjustment as your portfolio expands or shifts direction—whether toward residential sales or commercial leases. Setting quarterly reminders within Excel will keep this review process on track.

In summary, mastering insurance and liability management through Excel empowers real estate agents with the tools necessary for comprehensive risk assessment and proactive strategy implementation. By efficiently organizing vital documents, visually tracking critical deadlines with conditional formatting, analyzing historical claims data through pivot tables, effectively communicating with clients via mail merge capabilities, and fostering continuous learning about industry regulations, you enhance operational efficiency and build a resilient business model ready to navigate the inherent challenges of the real estate market.

Regulatory Compliance and Reporting

Understanding regulatory compliance and reporting is crucial for real estate agents. It not only helps avoid legal pitfalls but also fosters credibility and trust with clients. Compliance transcends mere adherence to laws; it involves cultivating a transparent environment where clients feel confident in your professional capabilities. Excel can be a powerful ally in navigating the complexities of compliance, allowing agents to streamline their reporting processes and meet necessary regulations efficiently.

Start by creating a comprehensive compliance checklist in

your Excel workbook. This checklist should detail all relevant regulations that impact your business, including local zoning laws, licensing requirements, fair housing regulations, and specific guidelines related to property management or sales transactions. Organize it with columns for status updates, deadlines, and notes on compliance procedures. For example, you might include a column for last review dates to track when updates were made, ensuring your practices stay current.

Next, structure your reporting framework by dedicating separate sheets to different aspects of compliance. One sheet could focus on environmental regulations affecting property listings, while another addresses financial disclosures required for sales transactions. This organization facilitates quick access to pertinent information during audits or client inquiries, enhancing operational efficiency.

To improve the accuracy of your recorded information, utilize Excel's data validation features. Create dropdown menus for key regulatory categories, ensuring consistency in data entry and minimizing errors. Take this example, when documenting client interactions regarding fair housing laws, predefined options can clarify expectations and reduce the risk of overlooking critical details.

Reporting is vital for demonstrating compliance. Excel's charting tools can visualize essential metrics related to regulatory adherence over time. By creating graphs that illustrate trends in compliance—such as tracking the number of completed training sessions on fair housing laws—you can identify areas needing improvement. Presenting this data visually helps communicate your commitment to compliance during team meetings or with stakeholders.

In addition to these strategies, consider incorporating automated reminders for critical reporting deadlines. Use Excel's formula capabilities to set alerts that notify you as these dates approach. For example, you could create a column with conditional formatting that highlights deadlines in red when they are within 30 days, prompting immediate action and ensuring timely submissions.

Another effective approach is developing a shared compliance dashboard within Excel for team members involved in various real estate transactions. This dashboard can feature live updates on each agent's progress in completing required training or documentation. Real-time collaboration fosters accountability and promotes a culture of transparency around compliance efforts.

To keep pace with changing regulations, dedicate a section of your workbook to tracking industry news and legislative changes relevant to real estate. Categorize these updates by date and impact level—high, medium, or low—to prioritize which changes require immediate attention or procedural adjustments.

Additionally, consider creating templates for routine compliance reports that can be easily updated as needed. These templates might include sections summarizing activities undertaken to adhere to regulations over specified periods. Take this example, if you need to report on the number of properties that underwent environmental assessments during a quarter, having a ready-to-use template streamlines the task and enhances efficiency.

Training staff on compliance best practices should be an ongoing process. Take advantage of Excel by designing training modules that incorporate scenarios related to regulatory challenges agents may encounter. Role-playing exercises can reinforce this training; for example, an agent might simulate responding to a client inquiry about zoning laws while referencing information from the compliance checklist.

In the end, mastering regulatory compliance and reporting through Excel equips real estate professionals with the structure necessary for operational excellence in a highly regulated environment. By maintaining organized checklists, utilizing data validation techniques, visualizing trends through charts, automating reminders for important deadlines, fostering collaboration via dashboards, diligently tracking legislative updates, and providing comprehensive training resources, you position yourself as not only compliant but also as a trusted advisor committed to ethical practices in real estate transactions.

Monitoring Risk with Real-time Dashboards

Effectively monitoring risk is essential for real estate agents who want to navigate the complexities of their industry. Given the market fluctuations and regulatory changes that can significantly impact operations, having real-time insights readily available is a strategic necessity. Excel offers robust tools for creating dashboards that not only visualize key metrics but also promote proactive decision-making.

To begin, identify the specific risks relevant to your business model. These could include market volatility, economic downturns, compliance issues, and operational inefficiencies. Clearly defining each risk within your dashboard enables you to track its status, assess potential impacts, and implement effective mitigation strategies. For example, if you are particularly concerned about fluctuations in housing prices, you might create a dedicated section in your dashboard for tracking local market trends, complete with historical data comparisons.

Once you've identified your risks, integrate data sources into your dashboard. Excel allows you to connect various datasets —whether they come from internal sales reports or external market analysis tools—creating a comprehensive view of your operational landscape. With Excel's Power Query feature, you can automate the importation of data from these different sources, ensuring that your dashboard always reflects current information without requiring manual updates. This automation not only saves time but also reduces the risk of errors associated with outdated data.

Next, take advantage of Excel's conditional formatting capabilities to highlight risks based on predefined thresholds. Take this example, if a specific metric related to property sales dips below a certain level—such as a 10% decrease in quarterly sales—you can set conditions that automatically change the cell color to red. This visual cue quickly alerts you to issues that need immediate attention. Conversely, using green for metrics that meet or exceed expectations creates an easy-to-read overview of your risk landscape.

Incorporating Key Performance Indicators (KPIs) into your dashboard can further enhance your risk monitoring efforts. If client acquisition rates are a major concern for you, consider including KPIs such as the number of new leads generated weekly or the conversion rate of those leads into actual sales. These indicators offer valuable insights into whether you're achieving healthy growth or if there are underlying issues that require resolution.

Another powerful tool at your disposal is scenario analysis within your dashboard. Excel's data tables allow you to simulate various scenarios based on changing inputs. For example, what would happen if interest rates were to rise by 2%? By adjusting relevant figures in your worksheet, you can model this scenario and observe its impact on projected sales or cash flow. This exercise not only prepares you for potential outcomes but also assists in developing contingency plans.

Engaging stakeholders in the risk monitoring process is equally crucial. Share access to your dashboard with team members across different areas of the business—marketing, finance, and compliance—to ensure everyone has visibility into current risks and can collaborate on mitigation strategies effectively. Since Excel allows multiple users to work on shared files simultaneously, fostering discussions around the insights gathered encourages transparency and collective responsibility.

Finally, regular reviews of your risk monitoring dashboard are vital for continuous improvement. Schedule periodic evaluations—perhaps monthly or quarterly—to assess whether identified risks remain relevant or need adjustments based on market shifts or internal performance changes. During these reviews, pay attention to emerging trends that may warrant more detailed analysis or proactive measures.

By leveraging Excel for real-time risk monitoring through dynamic dashboards, real estate agents position themselves to make informed decisions swiftly. The ability to visualize critical data points—enhanced by automated updates and team collaboration—enables you not just to identify threats early but also to capitalize on opportunities as they arise. With these tools at your disposal, you're not merely reacting to challenges; you're strategically steering your business towards stability and growth in an ever-evolving marketplace.

CHAPTER 16: USING EXCEL FOR TEAM COLLABORATION

Excel Online for Collaborative Work

E xcel Online offers a transformative platform for real estate agents, enabling seamless collaboration that transcends both time and distance. In today's fast-paced market, the demand for effective teamwork is greater than ever, making it essential to harness the capabilities of this powerful tool. Whether you are coordinating with colleagues across various locations or working alongside clients on property listings, Excel Online supports real-time collaboration and provides easy access to vital data.

To begin using Excel Online, simply log into your Microsoft account and either create new Excel files or upload existing ones. While the interface remains familiar, the real advantage lies in its cloud-based functionality. By saving your workbooks to OneDrive or SharePoint, any changes made are instantly updated for all users accessing the file, eliminating the confusion that often arises from multiple document versions circulating via email.

Consider a scenario where you're preparing a comparative market analysis for a client. With Excel Online, you can share the workbook with your team, allowing them to input their findings directly. This means you can see updates in real-time; for example, one agent may enter data about a recent sale while another reviews the pricing strategy. This immediate feedback loop not only enhances productivity but also ensures that everyone is aligned before presenting information to the client.

Collaboration extends beyond mere editing. Excel Online features commenting tools that enable users to leave notes directly within the spreadsheet. If there are questions about data entry or requests for clarification on specific calculations, team members can highlight the relevant cell and add a comment. This functionality reduces miscommunication and keeps discussions focused where they matter most.

To maximize effective collaboration, it's important to establish clear guidelines regarding team roles. Designating responsibilities—such as who handles data entry versus analysis—ensures that everyone understands their tasks and deadlines. This structured approach can streamline workflows when tackling large projects, like compiling property listings or conducting comprehensive investment analyses.

Integrating Microsoft Teams into your workflow can further enhance collaboration. You can embed your Excel Online files directly into Teams channels where discussions occur. Imagine discussing marketing strategies with your team while simultaneously reviewing budget sheets—all within the same platform. This integrated approach promotes transparency and efficiency in communication and data sharing.

Maintaining data integrity during online collaboration is crucial; leveraging Excel's version history feature allows you to track changes made by different users over time and revert back if needed. Take this example, if an error arises during a busy sales period, version history enables you to roll back to an earlier version before the mistake occurred, protecting against potential setbacks.

Visualizations play an essential role in collaborative efforts with Excel Online as well. Utilizing charts and graphs not only aids in presenting data but also facilitates discussions among team members. When evaluating property performance metrics, visual representations help everyone grasp trends quickly and collectively formulate action plans.

As you refine your collaborative efforts through Excel Online, consider how this tool aligns with your long-term goals as a real estate agent. The ability to collaborate closely with colleagues from anywhere opens new avenues for strategic partnerships and innovative client service approaches. As you navigate shared files and ongoing conversations, think about how these practices can enhance your brand reputation among clients seeking agile service providers.

By mastering the collaborative features of Excel Online, real estate agents position themselves not only as skilled technology users but also as leaders capable of fostering teamwork and innovation within their organizations. Embracing this tool goes beyond mere organization; it's about leveraging collective intelligence to make informed decisions swiftly—ultimately driving success in an increasingly competitive market landscape.

Sharing Workbooks Across Devices

Sharing workbooks across devices has become essential for effective collaboration in today's real estate landscape. With teams often spread across various locations and time zones, the ability to access and edit workbooks seamlessly on any device is crucial. This functionality, inherent to Excel Online, empowers agents to remain agile and responsive, ensuring that vital information is always at their fingertips.

To share a workbook, start by saving it to a cloud service

like OneDrive or SharePoint. Once saved, you can easily share the file with team members or clients by clicking the "Share" button within Excel Online. Here, you can specify whether recipients can edit or only view the document. This capability is particularly valuable for real estate agents who require quick feedback or approvals on listings or client analyses.

Consider a scenario where you're working on a financial analysis for a property investment while collaborating with an accountant in another city. As you make adjustments to cash flow projections, your colleague can simultaneously review those figures from her office—whether she's using a laptop or tablet. This immediate visibility of updates ensures that both of you remain aligned and can make informed decisions based on the most current data.

Beyond sharing capabilities, Excel Online enhances communication through its integrated commenting features. If someone identifies an inconsistency or has questions about specific figures in the workbook, they can simply click on the relevant cell to leave a comment. This targeted approach keeps discussions focused and organized, minimizing the miscommunication often associated with lengthy email threads.

To further streamline collaboration, establishing clear communication protocols is key. Take this example, defining which team members are responsible for specific sections of data entry helps reduce overlap and confusion. In complex scenarios—such as organizing an open house event where multiple team members might input their tasks into the same spreadsheet—clarity in roles promotes accountability and efficiency.

Integrating your Excel Online workbooks within collaboration platforms like Microsoft Teams adds another layer of efficiency. Imagine discussing marketing strategies during a team meeting while simultaneously analyzing budget forecasts directly within Teams. This seamless integration ensures everyone is looking at the same data, fostering an environment of collective problem-solving—crucial for driving successful outcomes.

Another important feature when sharing workbooks is version history. This function allows you to track changes over time, making it easy to identify who made specific edits. In fast-paced real estate transactions where accuracy is paramount, knowing you can revert to earlier versions serves as a safety net against costly mistakes. For example, if you accidentally overwrite important data while adjusting a commission structure during negotiations, you can quickly restore prior versions with confidence.

The data visualization capabilities within Excel Online also enhance collaborative discussions by providing clear graphical representations of trends and forecasts. When reviewing sales metrics with your team, charts depicting performance over time can facilitate deeper insights into market behaviors and support collaborative strategy development based on those insights.

As you integrate these collaboration tools into your daily workflows as a real estate agent, consider how they not only boost productivity but also strengthen client relationships. Providing timely updates and engaging clients through shared documents demonstrates responsiveness—a quality highly valued in today's service-oriented industry.

In the end, leveraging Excel Online's capabilities for sharing workbooks across devices positions real estate professionals as adaptable agents ready to tackle the complexities of modern transactions with finesse. The result is enhanced teamwork that leads to superior service delivery—something clients recognize and appreciate—solidifying your reputation as an indispensable partner in their real estate journey.

Co-authoring Documents in Real-Time

Co-authoring documents in real-time elevates collaboration, especially in the fast-paced world of real estate. Imagine working alongside colleagues or clients on a financial analysis while discussing strategies over the phone. This is where Excel Online truly shines, enabling multiple users to edit a document simultaneously, regardless of their physical location.

To get started with co-authoring, save your Excel file in OneDrive or SharePoint. Once uploaded, inviting collaborators is easy—just click the "Share" button and enter their email addresses. You can also customize permissions for each individual, deciding whether they can view or fully edit the document. This flexibility is essential for real estate teams that need to act quickly, particularly when finalizing a proposal for a prospective buyer.

For example, consider preparing a comparative market analysis (CMA) report for several properties in your area. You can share the workbook with a colleague who specializes in pricing strategies. While you update property details, she can analyze market trends and add insights directly into the same document. This synchronization speeds up the process and reduces errors that might arise from having multiple versions of the same file circulating.

Excel Online enhances this collaborative experience with its commenting feature. If you're uncertain about a specific figure —like an estimated closing cost—you can highlight that cell and leave a comment for your colleague to review. This direct communication within the document minimizes disruptions and keeps everyone focused on their tasks.

In addition to comments, using @mentions allows team members to notify each other about specific areas needing attention. Take this example, if you're analyzing property values and want input on historical data trends, simply type @ followed by their name in your comment. They'll receive an instant notification prompting them to check that section of the workbook.

Establishing clear collaboration guidelines is crucial for maximizing effectiveness during co-authoring sessions. Assign roles based on expertise: one agent may handle property evaluations while another focuses on financial projections or marketing strategies. This division of labor ensures clarity and accountability—especially important during high-stakes situations like preparing for an open house event.

Integrating Excel Online with Microsoft Teams can further enhance your collaborative efforts. Picture discussing marketing tactics during a team meeting while updating an Excel sheet in real-time; this creates a dynamic environment where decisions are made collectively rather than through delayed communications or follow-up emails.

Another important feature of co-authoring is the ability to track changes through version history—a built-in tool in Excel Online that shows who made edits and when those changes occurred. If an error arises from recent modifications—such as miscalculations in commission rates—you can easily revert to previous versions without losing significant progress.

And, Excel's graphical tools greatly enhance collaborative discussions. When evaluating sales performance over several quarters, charts illustrating these metrics provide immediate visual context that supports data-driven conversations among team members. These visuals clarify complex information and stimulate strategic thinking about future actions based on observed patterns.

As you incorporate these co-authoring features into your daily operations, you'll find they significantly boost efficiency while enriching client interactions. Allowing clients access to shared documents with real-time updates fosters transparency—an essential quality for buyers and sellers alike in today's marketplace.

In the end, co-authoring documents transforms how real estate professionals collaborate by fostering a culture of teamwork characterized by agility and responsiveness. The ability to work together seamlessly positions agents advantageously when navigating complex transactions or crafting compelling presentations—all while building strong relationships with clients rooted in trust and transparency.

Embracing this technology not only facilitates superior collaboration but also redefines client service standards, solidifying your role as a trusted advisor throughout their real estate journey.

Setting Permissions and Version History

Effective collaboration in real estate teams hinges on managing permissions and tracking version history in Excel, especially when multiple users access and edit the same documents. These features not only protect data integrity but also promote accountability among team members. By configuring these settings properly, you can significantly enhance your workflow.

First, consider how to set permissions. It's crucial to identify who should access your Excel workbooks and the level of access they need. Excel offers various options: users can be granted full editing rights, allowed view-only access, or given limited editing capabilities. For example, when preparing a property analysis sheet for clients, you may want to restrict them to view-only access while allowing your team members full editing rights. This approach prevents any unintended changes that could misrepresent the data.

To configure these permissions, open your workbook and go to the "File" tab. From there, select "Info" and click on "Protect Workbook." You'll find options like "Restrict Access" or "Encrypt with Password." Choosing "Restrict Access" enables you to specify which users can view or edit the document based on their email addresses within your organization. If a property report contains sensitive financial information, restricting access is essential to maintain confidentiality.

Consider this scenario: you're working on a market analysis report with two colleagues. By adjusting permission levels according to each member's role—one focusing on data collection and another on generating insights—you enhance both efficiency and security. The data collector might have full editing rights, while the analyst could be limited to suggesting changes without directly altering the core figures.

Version history is equally crucial in collaborative environments, especially when multiple parties contribute to documents. Excel's version history feature allows you to track changes over time, providing a clear overview of modifications and their contributors. This becomes invaluable when reflecting on decisions made during earlier project stages.

To access version history in Excel Online or newer desktop versions, click on the "File" tab, select "Info," and then choose "Version History." Here, you'll find a list of saved versions with timestamps. You can view any previous version by clicking on it, making it easy to compare against the current one. If something seems off in your latest update—perhaps a figure that doesn't add up or an inaccurate description—you can revert to an earlier version without starting from scratch.

Imagine you're crafting a client proposal that has gone through several rounds of edits based on feedback from both team members and clients. Utilizing version history allows you to identify when specific suggestions were incorporated or which revisions led to successful outcomes. This not only enhances transparency but also provides a helpful record for future reference—ideal for discussions about project evolution during meetings or client follow-ups.

In summary, mastering permissions and understanding version history in Excel can greatly improve collaboration among real estate teams. These practices empower professionals to share valuable information securely while maintaining clarity over modifications made throughout the process. Implementing them establishes a solid foundation for efficient teamwork and effective project management in a dynamic marketplace where precise data management is essential.

Integrating with Microsoft Teams

Integrating Excel with Microsoft Teams can transform the way real estate professionals collaborate, share information, and manage projects. Microsoft Teams acts as a central hub for teamwork, streamlining communication while ensuring that crucial Excel data is easily accessible and editable. This synergy boosts overall efficiency in real estate operations, leading to better decision-making and fostering a more collaborative environment.

To begin integrating Excel into your Microsoft Teams workspace, start by ensuring your files are stored in OneDrive or SharePoint. These platforms facilitate seamless access within Teams. Once your Excel documents are hosted online, open Microsoft Teams and navigate to the relevant channel for collaboration. Click on the "+" icon to add a new tab, then select "Excel" to link the desired spreadsheet for your team. This not only enhances visibility but also allows for real-time collaboration.

For example, consider a scenario where your team is working on a property listing sheet. Rather than emailing individual versions back and forth, you can upload the Excel file as a tab in a dedicated property listings channel. This way, everyone can view and edit the same document simultaneously. Team members can leave comments directly within Excel during their review process, promoting discussion without cluttering email threads. By utilizing this functionality, you eliminate confusion over which version of a document is the most current—an all-too-common challenge in collaborative projects.

Once integrated, Teams' chat feature can further enhance collaboration on specific sections of the Excel document. If a team member has questions about data analysis or needs clarification on figures presented in the spreadsheet, they can easily initiate a chat or call directly within Teams. Take this example, if someone identifies an anomaly in the sales figures while reviewing the spreadsheet, they can tag their colleague in a message with a reference to that specific section for immediate feedback.

Managing tasks also becomes more efficient with this integration. You can create task assignments related to items tracked within your Excel sheet using Microsoft Planner or To Do within Teams. This capability allows you to link specific tasks to data points or deadlines listed in your spreadsheet, ensuring that every team member understands their responsibilities based on current market analysis or client needs.

And, utilizing Power Automate—a tool integrated with both Excel and Microsoft Teams—can significantly enhance workflow automation. Imagine setting up triggers so that every time a new lead is added to an Excel sheet tracking potential clients, an automatic message is sent via Teams to notify team members about this update. This keeps everyone informed promptly and reduces the need for manual tracking efforts.

As meetings become routine in real estate practices, integrating your Excel data into Teams makes presenting findings more seamless. Instead of switching between applications during discussions, you can share your screen with live updates from your Excel document, keeping participants engaged and informed about new property listings or sales strategies derived from data analysis.

Another valuable benefit comes from using OneNote alongside this integration; it allows for supplementary documentation linked directly back to data analyses in your Excel files. When discussing insights from sales trends during team meetings in Microsoft Teams, capturing notes that connect directly to your dataset ensures nothing gets lost in translation.

This blend of tools creates an ecosystem where spreadsheets are not isolated but rather dynamic instruments of collaboration and insight generation across teams. The connection between Microsoft Teams and Excel is essential for modern real estate agents striving for efficiency amid increasing demands for quick turnaround times and accurate information management.

By effectively harnessing these integrations, real estate professionals can develop responsive workflows that not only save time but also enhance productivity across all aspects of their operations—from lead generation to contract negotiations—all grounded in robust data analysis practices powered by Excel.

Collaborative Task Lists and Schedules

Collaborative task lists and schedules are crucial for real estate teams aiming to enhance organization and efficiency. With multiple agents, administrative staff, and clients involved in each transaction, tracking responsibilities can quickly become overwhelming. By utilizing Excel within Microsoft Teams, teams can create dynamic task lists that promote collaboration and streamline workflows.

Consider the process of managing a new property listing. You need to ensure various tasks—such as scheduling showings, preparing marketing materials, and updating the MLS—are clearly assigned and monitored. Rather than relying on email reminders or separate documents that may be overlooked, an integrated Excel task list centralizes this vital information.

To create a collaborative task list in Excel, begin by setting up a table with columns for the task name, assigned team member, due date, status, and notes. This straightforward structure clarifies who is responsible for each task and when it is due. Your table might look like this:

| Task | Assigned To | Due Date | Status | Notes |

| Schedule Open House | Jane Doe | 10/15/2023| In Progress | Need confirmation from seller |

| Prepare Marketing Materials | John Smith | 10/14/2023| Not Started | Include digital brochures |

| Update MLS Listing | Sarah Johnson | 10/16/2023| Not Started | Check for recent changes |

After creating your table, upload it to a dedicated channel in Microsoft Teams where your team collaborates. Pinning this document as a tab allows all members easy access. Any changes made by one team member are instantly visible to others, ensuring everyone stays informed.

As team members complete their tasks or adjust deadlines based on client feedback or external factors, they can update the Excel sheet directly within Teams. This real-time collaboration reduces confusion about completed or pending tasks while eliminating version control issues associated with emailing files back and forth.

Setting reminders in Teams based on deadlines can further enhance accountability. If a task approaches its due date without updates, automated alerts prompt team members to check their progress. For example, if Sarah hasn't updated the MLS listing by October 15th as planned, an automatic reminder will be sent through Teams.

Integrating Excel with Microsoft Planner or To Do also allows you to create actionable task assignments linked to your collaborative list. You might connect specific tasks from your Excel sheet to Planner boards or individual assignments that team members can track. This integration reinforces responsibility while providing a visual overview of current workloads and priorities across the team.

As deadlines approach or changes occur—such as shifting market conditions—collaborative lists facilitate quick adaptations. Take this example, if new properties enter the market that may influence your open house strategy, revisiting the shared document allows the entire team to reassess priorities swiftly and discuss adjustments during scheduled meetings via Teams.

Additionally, using shared calendars within Teams alongside your Excel sheets helps coordinate schedules efficiently. For example, aligning everyone's availability for a client meeting or showing while tracking ongoing tasks becomes more manageable with a shared calendar integrated into your workspace.

Encouraging continuous feedback enhances this collaborative model further. Team members can leave comments directly in the Excel file regarding specific tasks or timelines. This practice fosters open dialogue and promotes a culture of teamwork where everyone feels engaged in driving the project forward.

In the end, implementing collaborative task lists and schedules through Excel within Microsoft Teams ensures real estate professionals stay organized amid busy workloads and dynamic market conditions. With clear communication channels and easily accessible information at hand, teams can focus on what matters most—effectively serving clients while maximizing productivity across operations. These practices not only facilitate seamless management of daily responsibilities but also strengthen partnerships among colleagues as you work together toward shared goals in real estate success.

Feedback and Communication Tools

Effective feedback and communication tools are vital for real estate teams looking to maintain clarity and foster collaboration. In the fast-paced real estate environment, where each transaction involves multiple stakeholders, ensuring everyone is aligned can be challenging. By utilizing Excel in tandem with integrated communication platforms like Microsoft Teams, teams can streamline this process and boost productivity.

One of the simplest ways to facilitate feedback is by embedding comments directly within Excel sheets. As agents update property listings or conduct market analyses, they can add comments to specific cells, allowing team members to ask questions or provide insights without cluttering the main document. For example, if John adjusts a property's price, he might leave a comment explaining the recent market trends that justify this change. Sarah could then respond directly in the cell, seeking clarification or sharing her thoughts on the potential impacts. This ongoing dialogue keeps discussions organized and contextually relevant.

In addition to in-document feedback, integrating Microsoft Teams offers a platform for real-time communication. Creating dedicated channels for specific projects or properties enables agents to discuss details without overwhelming their email inboxes. Take this example, if your team is preparing for an open house, establishing a dedicated channel for that event allows members to share ideas about staging, marketing materials, and last-minute logistics while referencing the relevant Excel sheet where tasks are tracked. This centralized approach minimizes miscommunication and fosters camaraderie as everyone works toward a common goal.

To further enhance engagement and accountability, consider utilizing polls or surveys within Teams for project decisions. If your team needs to choose between two marketing strategies for a new listing, creating a poll ensures that everyone's voice is heard quickly and effectively. The results can then guide decision-making while keeping all members actively involved in the process.

Additionally, leveraging task management features available in Teams can simplify tracking responsibilities related to ongoing projects. Assigning tasks linked directly to specific actions outlined in your Excel sheet clarifies who is responsible for what and by when. When tasks are completed, notifications keep everyone informed about progress without necessitating constant check-ins.

Regular check-in meetings can also benefit from these tools. Scheduling recurring meetings allows teams to collaboratively review completed tasks and address any outstanding issues. During these sessions, agents can display the shared Excel document on screen and walk through updates together in real time, making discussions more dynamic and engaging.

Encouraging feedback reinforces a culture of continuous improvement within your team. After completing major projects or transactions, take the time to solicit input from all members about what worked well and what could be improved next time. This practice not only strengthens teamwork but also provides invaluable insights that drive future success.

As teams become accustomed to these feedback mechanisms —whether through direct comments in documents, chat channels in Teams, or polls—they will find their collaboration becomes increasingly fluid over time. A well-structured approach reduces misunderstandings while enhancing responsiveness among team members.

By fostering open lines of communication through these integrated tools and practices, real estate professionals can navigate their complex responsibilities with greater ease and confidence. In the end, this collaborative environment not only enhances performance but also nurtures stronger relationships among colleagues as they collectively strive for excellence in client service and operational efficiency.

Tracking Team Performance

Tracking team performance in real estate is essential for achieving goals and ensuring that every team member contributes effectively to the organization's success. Excel provides powerful tools for monitoring, analyzing, and enhancing performance metrics across various facets of your real estate operations.

The first step is to establish a clear set of performance indicators. These metrics should align with your team's specific objectives, such as the number of properties sold, client satisfaction ratings, or lead conversion rates. Take this example, if your goal is to increase sales, you might track metrics like the average time taken to close a sale or the conversion rate of leads to clients. Once you've identified these indicators, you can organize them in a dedicated Excel spreadsheet.

Creating a worksheet titled "Team Performance Dashboard" within your Excel workbook can serve as a central hub for tracking these key metrics. Start by listing your chosen performance indicators in one column, then allocate additional columns for each team member's data inputs. As you gather data—whether through direct entry or integration with other systems—you will gain a clear visual representation of each member's performance against established benchmarks.

Excel's capability to handle large datasets comes into play here. Functions like SUM and AVERAGE allow you to quickly calculate totals and averages for various metrics across your team. For example, to find the total number of listings handled by each agent over a specific period, simply use the formula =SUM(range), where "range" refers to the cells containing individual contributions. This immediate feedback enables managers to pinpoint strengths and identify areas needing improvement without extensive manual calculations.

Visual representations of data through charts can further enhance understanding. By converting performance metrics into graphs—such as bar charts or line graphs—you can easily spot trends and patterns. Take this example, if one agent consistently outperforms others in sales volume, a graphical representation makes it simple to identify leading performers and initiate discussions about best practices during team meetings.

To maintain the effectiveness of your dashboard, regular updates and reviews are vital. Set aside time during weekly or bi-weekly meetings to collectively review these performance indicators with your team. This practice not only fosters accountability but also creates an environment where success is recognized and shared. If one agent achieves notable results, discussing their strategies can inspire others to adopt similar approaches.

Incorporating conditional formatting in Excel adds another layer of functionality when monitoring performance metrics. By applying color scales or icons based on performance thresholds—such as green for exceeding targets and red for those falling short—you provide instant visual cues that prompt further investigation or discussion.

Additionally, consider implementing feedback loops by allowing agents to self-report their challenges or successes related to their performance metrics directly in the spreadsheet comments section or through a linked survey form. This encourages communication about any roadblocks they may be facing while offering insights into how they perceive their contributions toward team goals.

Engaging in periodic analysis beyond mere number crunching can reveal deeper insights into underlying trends affecting team efficiency. For example, if certain periods show diminished productivity correlated with specific market fluctuations, it may be necessary to discuss strategic shifts.

Utilizing Excel's built-in functionalities like pivot tables facilitates deeper dives into your data without requiring complex formulas or setups. By effortlessly summarizing large volumes of information and dynamically filtering through variables—such as property types or geographic areas—you gain nuanced insights that inform decision-making processes at both operational and strategic levels.

As teams become accustomed to using these tracking methods within Excel while refining their focus on defined performance indicators over time, performance management will become more intuitive and seamlessly integrated into daily operations rather than an afterthought when targets are missed.

This structured approach not only cultivates accountability but also enhances collaboration as teammates openly share strategies for improvement based on real-time data insights. In doing so, everyone becomes invested not just in their personal success but also in uplifting the entire team's collective performance—ultimately driving sustained growth and excellence in service delivery within a competitive real estate landscape.

CHAPTER 17: DATA SECURITY AND BACKUP IN EXCEL

Understanding Data Security Risks

Data security risks in real estate are complex and require careful attention. As an agent, you manage sensitive information daily—ranging from client details to financial data related to property transactions. Recognizing these risks is the first step in safeguarding both your clients and your business. Data breaches can lead to significant reputational damage, financial loss, and legal consequences. By understanding the vulnerabilities within your systems, you can implement proactive measures to mitigate potential threats.

One of the most pressing risks stems from inadequate password protection. Weak or shared passwords can easily allow unauthorized individuals to access confidential files. For example, if multiple team members rely on a generic password for a shared Excel workbook, the chance of an accidental breach dramatically increases. To counter this risk, enforce a policy that mandates complex passwords—combinations of letters, numbers, and special characters are essential. Additionally, regularly changing these passwords can bolster your security.

Phishing attacks pose another serious threat to data integrity. In these incidents, malicious actors impersonate legitimate entities—such as banks or fellow real estate professionals —to deceive agents into revealing sensitive information. A common tactic involves sending emails that appear credible but contain links to counterfeit websites designed to harvest personal data. It is crucial to train your team to identify phishing attempts; implementing a multi-factor authentication system adds an extra layer of protection.

And, physical security should not be underestimated. Data remains vulnerable not just when stored digitally but also when printed or saved on unsecured devices. Leaving printed property reports unattended at open houses can expose sensitive client information to theft or misuse. To mitigate this risk, establish secure disposal protocols for sensitive documents and encourage team members to store physical materials in locked cabinets when not in use.

Malware attacks represent another significant risk in today's digital environment. These attacks often occur when users inadvertently download harmful software that compromises their systems and data integrity. Ensuring that all devices used by your team have up-to-date antivirus software is essential for minimizing this risk. Regular updates can protect against newly developed malware strains that exploit vulnerabilities in outdated systems.

While cloud storage solutions offer convenience, they also come with their own risks if not properly managed. Although these services facilitate easy file sharing among team members, they can also attract cybercriminals seeking valuable data repositories. Conduct thorough research before selecting a cloud provider; ensure they comply with industry-standard security protocols and offer encryption options for stored data.

Understanding how third-party applications integrate with Excel is equally critical for maintaining data security. Many real estate agents utilize various tools—like CRM systems or property management software—to enhance productivity; however, integrating these applications without proper oversight can create vulnerabilities in your workflow. Always review the permissions and access rights granted to external applications linked with your Excel workbooks, ensuring they only have the necessary access required for functionality.

Regular training sessions focused on data security best practices are invaluable for keeping your team informed about evolving threats and prevention techniques. Fostering a culture of awareness within your organization encourages proactive behavior regarding the protection of sensitive information.

Establishing robust backup procedures is equally important; it safeguards against potential data loss due to cyber incidents or hardware failures. Implement automated backups for critical files stored in Excel, ensuring these backups occur frequently enough to minimize any loss in case of an incident.

As you deepen your understanding of the specific data security risks within the real estate sector, you empower yourself and your team to take informed actions effectively. By instituting protective measures around password management, recognizing phishing attempts, securing physical documents, utilizing antivirus protections on devices, carefully evaluating cloud storage solutions, overseeing third-party application integrations diligently, engaging in ongoing training focused on security awareness, and maintaining rigorous backup protocols—you can create a resilient framework that protects sensitive information while fostering productivity and collaboration among colleagues.

By addressing these vulnerabilities proactively today, you lay the foundation for a more secure tomorrow—one where client trust remains intact and your business thrives amidst an ever-evolving digital landscape.

Using Password Protection for Files

In the realm of data security, password protection is your first line of defense. Real estate agents handle sensitive information, including financial records, client details, and transaction documents, making robust password protocols essential. A weak password can be an open invitation to cybercriminals, which underscores the importance of creating strong, unique passwords for every file and system.

A strong password typically consists of at least 12 characters, combining uppercase and lowercase letters, numbers, and special symbols. For example, instead of using "password123," consider a more complex phrase-like password such as "R3alEstate#2023!" This approach not only enhances security but also aids in memorization. Encouraging your team to adopt this strategy can significantly reduce the risk of unauthorized access.

In addition to crafting strong passwords, it is crucial to establish a routine for regular updates. Setting a schedule to change passwords—every 90 days, for instance—can help mitigate potential threats from lingering vulnerabilities. Remind your team that reusing old passwords across different platforms dramatically increases security risks. Utilizing a password manager can streamline this process by securely storing complex passwords, allowing users to maintain high security without the burden of memorization.

Implementing multi-factor authentication (MFA) is another vital step in safeguarding your Excel files. MFA adds an additional layer of protection by requiring users to provide two or more verification factors before accessing a file or system. Take this example, after entering their password, users may receive a text message with a one-time code that they must input to proceed. This way, even if a password is compromised, unauthorized individuals face additional barriers when attempting to access sensitive information.

It's also important to differentiate between shared files and personal documents within your Excel workbooks. By setting permissions based on user roles, you can ensure that team members only access files relevant to their work functions. For example, if you're collaborating on property listings while keeping financial records confidential, adjust the settings so that only designated individuals can view or edit specific sheets within your workbook.

Educating your team on recognizing phishing attempts is another critical aspect of password security. Regular training sessions can equip agents with the skills necessary to identify suspicious emails or messages that request personal information or contain direct links prompting them to log into accounts. Remind them always to verify the source before providing any credentials and encourage skepticism regarding unsolicited requests.

Leveraging Excel's built-in features for file protection can further enhance data security. You can easily set passwords on individual workbooks or specific worksheets within a workbook. To do this, navigate to the 'File' menu and select 'Info.' From there, choose 'Protect Workbook,' where you'll find options like 'Encrypt with Password.' Once you input a password and save the file, it will require that password upon opening—a straightforward yet effective way to protect sensitive content.

As you manage shared files among colleagues or clients using cloud storage solutions like OneDrive or SharePoint, understanding their built-in security options becomes equally important. These platforms often offer additional safeguards for shared content. Ensure that all team members are familiar with these features and encourage them to utilize available controls related to access permissions when sharing sensitive documents.

When considering remote work arrangements or collaborative projects through shared networks and devices, device security practices must also be prioritized. Encourage team members who access company files on personal devices or unsecured networks (like public Wi-Fi) to utilize VPNs (Virtual Private Networks) that encrypt internet traffic and enhance privacy.

In the end, fostering a culture centered around data protection within your organization is vital as threats continue to evolve in our digital landscape. Engage in regular discussions about password security and emphasize that protecting client data isn't solely an IT responsibility—it's everyone's job within your real estate practice.

Establishing comprehensive protocols for password management not only safeguards sensitive information but also reinforces client trust. Clients are more likely to feel secure knowing their data is protected by diligent professionals who prioritize confidentiality as part of their service ethos. By reinforcing these practices daily within your workflow, you're not just protecting files; you're building a reputation rooted in reliability and professionalism in an increasingly complex industry landscape.

Implementing Data Encryption

Data encryption is a crucial strategy for protecting sensitive information in your Excel workbooks. As a real estate agent, you frequently handle confidential documents, including client contracts, financial statements, and transaction records. By implementing strong encryption methods, you ensure that even if unauthorized access occurs, your data remains unreadable and secure.

To get started with data encryption in Excel, it's important to familiarize yourself with the software's built-in features.

Encrypting a workbook allows you to set a password that must be entered to access the file, providing an immediate layer of security. To encrypt a workbook, navigate to the 'File' tab, select 'Info,' then click on 'Protect Workbook.' From there, choose 'Encrypt with Password.' A dialog box will prompt you to enter your chosen password; make sure it's strong—ideally a mix of letters, numbers, and symbols—to enhance security.

Imagine this scenario: you've just completed a thorough analysis of a property investment and are preparing to share it with potential clients. Before sending the file, take the precaution of encrypting it to prevent unauthorized access to sensitive financial projections. Once encrypted, anyone attempting to open the workbook without the password will encounter only a prompt for it—effectively locking out prying eyes.

However, simply encrypting files is not enough; you also need to develop responsible habits for managing them. Regularly review and update your passwords, steering clear of easily guessable phrases or common words. If you often work in teams or collaborate with others, consider using a shared password manager that securely stores passwords and allows for designated access levels among users.

And, data encryption should extend beyond individual files. When dealing with larger projects that involve multiple spreadsheets or integrated datasets from various sources, think about encrypting these files at the source level as well. Take this example, when pulling data from external databases or APIs into your Excel sheets, ensure that your data transfer methods utilize encryption protocols like SSL (Secure Sockets Layer) to protect your information both during transit and at rest.

In addition to file encryption, consider options for encrypting specific cells or ranges within your spreadsheets that contain sensitive information. While Excel doesn't offer direct cell encryption capabilities like some other software might, you can implement techniques such as hiding sensitive information behind locked cells that require a password for access. To do this, select the cell or range you want to protect, right-click to access 'Format Cells,' go to the 'Protection' tab, and check 'Locked.' Don't forget to protect the sheet afterward by selecting 'Protect Sheet' from the Review tab.

Understanding how data encryption interacts with backup systems is another critical aspect of your security protocol. Regularly back up encrypted files onto secure drives or cloud services that have additional encryption layers. This way, even if your physical device is compromised or lost, your vital data remains protected.

When discussing encryption with clients or stakeholders, clarity is essential. Many people may not fully grasp what data encryption involves or its significance in safeguarding their personal information. Use simple analogies; for example, compare it to locking valuable items in a safe. Convey that while you take extensive precautions—encryption being one of them—to secure their data digitally, they can rest easy knowing their sensitive information isn't stored haphazardly.

Fostering a culture of awareness around data encryption practices within your team is equally important. Schedule training sessions where everyone can learn about various encryption methods and tools available beyond Excel itself. There are third-party solutions specifically designed for enhanced data security that can integrate seamlessly with Excel workflows.

As cyber threats evolve alongside technological advancements, remaining proactive about data encryption becomes essential for real estate professionals like you. Emphasizing these protective measures not only secures client information but also enhances your reputation as a trustworthy agent who values confidentiality.

By adopting these strategies for effective data encryption within your organization—utilizing Excel's built-in functionalities and supplementary tools—you create an environment where sensitive information is handled with care and integrity. In the end, this commitment reflects positively on your professionalism and dedication to protecting client information in an increasingly complex digital landscape.

Creating Regular Backup Systems

Creating a reliable backup system for your Excel workbooks is crucial for safeguarding your data against unexpected events like hardware failures, accidental deletions, or cyberattacks. In the fast-paced real estate industry, where timely access to information can be the deciding factor between closing a deal and losing it, a solid backup strategy is non-negotiable.

To begin, establish a routine for backups. Rather than waiting for a crisis to strike, proactively schedule regular intervals for saving copies of your important files. Depending on how frequently you update your data, this could mean daily, weekly, or even bi-weekly backups. Utilize Excel's version history feature to track changes made to your workbooks. This capability allows you to revert to previous versions if needed, ensuring that even minor mistakes can be corrected without major setbacks.

In addition to routine backups, consider implementing both local and cloud-based solutions for maximum data security. Storing copies on an external hard drive or USB flash drive gives you physical control over your data. However, when combined with a cloud-based solution like Microsoft OneDrive or Google Drive, you gain redundancy. Cloud storage protects against local hardware failures and offers the added benefit of remote access to your files—a crucial advantage in the mobile real estate sector.

Imagine this scenario: you've meticulously gathered and

analyzed data for an important property listing. One morning, as you try to open your Excel file, your computer fails to boot up. Panic might set in, but if you've established an automatic backup schedule that saves files to the cloud daily, you can quickly retrieve the most recent version from another device without losing hours of work.

Another essential element of your backup system is effective data organization. Create a clear folder structure for your files to ensure that backups are efficient and easily navigable when needed. For example, categorize folders by client names, project types, or property categories. This organization not only streamlines the backup process but also simplifies data retrieval when necessary.

Once you've established a backup routine and organizational system, it's wise to periodically test your backups. Regularly checking that they function correctly will assure you that your data can be recovered when required. A good practice is to select a few critical files and attempt restoring them from both local and cloud backups at least every couple of months. Confirming that these files open properly and contain the most recent data will provide peace of mind and validate your backup strategy.

As you develop this system, consider sharing access with relevant team members to enhance collaboration while maintaining security protocols. Setting up shared folders in cloud services allows your team to access essential documents while ensuring that everyone has access to the latest versions of those files. This cooperative approach fosters teamwork and mitigates risks associated with multiple people working off different versions.

Lastly, don't underestimate the importance of educating yourself and your team about best practices in data backup and recovery. Regular discussions about technological updates can help manage backups more effectively and introduce new tools that simplify the process. Cultivating awareness around data management ensures that everyone understands their role in protecting sensitive information.

By incorporating these strategies into your workflow, you'll establish a resilient backup system tailored for the demands of real estate professionals. With organized processes in place and proactive measures taken, you'll find reassurance in knowing that your valuable data is secure and readily accessible whenever needed. This commitment not only protects your business but also enhances client trust by demonstrating a serious dedication to safeguarding their information.

Managing Cloud Storage Solutions

Effectively managing cloud storage solutions is crucial for real estate professionals seeking to streamline their workflows while ensuring data security and accessibility. The transition to cloud-based storage has transformed how agents handle documents, spreadsheets, and presentations, facilitating real-time collaboration and immediate access to essential information from anywhere.

To start, choose a cloud storage provider that aligns with your specific needs. Options like Microsoft OneDrive, Google Drive, and Dropbox offer distinct features tailored for various users. For example, if you frequently work within the Microsoft ecosystem, OneDrive's seamless integration with Excel allows you to save your work directly from the application. This not only simplifies your workflow but also ensures that changes are automatically saved to the cloud in real time.

After selecting a provider, establish a clear organizational structure for your files that reflects your real estate workflow. An intuitive structure will make it easier to retrieve documents quickly. Consider creating main folders labeled by clients, property listings, or project categories. Within these main folders, you can organize documents into subfolders based on transaction stages or types of analysis, such as "Market Analysis," "Client Contracts," or "Financial Reports." This approach enhances efficiency when searching for past documents or preparing reports.

Another effective strategy is to leverage collaborative features available on most platforms. These allow you to share files with specific permissions, giving you control over who can view or edit sensitive information. Take this example, when collaborating on a property proposal with your team, you can share only the relevant folders while keeping confidential client data secure. This not only protects sensitive information but also fosters teamwork through shared resources.

Additionally, take advantage of version control offered by cloud services. Many platforms maintain a history of changes made to files, enabling you to revert to earlier versions as needed. This feature is especially useful in real estate transactions where multiple revisions occur during negotiations or project developments. For example, if you realize there's a significant mistake in a financial analysis report, you can easily restore a previous version without sifting through backup files.

Security should remain a top priority when managing cloud storage solutions. Activate two-factor authentication (2FA) for an added layer of protection on your accounts. This extra step requires users to provide additional verification—such as a code sent to their mobile device—making unauthorized access significantly more difficult. Regularly updating passwords and educating your team about phishing scams further fortifies defenses against potential breaches.

Monitoring and managing your storage capacity is also essential. As a real estate professional dealing with numerous transactions and large datasets—including property photos, contracts, and financial documents—it's easy to reach the limits of your cloud storage plan. Periodically review which files are necessary for active use and consider archiving older files that may not require immediate access but still hold value for historical analysis or reference.

Integrating cloud solutions with other tools can enhance overall productivity. Many CRM systems offer direct connections with cloud storage services, allowing for automatic document uploads when new leads are entered or client profiles are updated. This streamlining saves time and ensures that all important documents are consistently stored in one centralized location.

As you become more comfortable managing your cloud solutions, explore additional features such as automated workflows or third-party apps that connect with your cloud service. Many platforms provide integrations with task management tools that help organize projects or deadlines associated with property sales, keeping everything aligned and minimizing miscommunication.

By incorporating these strategies into your daily practice, you'll elevate your document management within the real estate sector while ensuring smooth operations amidst the industry's fast-paced nature. Leveraging effective cloud storage management techniques will create an agile framework that supports collaboration and enhances your ability to serve clients efficiently while safeguarding their sensitive data along the way.

Controlling Access to Sensitive Data

Controlling access to sensitive data is essential in the real estate industry, where client trust and confidentiality are paramount. When dealing with sensitive information —such as financial records, client contracts, and personal identification details—implementing robust access controls not only protects your data but also enhances your professional reputation.

To start, it's important to establish a clear policy outlining who can access different types of data. Consider categorizing information by its sensitivity level. For example, you might classify financial data and client contracts as high-sensitivity, while general property listings could be deemed low-sensitivity. This classification helps you determine appropriate access levels for team members, ensuring that only those who need specific information for their roles can access it.

Next, leverage the sharing settings offered by your cloud storage solution. Most platforms allow you to set permissions that control whether a user can view, comment on, or edit a file. When sharing documents with clients or collaborators, carefully review these permissions to prevent unauthorized alterations or access to sensitive information. Take this example, when sharing a financial analysis report with a client, consider granting them view-only access while retaining editing rights for yourself and your team.

In addition to specific permissions, implementing role-based access controls (RBAC) can further enhance security. This approach assigns permissions based on an individual's role within the organization. A junior agent may need access to property listings and marketing materials but shouldn't have the same level of access to financial documents or client contracts as a senior agent or manager. By clearly defining roles and associated permissions, you create a structured framework that minimizes the risks of unauthorized access.

Regularly reviewing who has access to sensitive data and updating permissions as needed is another effective measure. Staff turnover is common in real estate; when employees leave or change roles, their access should be promptly revoked or adjusted. Conducting periodic audits of user permissions helps maintain oversight and ensures that only current employees have access to confidential information. Establish a routine—perhaps quarterly—to assess these permissions and keep your data secure.

Training your team on data security protocols is equally vital. Ensure they understand the importance of protecting sensitive information and how to recognize potential threats such as phishing attempts or social engineering tactics. Regular training sessions can reinforce best practices and foster a culture of vigilance when handling confidential client data. Incorporating real-life scenarios into these sessions—such as discussing past security breaches and how they could have been avoided—can make the training more engaging.

For additional security, consider encrypting sensitive files before sharing them with clients or other parties. Encryption scrambles the contents of a document so that only authorized users with the correct decryption key can view it, providing another layer of protection—especially when transferring files via email or cloud services that may lack stringent security measures.

And, implementing two-factor authentication (2FA) enhances your defense against unauthorized access. By requiring a second form of verification—like a code sent to a mobile device —you ensure that even if someone obtains login credentials, they cannot gain entry without this additional step. Adopting 2FA across your organization promotes a proactive approach to security.

Finally, establish protocols for reporting potential security breaches or suspicious activity. Encourage team members to speak up if they notice anything unusual regarding data access or handling. Quick reporting can mitigate risks before they escalate into major issues. Fostering an open line of communication about security creates an environment where everyone feels responsible for protecting sensitive information.

By implementing these strategies, you will not only effectively control access to sensitive data but also build a resilient framework for data management within your real estate practice. Being diligent about safeguarding client information nurtures trust and lays the groundwork for lasting professional relationships.

Compliance with Data Regulations

Compliance with data regulations is a crucial consideration for real estate agents operating in an increasingly intricate legal environment. Given the industry's handling of vast amounts of sensitive information—such as financial records, personal identification, and transaction histories—agents must be well-versed in relevant regulations. Adhering to these laws not only protects clients but also maintains your agency's reputation.

To begin ensuring compliance, familiarize yourself with the applicable laws and regulations. In the United States, for instance, the Gramm-Leach-Bliley Act (GLBA) requires financial institutions, including real estate agencies, to safeguard the confidentiality and security of customer information. Additionally, the Fair Housing Act prohibits discrimination based on factors like race, color, religion, sex, or national origin. Understanding these laws will help you create a framework for managing data responsibly.

In addition to federal regulations, individual states often have specific laws governing data protection. For example, California's Consumer Privacy Act (CCPA) grants consumers rights over their personal information, including the right to know what data is collected and how it is used. Familiarizing yourself with your state's unique requirements can guide you in establishing processes that not only ensure compliance but also build client trust.

Implementing robust data management practices is vital for maintaining compliance. Start by developing a comprehensive privacy policy that outlines how client information is collected, used, and protected. This policy should be easily accessible to clients so they can understand their rights regarding their personal data. Transparency fosters trust and clarifies what clients can expect from your agency.

Another key aspect to consider is adopting a data minimization approach. This means collecting only the necessary data required for your business operations. Over-collection can increase liabilities and complicate compliance with regulations concerning the storage and processing of personal information. Take this example, when conducting market analysis, focus on gathering only relevant property details instead of extraneous personal information about clients.

Training your staff on compliance protocols is essential as well. Regular training sessions equip team members with the knowledge needed to handle client data responsibly and recognize potential compliance issues. Incorporating scenarios related to data breaches or mishandling prepares your team for real-world challenges while reinforcing the importance of adhering to regulations.

Conducting regular audits of your data management practices ensures ongoing compliance. Establish a routine review process—perhaps semi-annually or annually—to assess how well your agency adheres to established policies and legal requirements. During these audits, evaluate both the effectiveness of current procedures and areas where improvements could be made.

Documentation plays a critical role in demonstrating your compliance efforts. Keep thorough records of all data handling practices, employee training sessions, and audits conducted. Should regulatory inquiries arise or if there's ever a breach incident, having comprehensive documentation will provide evidence that appropriate measures were taken to protect client information.

Additionally, consider investing in technology solutions designed to support your compliance efforts. Many software options offer features that help automate aspects of data management—such as access controls or encryption—making it easier to remain compliant without overwhelming your team with manual processes. Tools like Excel can assist by organizing records and tracking interactions with sensitive information through structured databases.

Understanding the implications of non-compliance is equally important. Violations can result in significant fines—not just financially but also in terms of reputational damage. Cultivating a culture of compliance within your agency not only shields you from penalties but also positions you as a responsible player in the real estate market.

By prioritizing compliance with data regulations through education, transparent practices, and effective management strategies, you reinforce your business's integrity while fostering long-lasting relationships with clients built on trust and professionalism.

CHAPTER 18: USING EXCEL WITH OTHER REAL ESTATE SOFTWARE

Integrating Excel with
Accounting Software

I ntegrating Excel with accounting software can significantly transform how real estate agents manage their finances and streamline their workflows. As you handle numerous transactions and financial reports, establishing a seamless connection between these tools is crucial for maintaining both efficiency and accuracy. This integration empowers you to utilize the advanced analytical capabilities of Excel alongside the specialized features offered by accounting software.

To embark on this integration journey, start by selecting the accounting software that aligns best with your specific needs. Popular choices in the real estate sector include QuickBooks, FreshBooks, and Xero, each offering unique functionalities designed for different business sizes and requirements. Take this example, QuickBooks is well-regarded for its comprehensive reporting capabilities and user-friendly interface, making it an excellent choice for many real estate professionals. After identifying the right software, investigate how it can export data into Excel.

Most modern accounting applications come equipped with built-in features that simplify data export. You'll typically find options to download reports in formats like CSV or Excel directly from the software's dashboard. For example, if you're using QuickBooks, head to the "Reports" section where you can customize essential financial reports such as Profit and Loss statements or Balance Sheets before exporting them. This level of flexibility allows you to concentrate on datasets most relevant to your real estate transactions.

Once you've exported your data into Excel, you can leverage its advanced analysis tools. This includes creating pivot tables that summarize financial performance across various properties or clients. If you manage multiple listings with different rental incomes, a pivot table can quickly highlight which properties yield the highest returns over time.

Visualizing your data also becomes easier in Excel. Use its built-in charting functions to create dynamic graphs that illustrate trends in income or expenses over specified periods. For example, a line graph depicting monthly earnings from different properties can offer valuable insights into seasonal trends and performance fluctuations.

Automation is another advantage of integrating these systems. Tools like Zapier enable automated workflows between your accounting software and Excel. Imagine setting up an automation that updates an Excel sheet every time a new transaction is recorded in your accounting system—this not only saves time but also reduces errors related to manual data entry.

Additionally, consider developing templates within Excel that align with your accounting processes. Standardized templates for invoices or expense tracking ensure consistency and simplify later data imports into your accounting software. By establishing these templates, you can streamline recurring tasks such as generating monthly expense reports or tracking commissions from sales.

To maintain efficiency in all integrated processes, regular maintenance is essential. Schedule periodic reviews of both your accounting software settings and any automated workflows created with Excel. This practice will help identify areas for improvement and ensure everything operates smoothly without disruptions.

Training staff on how to effectively utilize these integrated systems will further enhance team productivity. Offer training sessions that focus on best practices for entering data into both platforms while ensuring compliance with relevant financial regulations specific to real estate transactions.

In the end, integrating Excel with accounting software fosters a powerful synergy that enhances financial management while allowing you to prioritize what truly matters: serving your clients effectively and sustainably growing your business. By embracing this integration, you gain sharper insights into financial performance while positioning yourself as a tech-savvy professional ready to navigate the fast-paced world of real estate challenges head-on.

CRM and Lead Management Integration

Integrating Excel with Customer Relationship Management (CRM) and lead management systems is a transformative step for real estate agents. This integration facilitates a seamless flow of information, ensuring that no lead slips through the cracks while offering valuable insights to refine your sales strategies. By streamlining communication, automating follow-ups, and organizing client data effectively, you enhance both accessibility and usability.

To get started, it's important to clarify your goals for CRM integration. Whether you're using a widely recognized platform like Salesforce or a specialized real estate CRM, understanding what you want to achieve is essential. For example, if your objective is to consolidate lead information for quick reference during client meetings, your focus should be on data synchronization. This involves connecting fields in your CRM—such as contact details, property interests, and interaction history—with corresponding cells in your Excel spreadsheets.

Let's explore how to implement this integration practically, using a common scenario: exporting lead data from your CRM into Excel for analysis or reporting. Most CRMs offer an export function that typically generates a CSV (Comma-Separated Values) file. Here's a straightforward guide to facilitate smooth integration:

1. Exporting Data: Start by accessing your CRM's dashboard and locating the export feature. Select the lead list you wish to analyze—this can include all leads or filtered segments based on criteria like location or purchase intent. Opt for the CSV format to ensure compatibility with Excel.

2. Opening in Excel: After downloading the CSV file, open Excel and use the "Open" dialog to locate your file. Excel will recognize the format and prompt you to specify how to import the data; be sure to verify that it aligns correctly with columns such as "First Name," "Last Name," and "Email.

3. Data Cleanup: Once imported, take a moment to review the data carefully. Use Excel's built-in "Remove Duplicates" feature found under the Data tab to eliminate any duplicates. This step is crucial for maintaining unique leads, which is vital for accurate tracking and follow-up.

4. Analysis: With clean data in hand, leverage Excel functions like COUNTIF or AVERAGE to analyze trends among your leads. Take this example, if you're curious about how many leads originate from referrals versus online ads, you can create formulas that count entries based on their source.

5. Visual Representation: To gain deeper insights into patterns within your lead generation efforts, consider creating charts or graphs directly from your dataset. Visual representations can help pinpoint which strategies are yielding the best results.

6. Automating Updates: To streamline this process for future cycles, explore using Power Query—a robust tool within Excel that can connect directly to your CRM's database if supported. Power Query automates the import process, allowing you to update your lead list regularly without manual effort.

The advantages of integrating Excel with CRM systems extend beyond mere lead management; they provide deeper insights into customer behavior and sales patterns over time. Take this example, after establishing this connection, you might uncover trends indicating that certain demographics are more likely to engage with specific properties or marketing campaigns.

Many agents have reported significant success through this integration, noting increased efficiency and higher conversion rates due to improved organization of client interactions and tailored follow-ups based on comprehensive analyses of their lead data.

In summary, mastering this integration not only simplifies daily operations but also strategically positions you within a competitive market landscape—equipped with actionable insights derived from streamlined data management practices designed specifically for success in real estate.

GIS and Mapping Tools

Integrating Geographic Information Systems (GIS) and mapping tools with Excel can significantly transform how real estate agents visualize and analyze data. This combination enables agents to interpret spatial information alongside their datasets, enhancing decision-making and enriching client presentations. By leveraging geographic data, agents can identify market trends, evaluate property locations, and refine marketing strategies.

To get started with GIS in Excel, first identify your specific needs. Are you interested in analyzing property values based on location? Or do you want to visualize how close properties are to schools or public transport? Once you clarify your objectives, you can explore the various GIS tools that align with your requirements. Popular platforms like ArcGIS and QGIS can be integrated with Excel to create a powerful synergy of data analysis and geographic insight.

A typical workflow involves exporting property data from Excel into a GIS platform. Here's a step-by-step guide to facilitate this process:

1. Prepare Your Data: Begin by ensuring your Excel spreadsheet contains relevant fields for mapping. Essential columns may include property addresses, zip codes, listing prices, and any other categorical or numerical data that could influence location-based analysis.

2. Exporting Data: Once your spreadsheet is organized, save it as a CSV file. Most GIS platforms support CSV imports, making it easier to transition your property data into the mapping environment.

3. Importing into GIS: Open your chosen GIS software and locate the import function. Follow the prompts to upload your CSV file, paying attention to how

the software recognizes the fields in your dataset—proper alignment is crucial for accurate mapping.

4. Geocoding Addresses: After importing, geocode the addresses in your dataset if they aren't automatically mapped. Geocoding converts addresses into geographic coordinates (latitude and longitude), enabling precise placement on a map.

5. Visualizing Data: Use the mapping features in your GIS tool to visualize your properties geographically. Create layers that display different attributes—such as average listing prices or types of properties—to gain a nuanced understanding of market trends across various areas.

6. Analyzing Spatial Patterns: With your data visualized on a map, take advantage of spatial analysis tools offered by most GIS applications. You might analyze clusters of high-value properties or assess how proximity to amenities influences pricing trends.

7. Exporting Insights Back to Excel: After conducting analyses within the GIS platform, export visualizations or analytical results back into Excel for reporting purposes. This approach creates a comprehensive narrative that combines quantitative data from Excel with qualitative insights derived from geographic analysis.

By adopting these practices, real estate professionals can craft compelling visual narratives for client meetings and marketing efforts—not only showcasing listings but also contextual factors that influence buyer decisions. Take this example, using heat maps to highlight areas of high activity can direct prospective clients toward neighborhoods they may not have previously considered.

Agents who incorporate GIS tools report a heightened understanding of local markets, enabling them to make more informed recommendations based on spatial analytics alongside traditional market metrics. Knowing which neighborhoods have rising home values while remaining close to essential services provides substantial leverage in negotiations.

Integrating GIS into your workflow enhances not only presentations but also supports strategic decision-making rooted in comprehensive spatial analysis—a vital asset in today's competitive real estate landscape where data-driven insights lead directly to improved client outcomes and increased sales success.

Property Management Systems

Effectively managing real estate properties goes beyond cultivating strong relationships with tenants and owners; it requires a comprehensive framework for tracking all aspects of property management. Property Management Systems (PMS) play a crucial role in streamlining operations, from tenant screening to maintenance requests. By integrating these systems with Excel, real estate agents can optimize their workflows and enhance their overall efficiency.

To start, it's important to familiarize yourself with the key functionalities offered by a PMS. These typically include tenant management, lease tracking, financial reporting, and maintenance management. When combined with Excel's powerful data analysis capabilities, you can create tailored reports that provide insights specific to your property portfolio.

Let's explore how to establish a seamless workflow using Excel alongside your Property Management System. The first step is exporting your tenant and property data from the PMS into Excel. Here's how to do this effectively:

1. Export Data from PMS: Most Property Management Systems offer options to export tenant information, lease agreements, and financial transactions in formats like CSV or Excel files. Select the format that best meets your needs and download the data.

2. Organizing Your Spreadsheet: Once you've exported the data, open the file in Excel and organize it into clearly defined columns—such as Tenant Name, Lease Start Date, Rent Amount, Payment Status, and Maintenance Requests. Using headers will enhance clarity and ensure each piece of information is placed correctly.

3. Using Formulas for Tracking: Excel's formula capabilities allow you to automate various processes. For example, you can apply conditional formatting to highlight overdue rent payments by creating rules that change the background color of cells based on payment status. This visual cue helps you quickly identify which tenants need follow-ups.

4. Calculating Financial Metrics: To effortlessly monitor income and expenses, create a summary table in your spreadsheet that uses functions like SUM or AVERAGE to calculate total rent collected versus outstanding payments over specified periods. This provides an easily updated snapshot of cash flow, enabling informed decision-making.

5. Tracking Maintenance Requests: Efficiently handling maintenance requests is a common challenge in property management. Set up a dedicated section in your Excel workbook for tracking these issues, where each row corresponds to a request. Essential columns might include Tenant Name, Date Reported, Issue Description, Status, and Completion Date. Regularly updating this table will help ensure that no request

falls through the cracks.

6. Generating Reports: Utilize pivot tables to summarize tenant payment statuses or maintenance requests by property type or location. By dragging and dropping relevant fields into the rows and values sections of the pivot table setup menu, you can quickly create detailed reports without manual sorting.

7. Integrating with Financial Software: If you use accounting software like QuickBooks or Xero alongside your PMS, consider linking these platforms with Excel to import financial transactions directly into your spreadsheets. This integration reduces data entry errors and saves time during reconciliation tasks.

8. Visualizing Data: Excel's robust visualization tools can help you better understand trends over time. Take this example, consider using line graphs to track rental income fluctuations or bar charts to compare maintenance costs across properties over different periods.

For real estate agents managing multiple properties simultaneously, leveraging these features within a Property Management System integrated with Excel can lead to significant operational improvements. The insights gained from analyzing this data empower proactive strategies—such as anticipating potential vacancies or planning budget allocations for upcoming maintenance projects.

And, automating routine tasks within this framework allows agents to dedicate more time to nurturing client relationships rather than getting bogged down by administrative duties. Effectively engaging clients involves not just showing properties but also promptly addressing their concerns—efficient management provides agents with a competitive edge.

By seamlessly combining the functionalities of PMS with Excel's analytical capabilities, real estate professionals can position themselves not only as property managers but also as strategic advisors capable of delivering nuanced insights backed by data analysis. In today's fast-paced market, where agility often determines success, this approach is essential for thriving in the industry.

Data Export and Import Workflows

Data management in real estate requires a smooth and efficient flow of information across various platforms. Effective data export and import processes not only boost productivity but also reduce the errors that can arise from manual data entry. By grasping the workflows involved in data transfer, real estate professionals can maintain both efficiency and accuracy in their operations.

For exporting data, many systems—such as Customer Relationship Management (CRM) tools, Property Management Systems (PMS), and accounting software—provide built-in features that allow users to download essential information in formats like CSV or Excel. Take this example, if you're using a PMS to manage tenant details, you'll typically find an export function on the main dashboard. By selecting the specific fields you need, such as tenant names, lease dates, and payment statuses, you can customize your dataset to suit your current analysis requirements.

Once you've successfully exported your data, the next step is to import it into Excel for further manipulation or analysis. Open Excel and head to the "Data" tab where you'll find the "Get Data" option. This feature enables you to pull data from various sources, including files on your device or even directly from databases for larger datasets. To import standard exports, choose "From Text/CSV," which guides you through the process of importing your downloaded file smoothly.

After importing, focus on organizing your data. Utilize Excel's features to address any inconsistencies that may have occurred during the export process. Common issues include misaligned columns or varying formatting styles between different systems. Employ sorting functions to group similar entries together and filtering options to easily view specific subsets of data.

A practical approach is to use Excel's built-in functions for validation checks once your data is imported. Take this example, consider applying conditional formatting to automatically highlight duplicate entries or incomplete records. This step ensures that your dataset is accurate and actionable before you begin analysis or reporting.

After cleaning your dataset, explore how formulas can enhance your analytical efficiency. If you manage properties across different regions and have imported sales data, using functions like SUMIFS allows you to calculate total sales volumes based on multiple criteria—such as property type or location—without manually sifting through each entry.

Integrating these workflows with financial applications can further improve accuracy and efficiency in financial reporting. For example, when syncing transactions from accounting software like QuickBooks into Excel, make sure all relevant accounts align properly. Set up automated import routines using Excel's Power Query tool, which enables you to define transformation rules for each import. This way, when new data is available in QuickBooks, it updates in Excel automatically without requiring manual intervention.

Regularly backing up your datasets is also vital for protecting sensitive client information and transaction histories. Establish a routine for exports—weekly or monthly based on operational needs—to ensure access to historical performance without overloading resources during peak business periods.

Visualizing exported data can offer immediate insights

into market trends. Tools like pivot tables allow you to quickly aggregate and analyze complex datasets; for example, breaking down rental income by neighborhood can reveal lucrative opportunities or areas that need attention.

Streamlining these export-import workflows encourages a more proactive approach to managing real estate operations effectively. By saving time and enabling timely insights derived from comprehensive datasets, agents are empowered to make informed decisions.

In the end, refining how you handle data transfers lays a strong foundation for strategic decision-making in real estate ventures. By ensuring that information flows seamlessly between systems while maintaining high standards of accuracy and visualization capabilities within Excel, agents are better equipped to adapt swiftly in an ever-evolving market landscape.

Automating with APIs

In the real estate sector, enhancing operational efficiency through automation can yield substantial benefits. A powerful tool for achieving this is the use of Application Programming Interfaces (APIs), which facilitate seamless communication between different software systems. By incorporating APIs into your Excel workflows, you can optimize data management, increase accuracy, and save precious time.

Consider the scenario where you're using a Customer Relationship Management (CRM) tool alongside Excel to monitor client interactions and property listings. Manually entering data can introduce errors and inconsistencies, but integrating an API allows you to automatically transfer client information from your CRM directly into Excel. For example, if you need to generate reports on leads, the API enables Excel to pull in the latest data without the need for manual updates. This direct connection ensures that your reports are always based on the most current information.

Setting up this integration is typically a straightforward process. Many popular CRM systems, such as Salesforce and Zoho, offer API documentation and support for connecting with other applications. To link Salesforce with Excel using its API, you'll first need to obtain your API key from Salesforce. Then, within Excel, you can utilize Power Query or VBA (Visual Basic for Applications) to establish a connection. Here's a simple guide to help you get started:

1. Open Excel and navigate to the "Data" tab.

2. Select "Get Data" > "From Other Sources" > "From Web."

3. Input the API endpoint URL provided by Salesforce along with your API key.

4. Once connected, use Power Query's data transformation tools to filter or rearrange the data before loading it into your worksheet.

This method not only brings in fresh data but also allows you to refresh it effortlessly whenever needed.

APIs can also be used effectively to import market data or property listings from external databases into Excel for analysis. Many real estate websites provide public APIs that grant agents access to extensive datasets regarding property prices, trends, and buyer demographics. By connecting these APIs to Excel, you can create live dashboards that automatically update with current market conditions, eliminating the need for constant data re-entry.

Take this example, if you're tracking housing prices across various neighborhoods, using an API from a local real estate platform could automate this process efficiently. With just a few lines of code in VBA or through Power Query's settings, you could schedule Excel to refresh its data weekly:

```vba
```

```
Sub RefreshAPIData()

Dim ws As Worksheet

Set ws = ThisWorkbook.Sheets("MarketData") ' This sheet
contains your data


' This line triggers a refresh for any connections linked via API

ThisWorkbook.RefreshAll


MsgBox "Market data refreshed!

End Sub
```
` ` `

Beyond direct integrations with CRMs or market databases, APIs can also streamline reporting and analysis processes. If your office conducts regular performance reviews based on key performance indicators (KPIs) like sales figures or lead conversion rates, consider automating reports that aggregate these metrics across different platforms.

For example, if you're using QuickBooks for financial management alongside Excel for reporting, you could automate the extraction of monthly sales data by configuring QuickBooks' API connection within Excel. This setup would compile income statements or expense reports without manual entry, ensuring that figures are up-to-date during meetings.

While automating tasks through APIs greatly enhances efficiency, it's crucial to prioritize security when handling sensitive client information. Implementing OAuth 2.0 for secure authentication provides an additional layer of protection when accessing third-party APIs.

And, automation significantly boosts your analytics

capabilities. If you're leveraging machine learning algorithms for predictive analytics in real estate trends, having live data directly integrated into your analysis model enhances forecasting accuracy and informs better decision-making.

By embracing automation through APIs, real estate professionals can transform how they manage workloads and analyze critical data points quickly and accurately. The resulting increase in productivity not only frees up time for agents to cultivate relationships but also empowers them to respond rapidly to market changes with reliable insights at their fingertips.

Customizing Excel for Specialized Needs

Customizing Excel to suit your specific needs can greatly enhance your efficiency and effectiveness as a real estate agent. Each professional operates within a unique context shaped by their market, clientele, and workflows. By tailoring Excel to meet these demands, you not only streamline your processes but also present data in ways that resonate with clients and stakeholders.

Start by personalizing your Excel environment. A key first step in customization is adjusting the Ribbon—the toolbar at the top of Excel. You can add or remove tabs based on the tasks you perform most frequently. For example, if financial analysis or property management functions are part of your daily routine, consider creating a custom tab that includes these functions for quick access. To do this, right-click on the Ribbon and select "Customize the Ribbon." From there, you can create a new tab and drag relevant commands into it. This simple adjustment can save you valuable time spent navigating through menus, allowing you to focus more on analysis rather than searching for tools.

Next, think about modifying templates for specific projects or listings. Real estate transactions often require standardized documents such as property valuation reports or client presentations. By creating an Excel template that includes all necessary fields and calculations, you simplify the process of generating reports for future use. Take this example, design a property analysis template with sections for property details, pricing strategies, comparative market analysis data, and financial metrics like ROI and cash flow projections. This way, each time you evaluate a new property, you can easily fill in the blanks without starting from scratch.

Excel's formatting capabilities can also be customized to enhance readability and impact. Use conditional formatting to highlight key performance indicators (KPIs) or trends within your datasets. For example, when tracking monthly sales performance, set rules to change cell colors based on sales thresholds—turning cells green for targets met and red for those missed. This visual cue allows for quick assessments at a glance and helps identify areas needing attention without wading through extensive rows of data.

In addition to visual customization, leveraging named ranges can further streamline your work in Excel. Named ranges let you assign descriptive names to specific cells or ranges of data instead of relying on traditional cell references like A1 or B2. For example, if you have a range containing average home prices in various neighborhoods, naming it "AvgHomePrices" makes formulas clearer and easier to understand. Using names in formulas—such as =AVERAGE(AvgHomePrices)—clarifies what the formula represents, reducing errors and simplifying collaboration.

Integrating external data sources into your customized setup will significantly expand Excel's functionality. Tools like Power Query allow you to pull data from online real estate databases directly into your worksheets. By setting up queries, you can ensure real-time updates; thus, your market analysis always reflects current conditions automatically. Imagine pulling recent sales figures from a local MLS (Multiple Listing Service) database every morning before meeting clients—this ensures you're always armed with the latest information when discussing properties.

Another valuable area for customization is dashboard creation. Dashboards serve as powerful visualization tools that condense complex datasets into digestible insights. Design interactive dashboards that showcase key metrics such as monthly sales trends, active listings by price range, or client engagement levels over time. Utilizing features like slicers enables users to filter data dynamically—providing tailored views depending on what stakeholders wish to analyze at any moment.

Finally, don't overlook Excel's automation capabilities through VBA (Visual Basic for Applications). Custom scripts can automate repetitive tasks such as sending reports via email or formatting documents according to specific standards. Take this example, if generating monthly performance summaries for team meetings is part of your workflow, writing a VBA script could automate this entire process—from data gathering through report generation—ensuring timely delivery without manual intervention.

By implementing these customizations, you'll empower yourself as a real estate professional, enhancing productivity while minimizing manual errors. As you adapt Excel to fit specialized needs—whether through tailored templates or dynamic dashboards—you'll find yourself better equipped to provide high-quality service while navigating the complexities of real estate transactions effectively. The result? A more organized workflow that not only meets but exceeds client expectations in an increasingly competitive marketplace.

CHAPTER 19:
CONTINUOUS
LEARNING AND
EXCEL RESOURCE
MANAGEMENT

Keeping Up with Excel Updates

Excel is a dynamic tool that frequently updates, making it essential for real estate professionals to stay informed about these changes in order to fully leverage its capabilities. Understanding new features, enhancements, and best practices can significantly streamline your workflows and enhance your analytical skills. By embracing Excel's continuous evolution, you not only maintain a competitive edge but also deliver greater value to your clients.

To begin, actively checking for updates is crucial. Excel regularly releases patches and new functionalities designed to enhance user experience and efficiency. Microsoft simplifies this process by allowing you to access updates directly within the application. Simply navigate to the "File" menu, select "Account," and click on "Update Options." By choosing "Update Now," you can manually check for the latest version. This small habit ensures you benefit from improvements like enhanced data analysis tools and new charting options as soon as they are available.

In addition to keeping track of technical updates, it's important to familiarize yourself with the capabilities introduced or optimized in newer versions. For example, the introduction of dynamic arrays has transformed how Excel handles data manipulation, enabling users to perform complex calculations more effortlessly than before. Understanding these features can significantly reduce the time spent on tasks that previously required extensive formulas or manual adjustments.

Engaging with online communities and resources dedicated to Excel can also help you stay informed about the latest best practices and applications relevant to your work in real estate. Websites like Microsoft's official blog provide insights into upcoming features, while forums such as Reddit's r/excel allow users to share their experiences with new functionalities. Additionally, platforms like LinkedIn host professional groups where industry experts discuss not only updates but also tips on maximizing productivity using Excel in real estate contexts.

Participating in online courses or webinars can further enhance your understanding of new tools and methods introduced in Excel. Many platforms, including Coursera and Udemy, offer targeted lessons specifically about Excel updates tailored for various professions, including real estate. By investing time in these educational resources, you can quickly adapt to changes while acquiring practical skills directly applicable to your work.

Experimenting with new features is equally important. After familiarizing yourself with an update through tutorials or community feedback, test these functionalities in your existing projects. Create sample spreadsheets or apply them in low-risk scenarios to observe their impacts firsthand. For example, if a new chart type has been introduced, try incorporating it into your property analysis reports to see how it enhances data visualization. This hands-on approach not only solidifies your understanding but also boosts your confidence in using these tools during client interactions.

Seeking feedback from clients or colleagues about their experiences with any new functionalities you've adopted can provide valuable perspectives on how these updates affect workflows and decision-making based on presented data. Their insights may lead you to discover further enhancements or alternative methods that better align with client expectations.

Lastly, consider creating a checklist for periodic reviews of your Excel skills and knowledge base. A simple document outlining critical features or shortcuts you've learned, along with any newly introduced functions since your last review, can be an effective way to stay organized and ensure you're consistently leveraging Excel's capabilities. Regularly updating this checklist will not only motivate you but also serve as a quick reference guide when tackling specific tasks.

Staying abreast of Excel updates ensures that you're not just keeping pace but are also a step ahead in an industry that thrives on efficiency and innovation. Adapting to these changes equips you with tools that make analyzing complex datasets more manageable while improving overall productivity and client satisfaction. Proactively pursuing knowledge allows you to navigate the multifaceted world of real estate with agility—this continuous quest for improvement will undoubtedly distinguish you as an adept professional ready for any challenges that may arise.

Utilizing Online Courses and Tutorials

Harnessing the power of online courses and tutorials can significantly enhance your Excel skills, especially in the realm of real estate. These resources offer tailored instruction, enabling you to learn at your own pace and focus on the skills most pertinent to your career. Whether you're a beginner eager to understand the basics or an experienced user looking to master advanced techniques, a wealth of knowledge is readily available.

To begin, identify your specific learning needs. If financial analysis in Excel is a challenge—an essential skill for evaluating property investments—seek out courses that specialize in financial modeling or real estate analytics. Platforms like Coursera and Udemy provide a variety of courses covering everything from fundamental formulas to sophisticated data visualization techniques. Many of these programs are designed by industry experts, ensuring that you gain practical insights that can be directly applied to your work.

In addition to formal courses, consider exploring free tutorials on platforms like YouTube. Channels dedicated to Excel often simplify complex concepts into digestible segments, offering step-by-step instructions that cater to visual learners. Take this example, a tutorial on creating amortization schedules might guide you through the process—from setting up your worksheet to applying formulas that automatically calculate payment schedules based on varying interest rates. Engaging with such content allows you to see how each function operates in real-world scenarios.

Don't overlook the benefits of interactive learning environments. Websites like ExcelJet provide concise lessons accompanied by practice exercises that reinforce your understanding. Completing these exercises after watching instructional videos helps solidify your knowledge and builds confidence as you witness your skills develop in real time.

The instant feedback you receive is invaluable, helping you pinpoint areas where further practice may be necessary.

Networking within these educational communities can also enhance your learning experience. Join discussion forums or groups related to the courses you take; sharing insights and asking questions not only enriches your understanding but also connects you with fellow professionals who may have encountered similar challenges in applying Excel to real estate tasks. These connections can lead to collaborations or mentoring opportunities, offering support as you refine your skills.

As you delve into online courses, actively engage with the content. Take notes while watching videos or following along with tutorials; this practice reinforces your learning and creates a personalized reference for future use. Don't hesitate to pause and experiment with what you're learning directly in Excel. For example, if a tutorial explains how to use VLOOKUP for property comparisons, apply it immediately to your own listings or client data sets. This hands-on approach transforms abstract concepts into tangible skills.

After completing a course, periodically review what you've learned. Challenge yourself with mini-projects that utilize your new skills—such as constructing a comprehensive budget model for managing client properties or developing a sales forecast spreadsheet based on historical data trends. This practice not only reinforces your knowledge but also demonstrates your growing expertise to clients and colleagues.

Finally, stay proactive about seeking out new resources as they become available. As technology evolves, so too do the tools and strategies for real estate analysis through Excel. Subscribing to newsletters from leading Excel educators or following influential bloggers can help keep you informed about new courses and innovative techniques that emerge within the community.

Leveraging online courses and tutorials is not merely about acquiring knowledge; it's about fostering a mindset of continuous learning that enhances your professional capabilities and the value you bring to clients. Embracing this approach equips you with advanced tools necessary for navigating complex datasets efficiently while enabling smarter decision-making in your real estate career. Your commitment to self-improvement through these resources will undoubtedly position you as a knowledgeable leader in a competitive industry landscape.

Community Forums and Online Groups

Engaging with community forums and online groups can significantly benefit real estate professionals aiming to improve their Excel skills. These platforms foster an environment where individuals can exchange knowledge, share experiences, and collaboratively solve problems. While the learning curve for Excel may seem daunting, connecting with a community makes the process more manageable.

Begin by identifying active forums tailored to real estate professionals and Excel enthusiasts. For example, platforms like Reddit host dedicated subreddits such as r/Excel and r/RealEstate, where users post inquiries ranging from basic formula usage to advanced data analysis techniques. Within these communities, you'll find discussions that not only tackle specific issues but also provide insights into best practices. If you're grappling with VLOOKUP to compare property data, chances are someone has already shared a solution that directly addresses your query.

Active participation is crucial. Instead of merely observing, engage with the content. When faced with a challenge—such as setting up an amortization schedule for your clients—don't hesitate to ask for advice or examples from others who have dealt with similar tasks. You'll often receive practical suggestions along with resources that clarify complex concepts. This collaborative approach not only deepens your understanding but also builds confidence as you see how others apply their skills in real-world scenarios.

In addition to seeking help, consider sharing your own insights. If you've recently mastered a particular function or discovered a time-saving shortcut for data entry, share it within the community. Teaching others reinforces your own learning and positions you as a valuable member of the group. Explaining concepts helps solidify your understanding while positively contributing to the community's growth.

Networking through these forums can lead to meaningful professional relationships as well. Connecting with other real estate agents or Excel experts opens avenues for collaboration beyond simple Q&A interactions. You might discover someone who shares your interests in financial modeling or market analysis techniques, paving the way for mentorship opportunities or joint projects. Take this example, if you and another agent both explore using Excel for predictive analytics, collaborating on templates could enhance both of your practices.

Another benefit of engaging in online communities is access to curated resources shared by members. Users frequently post links to webinars, online courses, or articles that delve deeper into specific Excel functionalities relevant to real estate analysis. These resources can be invaluable for expanding your skill set without wading through unrelated materials elsewhere.

As you immerse yourself in these discussions and interactions, be on the lookout for local meetups or virtual events organized by forum members. Participating in these gatherings provides opportunities for face-to-face networking and allows you to learn directly from industry peers who share firsthand accounts of successful strategies they've implemented using

Excel.

Consistency is key when utilizing these forums effectively. Dedicate time each week to check in on discussions that align with your interests—whether those involve property analysis techniques or tips for automating reports with macros. Regular engagement keeps you updated on new trends and tools while reinforcing connections with other professionals who share your goals.

Community forums and online groups are dynamic ecosystems where knowledge thrives through shared experiences and collaboration. By actively participating in these spaces, you position yourself not only as a learner but also as a contributor—an essential role that enhances both personal growth and professional development within the competitive real estate landscape.

Committing to leverage these communities will undoubtedly enrich your understanding of Excel's capabilities while providing practical insights that elevate your practice as a real estate agent. Embrace this collaborative spirit; it transforms isolated learning into collective success, propelling you toward greater proficiency and effectiveness in your career.

Attending Excel Workshops and Seminars

Attending Excel workshops and seminars offers real estate professionals a valuable opportunity to enhance their understanding of the software while building connections with peers. These events typically feature expert-led sessions that delve into a wide range of topics, from basic functionalities to advanced data analysis techniques tailored for the real estate market. By immersing yourself in this dynamic environment, you gain access to hands-on learning experiences and insights that can be applied directly to your daily operations.

When selecting workshops, prioritize those that emphasize practical applications relevant to real estate. Take this example, some workshops may include sessions on creating financial models in Excel to evaluate property investments. This focused training not only equips you with new skills but also allows you to apply them to scenarios you encounter regularly in your work, which is especially beneficial when dealing with complex calculations or analyzing market trends. Engaging with instructors can clarify uncertainties and deepen your understanding of challenging concepts.

Networking is another significant advantage of attending these events. Connecting with fellow real estate professionals can lead to valuable collaborations and partnerships in the future. During breaks or informal networking sessions, you have the opportunity to exchange experiences and strategies with others facing similar challenges. For example, discussing your methods for managing client data through Excel can spark insightful conversations that introduce you to innovative approaches you may not have considered.

In addition to learning from experts and networking, many workshops incorporate group activities or case studies. These collaborative exercises often simulate real-world challenges, allowing participants to tackle problems together. Working alongside others provides diverse perspectives on issues like property management or sales forecasting, leading to unexpected solutions that enhance your understanding and application of Excel in your practice.

Be proactive in seeking feedback during these sessions. If you're working on a project such as a marketing analysis report, share your approach with the group and invite input on specific aspects of your Excel usage. Constructive critiques from experienced colleagues can reveal areas for improvement and inspire new methods for effectively presenting data.

And, workshops often provide resources that extend beyond the event itself. Many instructors share materials, templates, and additional reading resources that enable continued learning after the session concludes. This ongoing access ensures you remain engaged with the content and can revisit complex topics at your own pace. For example, if a session covers advanced charting techniques, having reference materials allows you to practice those skills later when preparing client presentations.

As you explore available workshops, consider both local and virtual options. While in-person events may facilitate more personal interactions, online seminars offer expanded accessibility, enabling participation from anywhere in the world. This flexibility allows you to choose from a wider array of topics at various times, ensuring you find something that fits your schedule and learning preferences.

Consistency in attending these workshops is essential for long-term success. Aim to seek out new opportunities quarterly or biannually. The ever-evolving nature of Excel means there's always something new to learn—whether it's updates in functionality or emerging best practices within the real estate sector. Committing to continuous education not only sharpens your skills but also positions you as an informed leader among your peers.

In the end, investing time in workshops and seminars fosters both professional expertise and confidence in utilizing Excel as a powerful tool in real estate. Embrace every opportunity to learn; this commitment will yield dividends not only in enhanced capabilities but also in enriched professional relationships that strengthen your career trajectory over time.

Accessing Blogs and Newsletters

Staying updated with advancements in Excel and best practices can greatly benefit from regularly engaging with blogs and newsletters specifically designed for real estate professionals. These platforms offer a wealth of information, covering everything from basic functionalities to complex data analytics tailored to the industry. By following reputable sources, you can access practical advice that helps keep your skills sharp and relevant.

Many industry-focused blogs explore case studies that showcase successful uses of Excel in real estate. For example, a blog post might illustrate how a real estate agent used pivot tables to analyze sales data, uncovering trends that informed property investment decisions. Engaging with these real-world examples not only deepens your understanding of Excel's capabilities but also encourages you to adopt similar strategies in your own work.

Newsletters are particularly valuable due to their curated content, often spotlighting the latest trends, tools, and techniques in Excel. They frequently include expert commentary that clarifies complex concepts. Take this example, a newsletter might explain recent updates to Excel features or offer step-by-step instructions on using new functions like XLOOKUP or dynamic arrays. By subscribing to these resources, you can stay informed without having to sift through overwhelming amounts of information.

To maximize your learning experience, actively engage with the content rather than simply reading it passively. Take notes as you navigate through blogs or newsletters; jot down ideas that resonate with your daily tasks. If you discover a formula or technique that seems beneficial, apply it to your projects right away. This hands-on approach will reinforce your understanding and help integrate new methods into your routine.

Participating in online discussions related to the content you consume can further enhance your comprehension. Many blogs feature comment sections or forums where readers share ideas and experiences. Contributing to these discussions not only broadens your perspective but also allows you to connect with other professionals who share similar interests. Sharing challenges related to data analysis or reporting may elicit helpful responses from those who have faced similar hurdles.

In addition to general Excel resources, consider seeking newsletters that focus specifically on real estate trends and analytics. These publications often address broader topics like market analysis and investment strategies while incorporating Excel applications within those discussions. Take this example, a newsletter might examine how emerging technologies influence property management decisions while providing guidance on creating effective dashboards in Excel for data visualization.

As you curate your list of blogs and newsletters, prioritize those offering actionable insights that align with your specific needs as a real estate professional. Subscribing to established sites like "ExcelJet" for quick tips or "The Real Estate Investing Blog," which merges investment insights with practical Excel applications, can be especially beneficial. Tailoring your information sources ensures that what you learn directly supports your professional objectives.

Regularly reviewing this material fosters an environment of continuous learning and improvement. Dedicate at least a few minutes each week to explore new content—whether it's reading an article during lunch breaks or skimming through newsletters on weekends. This commitment not only enhances your skills but also cultivates an ongoing curiosity about what's possible with Excel in your profession.

In the end, leveraging blogs and newsletters is an investment in your professional growth that pays off over time. Staying informed about the latest tools and techniques empowers you to tackle challenges with confidence and creativity, positioning yourself as an innovative thinker in the competitive real estate market. Embrace this resource-rich landscape; it's one of the most effective ways to ensure you remain at the forefront of what's achievable with Excel in real estate management and analysis.

Utilizing Excel Add-ins and Extensions

Excel is a powerful tool in its own right, but its functionality can be greatly enhanced through the use of add-ins and extensions. These additional features can streamline your workflow, introduce new analytical capabilities, and ultimately save you time—an invaluable resource in the fast-paced world of real estate.

One of the most popular add-ins is Power Query, which allows you to pull data from various sources, including databases, online services, and even other Excel files. For example, if you're responsible for compiling property data from multiple listings across different platforms, Power Query can simplify this process. Instead of manually importing each dataset, it enables you to connect directly to these sources and automate the data import. Once connected, you can clean and transform your data within the same interface before loading it into Excel for analysis. This not only saves time but also minimizes the risk of errors associated with manual entry.

Another valuable add-in is Power Pivot, which enhances Excel's data modeling capabilities. With Power Pivot, you can create complex data models that allow for sophisticated calculations using DAX (Data Analysis Expressions). Take this example, when analyzing sales trends across various neighborhoods, you can build a model that incorporates historical sales data alongside current listings to more accurately forecast future trends. By establishing relationships between different tables—such as properties, agents, and clients—you gain deeper insights through interactive reporting that standard Excel formulas may struggle to achieve.

Additionally, consider utilizing specialized add-ins tailored for specific real estate functions. Tools like Zillow or Realtor.com's Excel integration provide real-time property valuation estimates directly within your spreadsheets. When assessing potential investments or developing pricing strategies for listings, having current market data at your fingertips significantly enhances your analysis. Imagine being able to pull in property comparisons with just a few clicks rather than sifting through multiple websites; this efficiency can substantially improve your decision-making process.

For those who frequently work with financial modeling or require advanced statistical analysis, tools such as the Analysis ToolPak are essential. This add-in offers a suite of statistical functions, including regression analysis, t-tests, and histograms that can simplify complex calculations necessary for evaluating investments. For example, if you're assessing the viability of a new development project, using regression analysis could help predict future cash flows based on historical performance metrics.

Integrating third-party add-ins further expands Excel's capabilities. Platforms like Microsoft AppSource allow you to discover specialized solutions designed specifically for real estate professionals. These extensions often include unique features such as enhanced mapping tools or project management functionalities tailored to industry needs. Take this example, an app that integrates with mapping software could enable you to visualize property locations alongside demographic data—an insightful approach when presenting market analyses to clients.

To effectively utilize these add-ins, begin by identifying your specific needs and challenges within your workflow. Experimenting with different tools can help you assess how well they fit into your existing processes. Many add-ins offer trial versions; taking advantage of these can help you gauge their value before making any commitments. Additionally, incorporating training sessions or tutorials related to each add-in will maximize their benefits—understanding how to leverage their full potential is crucial for enhancing productivity.

Incorporating Excel add-ins not only boosts efficiency but also positions you as a knowledgeable professional who embraces technology to achieve results in real estate transactions. As these tools become integrated into your routine, you'll find they streamline tasks while empowering you with deeper insights and better data-driven decisions—an essential advantage in this competitive field.

Embracing these enhancements fundamentally transforms how you manage data in real estate. The next time you're faced with overwhelming datasets or complex analyses, remember that leveraging add-ins can simplify processes while providing rich insights that lead to informed decisions and successful outcomes.

Leveraging Expert Advice and Mentorship

Mentorship in real estate can be a transformative experience, offering valuable insights and guidance that accelerate your professional growth. As you navigate the complexities of the industry, seeking expert advice enhances not only your understanding of Excel but also your grasp of market dynamics. Whether through formal mentorship programs or informal relationships with seasoned colleagues, leveraging this expertise can significantly boost your success in real estate.

Start by identifying mentors who have achieved success in areas aligned with your goals. Look for individuals who effectively use Excel to analyze data, manage transactions, or develop marketing strategies. A mentor's experience with specific tools and techniques can provide you with shortcuts and advanced methods that may be otherwise overlooked. Take this example, a mentor skilled in financial modeling can offer unique perspectives on using Excel for investment analysis, teaching you how to apply functions like NPV (Net Present Value) and IRR (Internal Rate of Return) effectively.

Engaging with these experienced professionals creates an

environment of continuous learning. Regular discussions about real estate challenges can yield practical solutions. Consider scheduling weekly check-ins or monthly coffee meetings to discuss recent market trends, share insights from your analyses, and seek feedback on your use of Excel tools. This collaborative approach enriches your knowledge base and fosters a support network that encourages accountability and motivation.

Another effective way to leverage expertise is by participating in workshops or seminars led by industry leaders. These events present rich opportunities to learn cutting-edge Excel techniques directly from those at the forefront of real estate technology. When attending these sessions, take thorough notes and ask questions that relate to the challenges you're facing in your daily work. Engaging actively will help cement what you've learned and demonstrate your commitment to growth.

Additionally, consider joining professional organizations related to real estate and data analytics. Many of these groups provide access to resources such as online forums where members share their experiences and strategies regarding Excel usage in various contexts. By tapping into this collective wisdom, you can discover solutions to common issues—such as automating report generation or streamlining data entry processes—that might otherwise consume hours of your time.

Mentorship doesn't always have to be a one-on-one relationship; it can also involve learning from multiple sources simultaneously. Online communities and social media platforms like LinkedIn allow you to connect with experts around the globe. Engaging with their content— whether articles on effective spreadsheet management or video tutorials on advanced formulas—can broaden your knowledge and introduce new methodologies that enhance your efficiency.

Practical application is essential when absorbing new concepts from mentors and workshops. For example, after learning about a new financial modeling technique from a mentor or seminar leader, take the time to implement it into an ongoing project or mock scenario within Excel. This hands-on practice reinforces your learning and highlights its relevance in your work context.

Also, don't hesitate to share what you've learned with peers or junior colleagues. Teaching others is one of the best ways to solidify knowledge while establishing yourself as a knowledgeable figure within your team or organization. Consider leading small training sessions focused on specific Excel functionalities relevant to real estate operations—this not only fosters collaboration but also showcases both your expertise and leadership potential.

As you build relationships with mentors and engage with broader communities within real estate, remember that this journey is iterative; continuous feedback will enhance both your technical skills and overall business acumen. Taking the initiative to seek advice transforms not only how you use Excel but also elevates your performance within the competitive landscape of real estate.

In the end, this commitment to professional growth through mentorship empowers you as a real estate agent capable of harnessing data-driven insights for informed decision-making—a key differentiator for achieving long-term success in this dynamic field.

CHAPTER 20: THE FUTURE OF REAL ESTATE WITH EXCEL

*Emerging Trends in Real
Estate Analysis*

Emerging trends in real estate analysis are transforming the industry, presenting exciting opportunities for agents willing to adapt and innovate. One of the most significant shifts is the growing reliance on big data analytics. Real estate professionals are now tapping into extensive datasets that encompass everything from market trends to consumer preferences, enabling them to make informed decisions that drive success. Agents who effectively leverage data analytics can identify prime investment opportunities, refine pricing strategies, and enhance client experiences through personalized solutions.

Artificial intelligence (AI) is another pivotal force in this evolution. AI algorithms can analyze market patterns and predict future trends with remarkable precision. For example, predictive analytics tools utilize historical data to forecast property values, allowing agents to offer accurate advice to both buyers and sellers. Imagine being able to present clients with well-founded projections of how a neighborhood's value might change over the coming years based on comprehensive data analysis. These insights not only elevate your role as an advisor but also build trust with your clients.

In addition to AI, virtual and augmented reality (VR/AR) technologies are becoming increasingly important in real estate marketing and analysis. These tools provide potential buyers with the ability to explore properties from anywhere in the world, delivering immersive experiences that surpass traditional photos or videos. By incorporating VR tours into your listings, you can engage clients more effectively, showcasing properties in a dynamic manner that highlights their unique features and potential. This approach not only attracts more leads but also helps clients envision themselves living in these spaces.

Sustainability has also emerged as a crucial consideration for many buyers. Increasingly, individuals are seeking energy-efficient homes and properties that adhere to green building practices. Real estate agents who recognize this trend can position themselves as experts in eco-friendly properties, tapping into a growing market segment that prioritizes sustainability. By analyzing energy consumption data or carbon footprints associated with different properties, you can guide clients toward investments that align with their values while potentially saving them money over time.

The rise of remote work has further altered the real estate landscape. As more individuals look for homes that accommodate flexible work arrangements, understanding new buyer priorities has become essential. Features such as home office spaces, proximity to essential services, and outdoor areas have gained increased importance. By analyzing demographic shifts and preferences, you can tailor your marketing strategies to effectively meet the evolving needs of buyers.

Social media analytics are also playing an increasingly vital role by providing insights into consumer behavior and preferences. Monitoring engagement metrics across platforms like Instagram and Facebook allows agents to refine their marketing approaches to resonate better with potential clients. Take this example, if data reveals that certain types of posts—like before-and-after renovations—generate higher engagement rates, you can adjust your content strategy accordingly.

And, blockchain technology is emerging as a powerful tool for enhancing transparency and efficiency in real estate transactions. Utilizing blockchain for property records and contracts can significantly reduce fraud risks and streamline processes. This advancement not only fosters trust with clients but also simplifies complex transactions often involving multiple stakeholders.

To navigate these emerging trends successfully requires continuous learning and adaptation. Staying informed about technological advancements and market shifts will empower you to position yourself as a thought leader within your field. Attending industry conferences or participating in webinars can provide valuable insights into how other professionals are successfully navigating these changes.

As these trends continue to evolve, it becomes increasingly clear that adaptability will be crucial for real estate professionals aiming for success in an ever-changing landscape. Embracing new technologies and methodologies not only enhances your service offerings but also opens doors to new markets and client demographics eager for innovative real estate experiences.

The Role of AI and Machine Learning

The integration of artificial intelligence (AI) and machine learning into real estate analysis is profoundly reshaping the industry. Agents who embrace these technologies are not just keeping up with change; they are positioning themselves at the forefront of innovation. AI applications can analyze vast datasets, delivering insights that enable agents to make swift, data-driven decisions—an essential advantage in a market where timing can mean the difference between closing a deal and missing an opportunity.

For example, machine learning algorithms can sift through historical sales data to identify patterns that might elude human observation. By evaluating factors such as neighborhood demographics, economic indicators, and seasonal trends, these algorithms can predict future property values with remarkable accuracy. Imagine receiving a report indicating that a specific area is poised for appreciation due to emerging infrastructure projects or demographic shifts. Armed with this information, you can confidently advise clients, helping them capitalize on opportunities before they become widely recognized.

In addition to enhancing market analysis, AI also improves client interactions. Chatbots powered by AI can efficiently handle routine inquiries, providing potential buyers with immediate responses while allowing agents to concentrate on more complex matters. Take this example, when a prospective buyer visits your website and inquires about available properties in a particular area, an AI-driven chatbot can instantly pull up relevant listings and guide them through the next steps. This not only boosts client satisfaction but also increases your chances of converting inquiries into sales.

And, AI can significantly enhance personalized marketing strategies. By analyzing client preferences and behaviors through predictive analytics, agents can tailor their outreach efforts more effectively. Take this example, if you have data showing that certain clients are drawn to eco-friendly homes or properties close to public transportation, you can create targeted campaigns that highlight these features, leading to higher engagement rates. Such personalized approaches resonate deeply with clients, fostering loyalty and encouraging repeat business.

Machine learning algorithms also play a crucial role in risk assessment within real estate transactions. They can analyze market conditions and historical transaction data to evaluate potential risks associated with investments. For example, if an agent considers recommending a property to an investor, machine learning tools can identify potential red flags based on past price volatility or local economic downturns. This insight allows agents to provide comprehensive risk assessments and avoid pitfalls that could jeopardize client investments.

Data visualization becomes more accessible with AI-driven tools as well. Advanced software can transform complex datasets into intuitive visual formats like heat maps or infographics. These visuals enable agents to clearly present market trends during client meetings or open houses. When clients see compelling graphics illustrating market conditions or property value trends, it enhances their understanding and builds trust in your expertise.

As these technologies continue to evolve, it is crucial for real estate professionals to prioritize ongoing education in AI and machine learning applications relevant to their work. Engaging in online courses or participating in workshops focused on data analytics will significantly bolster your skill set, preparing you not only for current market demands but also for future challenges.

Collaboration among industry stakeholders is equally vital for effectively leveraging AI across the board. As more firms adopt these technologies, sharing best practices will cultivate a more informed ecosystem where agents learn from one another's experiences, fostering collective innovation.

In the end, the role of AI and machine learning in real estate transcends the realm of tools; they represent transformative forces that redefine how agents operate within the industry landscape. By fully embracing these technologies —understanding their capabilities while remaining adaptable —agents can ensure their relevance amidst rapid changes driven by data intelligence.

This technology-driven foundation opens up opportunities for enhanced decision-making capabilities at every level of your practice—where informed choices lead directly to successful outcomes for both you and your clients.

Enhancements in Big Data and Analytics

Big data has fundamentally changed the real estate landscape, providing agents with unparalleled access to a wealth of information that can inform strategic decision-making. With a myriad of data sources—ranging from public property records to social media insights and economic indicators— real estate professionals can now analyze market trends and consumer behaviors on an unprecedented scale. Mastering the use of this data is no longer just an advantage; it is essential for remaining competitive in today's market.

One of the most significant ways big data enhances real estate analytics is through predictive modeling. By employing algorithms that examine historical data in conjunction with current market conditions, agents can forecast future property values with remarkable accuracy. Take this example, an agent analyzing sales trends in a neighborhood over the past decade can integrate various data points such as average sales prices, sales frequency, and demographic shifts to create a model predicting future appreciation rates. This valuable insight enables agents to guide clients on the best timing for buying or selling properties, ultimately maximizing investment returns.

And, big data provides a deeper understanding of client preferences. Advanced analytics tools allow agents to segment potential buyers based on diverse criteria like income levels, lifestyle choices, and purchasing behaviors. For example, if an analysis shows that many clients searching for homes in a specific area prioritize proximity to schools and parks, agents can adjust their marketing strategies to highlight these features. This targeted approach not only boosts client engagement but also positions agents as informed advisors who truly understand their clients' needs.

Data visualization tools are essential in transforming complex datasets into clear, actionable insights. With user-friendly dashboards and visual representations of data trends, agents can present their findings in an engaging way during client consultations or team meetings. Picture showcasing a heat map that illustrates rising property values across different neighborhoods; such visual aids not only capture attention but also reinforce the narrative surrounding market opportunities. When clients see compelling evidence of trends backed by solid data, their trust in your expertise increases.

In addition to enhancing individual analyses, big data allows for comprehensive market evaluations by aggregating information from various sources, including real estate websites, social media platforms, and economic reports. By collecting and synthesizing this information, agents can spot emerging markets or potential investment opportunities before they become widely recognized. Take this example, if an agent learns about planned infrastructure developments in a previously overlooked area through city planning documents and online news articles, they can alert their clients to imminent opportunities for property acquisition at favorable prices.

The scalability of big data solutions means that even smaller agencies can access powerful analytics tools once limited to larger firms with extensive resources. Cloud-based platforms provide sophisticated analytics capabilities without necessitating hefty upfront investments in software or hardware. This democratization of technology empowers agents to compete effectively against larger players while delivering superior insights to their clients.

To fully leverage the benefits of big data, ongoing education is essential. Real estate professionals should focus on enhancing their analytical skills and becoming proficient in data interpretation techniques. Engaging with online courses on analytics software or attending industry workshops can significantly elevate one's ability to make informed, data-driven decisions. The knowledge gained will not only improve service offerings but also help establish agents as thought leaders within their communities.

As the flow of data continues unabated, it presents both challenges and opportunities; adapting to this evolving landscape is crucial for long-term success in real estate. With new technologies emerging and consumer expectations leaning toward more personalized experiences grounded in solid data insights, those who embrace these changes will find themselves ahead of the curve. The relationship between big data and real estate goes beyond mere access to information —it's about strategically utilizing that information to drive results for clients and build lasting relationships founded on trust and expertise.

With the right tools and knowledge at your disposal, you can transform raw numbers into actionable insights that shape your business strategy and foster client loyalty. As you integrate big data into your daily practice, view it not just as an analytical tool but as a cornerstone for innovation in your real estate endeavors.

Sustainability and Technology in Real Estate

The integration of sustainability and technology in the real estate sector is fundamentally changing how agents conduct business and connect with clients. As environmentally friendly practices gain traction, real estate professionals are not only adopting green building initiatives but also harnessing technology to bolster their sustainability efforts.

This evolution is more than just a passing trend; it reflects the growing demand from clients who are increasingly conscious of their environmental impact.

A key development in this transformation is the rise of smart buildings, which leverage advanced technologies to enhance energy efficiency and minimize carbon footprints. These buildings utilize Internet of Things (IoT) devices to monitor energy consumption, lighting, and climate control in real-time. For example, a smart thermostat can adjust heating and cooling based on occupancy patterns, leading to significant reductions in energy use. By understanding the features and advantages of these systems, real estate agents can effectively market properties that prioritize sustainability, appealing to buyers in search of energy-efficient homes.

Also, technology has simplified the assessment of a property's environmental impact. Tools such as energy modeling software allow agents to analyze how various design choices influence energy consumption and sustainability. Imagine utilizing a program that simulates energy use based on different materials or layouts; this information can be crucial when advising clients on renovations or new constructions. By showcasing a commitment to sustainable practices through technology, agents can establish themselves as informed advocates for eco-friendly living.

Sustainability also encompasses land use and urban planning. Agents can employ geographic information systems (GIS) to evaluate zoning regulations, environmental hazards, and community resources within potential neighborhoods. Take this example, by identifying areas with high walkability scores and access to public transportation, agents can provide clients with insights that align their lifestyle preferences with sustainable living options. This analytical approach not only enhances clients' understanding but also fosters trust through informed recommendations.

And, embracing sustainability involves the promotion of renewable energy sources. Real estate agents have the opportunity to educate clients about the advantages of solar panels or wind turbines as property upgrades. These installations not only lower electricity bills but also boost property values over time. When presenting a listing that features solar power capabilities, emphasizing long-term savings and potential tax credits can effectively attract eco-conscious buyers. This strategic marketing positions sustainability as a compelling selling point rather than an afterthought.

Incorporating sustainable practices into marketing strategies enhances brand reputation and appeals to socially responsible consumers. Highlighting properties that possess green certifications—such as LEED (Leadership in Energy and Environmental Design)—can draw in buyers who prioritize environmental stewardship. Utilizing platforms that emphasize green initiatives enables agents to reach a wider audience that values sustainability in their purchasing decisions.

Collaboration among stakeholders in the real estate ecosystem is vital for effectively promoting sustainable practices. By partnering with architects, builders, and local governments, agents can stay informed about upcoming projects that adhere to sustainability standards. Being at the forefront of these developments allows agents to guide clients toward opportunities that resonate with their values while building partnerships that strengthen their professional networks.

As technology continues to evolve, so does the potential for implementing more sustainable practices in real estate transactions. The advent of blockchain technology offers greater transparency by securely recording transactions and ownership histories. This level of trust is essential for buyers who may be cautious about greenwashing—

the practice of misleadingly presenting an organization as more environmentally friendly than it truly is. By leveraging blockchain in property transactions, agents can ensure that their claims about sustainability are verifiable and credible.

In the end, embracing sustainability through technology positions real estate agents not only as salespeople but as trusted advisors who grasp the complexities of modern living. As client awareness increases—driven by enhanced access to information and shifting societal values—agents who invest in understanding these trends will find themselves at a distinct advantage. By nurturing relationships grounded in transparency and shared values around sustainability, agents can foster loyalty among their clientele while contributing meaningfully to a greener future.

To harness these advancements, continuous education and adaptation are essential as new technologies emerge in response to environmental challenges. Actively engaging with resources that enhance your knowledge of sustainable practices within real estate will not only enrich your skillset but also signal your dedication to better serving your clients.

Incorporating sustainability into your business model transforms challenges into opportunities, ultimately paving the way for innovation and growth in an industry ripe for change.

Virtual Reality and Augmented Reality Solutions

Virtual reality (VR) and augmented reality (AR) have transitioned from the realm of science fiction to become essential tools in the real estate industry. These technologies are reshaping how agents showcase properties and interact with clients, providing immersive experiences that allow potential buyers to visualize homes without ever stepping inside. By integrating VR and AR into your marketing strategy, you can enhance client interactions and streamline property presentations.

Imagine a prospective buyer donning VR goggles and virtually walking through every room of a property as if they were actually there. This immersive experience allows them to appreciate the layout and flow of the home, helping them envision their lives within those walls. Take this example, companies like Matterport offer 3D scanning services that create detailed virtual tours, which agents can easily share on their websites or during open houses, significantly boosting engagement rates.

AR adds another dimension by overlaying digital information onto physical spaces using smartphones or tablets. With AR apps, you could showcase potential renovations or furnishings in an empty room. A client could simply point their device at a blank space and instantly visualize how their furniture would fit or see fresh paint colors applied to the walls. This capability not only aids clients in making informed decisions but also generates excitement about properties that might otherwise seem less appealing due to their current condition.

Implementing these technologies is more accessible than you might think; many user-friendly platforms allow real estate agents to create stunning virtual experiences with relative ease. For example, software like Zillow 3D Home or RoOomy enables agents to quickly produce high-quality virtual tours. As you incorporate these tools into your listings, focus on highlighting unique property features—such as a chef's kitchen or spacious backyard—through targeted virtual showcases that captivate buyers' imaginations.

The advantages of VR extend beyond showcasing properties; it also facilitates remote meetings with clients who may be unable to travel for in-person discussions. Picture conducting a walkthrough of multiple listings via VR while discussing each property's merits in real time with clients located halfway across the country. This innovative approach breaks down barriers and adds a personal touch that traditional video calls often lack.

Additionally, AR can enhance open houses by providing instant access to information about a property's history, nearby schools, or local amenities through interactive elements embedded in signage or brochures. Clients could scan QR codes at an open house that direct them to detailed insights about neighborhood demographics or recent sales trends—all without overwhelming them with paper handouts.

It's essential to recognize that these technological advancements particularly appeal to millennials and Gen Z buyers, who value convenience and immersive experiences when making significant decisions like purchasing a home. A study by the National Association of Realtors indicates that younger buyers are more likely to engage with listings featuring VR tours compared to those without such offerings. By aligning your marketing strategies with current preferences, you position yourself as an innovative leader in the competitive real estate landscape.

As you explore these opportunities, think about how you can seamlessly integrate VR and AR solutions into your existing workflows. Investing time in understanding various software options will empower you not only to attract more clients but also to enhance their experience throughout the buying journey.

However exciting these technologies may be, it's crucial that they complement—not replace—traditional marketing methods. Combining immersive virtual experiences with personal interactions creates a holistic approach that resonates deeply with clients. As you adapt your business model around these innovations, remember that nurturing genuine relationships remains paramount; technology should serve as an extension of your expertise rather than its replacement.

The rapid evolution of VR and AR offers ongoing opportunities for improvement within your practice. Regularly assessing new developments will ensure you're leveraging cutting-edge solutions effectively while meeting client expectations head-on.

Incorporating virtual and augmented reality into your real estate strategy not only enhances property presentations but also positions you at the forefront of industry innovation—a crucial advantage in today's competitive marketplace. By thoughtfully embracing these tools, you empower yourself to provide enriched client experiences that elevate your service offerings well beyond conventional approaches.

Developing Proactive Data Strategies

Data serves as the backbone of any successful real estate strategy. By developing proactive data strategies, you can transform your operations to be both efficient and insightful. Rather than merely reacting to market changes or client demands after they arise, a proactive approach enables you to anticipate trends and identify needs before they become apparent. This foresight not only enhances decision-making but also provides a competitive advantage.

To cultivate a proactive data strategy, start with a comprehensive assessment of your current data sources. Evaluate both quantitative and qualitative data, including sales records, client feedback, market trends, and property performance metrics. Take this example, if you observe that certain neighborhoods consistently outperform others in terms of sales or rental prices, these insights can inform your investment decisions and marketing focus. Organizing this information in Excel can create a streamlined database that facilitates easy analysis.

After establishing a solid foundation of data collection, it's crucial to analyze the information critically. Techniques such as segmentation can uncover valuable patterns within your clientele. By grouping clients based on demographics—such as age, income level, or family size—you can tailor your marketing strategies more effectively. For example, if you find that many of your buyers are young families seeking homes near schools, you can prioritize listings in those areas when reaching out to potential clients.

In addition to segmentation, predictive analytics can help forecast future trends. Excel's forecasting functions allow you to project future property values based on historical data. Using formulas like the FORECAST.LINEAR function, you can estimate sales prices or demand in various neighborhoods by analyzing past performance. Take this example, if you discover that properties near new development zones typically appreciate by 10% annually, you'll be well-equipped to guide clients in making informed investment decisions.

Visualization is another key element in developing proactive data strategies. Creating dashboards in Excel not only summarizes essential metrics but also enables quick comprehension at a glance. These dashboards can track critical indicators such as average days on market or price per square foot across different areas—information vital for positioning listings competitively. Engaging visuals during presentations or discussions enhance client understanding and involvement in the process.

Automation is essential for keeping your data strategies active without overwhelming yourself with manual tasks. Excel offers powerful features like Macros and Power Query that can streamline repetitive processes such as data entry and report generation. Take this example, if compiling monthly sales reports from various sources is necessary, setting up automated macros can significantly reduce labor while minimizing errors—a crucial factor in the fast-paced real estate environment.

To stay ahead in the market, consider integrating external

data sources into your analysis framework. Subscribing to real estate market reports or using APIs from platforms like Zillow or Realtor.com allows you to access live market conditions directly within Excel. Imagine the efficiency of automatically updating your listings with current MLS statuses or price changes; this adaptability boosts both your credibility and response times with clients.

Building strong relationships with local stakeholders—such as developers or city planners—can further enhance your data collection efforts by providing insights into upcoming projects that may significantly influence property values. Being aware of these developments not only allows you to inform clients better but also positions you as a knowledgeable industry leader who understands the complexities of market dynamics.

Lastly, adopt an iterative mindset toward improving your proactive strategies by continuously revisiting and refining them based on outcomes and feedback. Regularly assess how effective your insights have been in guiding decisions and adjust your approach when expectations aren't met; this agility will help you remain nimble in a fluctuating market landscape.

To wrap things up, a well-crafted proactive data strategy empowers real estate agents not just to react but to lead confidently within their markets. By effectively integrating these tactics into your daily practice with tools like Excel, you are not merely keeping pace; you are setting the standard for success that others will aspire to meet in their pursuit of excellence in the competitive world of real estate.

Adapting to Technological Advancements

Technological advancements are fundamentally transforming the real estate landscape, and staying competitive requires quick and effective adaptation. Excel, with its versatility, offers a multitude of ways to harness these innovations, enhancing your efficiency in the industry. By embracing technology, you not only optimize your workflow but also position yourself as a forward-thinking agent capable of delivering exceptional service to your clients.

Begin by exploring how data analytics can significantly improve your decision-making processes. Each day generates vast amounts of information—ranging from market trends to client interactions. Mastering Excel's analytical capabilities can provide you with a valuable edge. For example, utilizing advanced functions like pivot tables enables you to break down complex datasets into actionable insights. By categorizing data according to various criteria—such as property type or location—you can uncover patterns that may otherwise go unnoticed in raw figures. This level of analysis equips you with the intelligence necessary for making informed strategic decisions.

Also, integrating Excel with other software solutions can amplify its functionalities. Many real estate agents rely on Customer Relationship Management (CRM) systems to track client interactions and leads. By importing data from these systems into Excel, you can conduct deeper analyses that inform your marketing strategies and identify potential upsell opportunities. Leveraging functions like VLOOKUP or INDEX-MATCH allows you to correlate data between your CRM and Excel spreadsheets, providing nuanced insights into client behaviors and preferences.

Automation is another crucial component of adapting to technological change. Excel's macro functionality can help streamline repetitive tasks such as generating reports or updating listings. Take this example, if compiling monthly performance reports is a regular task for you, creating a macro to automate this process not only saves time but also minimizes the risk of human error. By automating routine tasks, you free up valuable time for strategic planning and client engagement rather than getting bogged down by administrative duties.

Additionally, mobile technology has revolutionized how real estate professionals operate in the field. With tools like Microsoft Excel available on mobile devices, you can access essential data anytime and anywhere—whether during an open house or a client meeting. Imagine being able to pull up comparable market analysis (CMA) data instantly while discussing property options with a prospective buyer; this responsiveness not only impresses clients but also underscores your commitment to transparency and informed decision-making.

Collaboration tools have also become vital in contemporary real estate practices. Utilizing cloud-based versions of Excel allows multiple team members to work on documents simultaneously without version conflicts. This is particularly beneficial for managing large projects that require input from various stakeholders. Co-authoring features facilitate seamless communication within teams, ensuring that everyone stays updated with the latest information without unnecessary delays.

And, embracing emerging technologies such as artificial intelligence (AI) can distinguish you from competitors who may be slower to adapt. AI-powered tools analyze market trends and predict future movements based on historical data—enhancing your advisory role significantly. Take this example, incorporating AI-generated insights into your presentations enables you to offer clients tailored forecasts aligned with their investment goals.

Adapting to these technological advancements necessitates not only acquiring technical skills but also fostering a mindset shift. Cultivating curiosity about new tools and techniques empowers you to integrate them effectively into your practice. Regularly engaging with online forums or attending workshops focused on real estate technology keeps you informed about trends that could impact your business strategy.

In the end, it's essential to remember that technology should enhance rather than replace personal relationships in real estate. While tools like Excel improve data management and analysis, the human elements of trust, rapport, and understanding are irreplaceable when it comes to building lasting client relationships. Use technology judiciously to augment your capabilities while ensuring genuine connections remain at the core of what you do.

Successfully adapting requires both strategic thinking and a commitment to continuous evolution alongside industry shifts. By integrating technological advancements into your everyday operations through powerful tools like Excel, you're not merely keeping pace; you're paving the way for innovation in real estate practices that will resonate throughout your career.

Excel as a Future-Proof Skill

In today's ever-evolving real estate landscape, Excel has become an essential skill that enhances daily operations and fosters long-term career resilience. As data-driven decision-making continues to gain traction among successful agents, the ability to analyze, interpret, and present data effectively is increasingly crucial. Mastering Excel provides professionals with a versatile toolkit that not only addresses current challenges but also anticipates future demands.

Consider the vast amount of data generated during real estate transactions—property values, market trends, client interactions, and financial metrics. This abundance of information can feel overwhelming; however, Excel allows you to navigate it with ease. Take this example, utilizing Excel's data visualization tools, such as charts and graphs, can transform complex market analyses into easily digestible presentations for clients. Imagine showcasing a sales performance graph during a listing presentation; these visual aids not only elevate your professionalism but also foster client trust by demonstrating transparency in your methods.

Excel's adaptability in integrating with various software solutions further solidifies its status as a future-proof skill. As new technologies—like CRM systems and advanced analytics platforms—emerge, the ability to import and analyze data within Excel remains invaluable. Functions such as VLOOKUP enable you to seamlessly connect disparate datasets, creating a comprehensive view of client profiles or property listings that informs strategic decisions. By mastering these functionalities now, you are effectively preparing your practice for the rapidly changing technological landscape.

In addition to data analysis, the growing emphasis on automation within the industry is another vital consideration. Professionals who leverage Excel's macro capabilities to automate repetitive tasks will find themselves with more time for relationship building and strategic initiatives. For example, rather than manually tracking transaction progress or compiling monthly reports, you can create macros to streamline these processes significantly. This not only boosts efficiency but also allows you to shift your focus from administrative tasks to enhancing client engagement and refining sales strategies.

The importance of adaptability in response to evolving industry standards cannot be overstated. As new regulations and market dynamics arise, proficiency in Excel empowers agents to respond proactively. The analytical skills gained through mastering Excel enable you to conduct scenario planning for various market conditions, ensuring you are equipped with insights that guide clients toward informed decisions.

And, committing to continuous learning will strengthen your expertise. In an environment where changes occur rapidly —whether due to regulatory updates or shifts in consumer preferences—staying updated on new features and best practices within Excel will keep you competitive. Online courses and community forums offer valuable opportunities for ongoing education, reinforcing your skills while exposing you to innovative approaches utilized by peers.

As you navigate your career path, embracing Excel as an essential skill rather than just a tool will set you apart in the marketplace. It's not merely about using functions; it's about cultivating a mindset focused on leveraging data for strategic advantage. Clients increasingly seek agents who can offer insights backed by solid analysis rather than instinct alone.

In the end, while other skills may fade with trends or technological advancements, the ability to analyze and present data effectively through Excel remains timeless. As you build your real estate career on this foundation, remember that technology is simply a tool—your expertise and interpersonal skills will always be what truly distinguishes you in the eyes of your clients.

In summary, investing time and effort into mastering Excel yields benefits far beyond immediate tasks; it enhances your capacity to thrive amid uncertainty while consistently delivering exceptional value. Embrace this journey of growth with confidence—Excel will be a steadfast ally as you advance in the dynamic world of real estate.

Mastering Excel goes beyond simply acquiring technical skills; it's about transforming your approach to the real estate profession. Throughout this journey, you've delved into a range of Excel functionalities specifically designed for the nuances of real estate operations. Each chapter has equipped you with tools that enhance your efficiency, improve your presentations, and enable you to provide data-driven insights for your clients.

Think about how this knowledge influences your daily

tasks. With the ability to swiftly analyze property trends using functions like AVERAGE or VLOOKUP, you can offer more precise valuations and market analyses. This expertise positions you as a trusted advisor, capable of confidently navigating the complexities of the market. Real estate is no longer just about showcasing properties; it's about crafting compelling narratives supported by data that resonate with your clients' needs.

The ever-evolving nature of real estate demands adaptability, and Excel serves as a powerful ally in this regard. Automating repetitive tasks with macros saves you time and minimizes errors, allowing you to devote more energy to cultivating meaningful client relationships rather than getting caught up in administrative details. Imagine having extra hours each week to strategize, network, or refine your marketing tactics—all thanks to the efficiencies gained through Excel.

Beyond these immediate benefits, consider the long-term implications for your career. As data becomes increasingly pivotal in real estate decision-making, those skilled in data analysis will stand out in a competitive landscape. You're not just learning to use software; you're fostering a mindset that values insight over instinct. This analytical perspective will distinguish you as a leader in your field.

In any profession—especially one as fast-paced as real estate—continuous improvement is crucial for maintaining relevance. Staying updated on Excel enhancements and leveraging resources such as online courses or community forums will keep you at the forefront of industry developments. This commitment demonstrates an awareness that the landscape will continue evolving; being informed empowers you to anticipate changes rather than simply reacting to them.

In the end, embracing Excel as a core skill not only enhances your professional toolkit but also enriches your interactions with clients. As you become more adept at interpreting data and providing actionable insights, you increase the value you deliver—building trust and loyalty among those you serve. Real estate is inherently relational; mastering Excel offers a pathway for deeper engagement through informed conversations that align with clients' aspirations and concerns.

As we conclude this exploration of Excel's applications in real estate, take a moment to reflect on how far you've come and envision where these skills can lead you next. Your journey doesn't end here; it marks the beginning of a new chapter filled with opportunities for growth and excellence in your career. With each spreadsheet navigated and each function mastered, you're constructing a future that's not only successful but sustainable—a future where you're empowered by data and driven by insights.

Approach this knowledge with confidence as you advance in your career—Excel will remain an essential tool that helps you thrive amidst challenges while consistently delivering exceptional service to your clients. Your commitment to excellence starts now; let these lessons inform your decisions today and shape your successes tomorrow.

- **Recap of Key Learnings**

Throughout our exploration of Excel's applications for real estate agents, you've discovered a wealth of insights and skills aimed at enhancing your efficiency and advancing your career. Let's take a moment to recap the key takeaways that will empower you to confidently navigate the complexities of this dynamic industry.

Essentially of your learning are foundational skills in Excel, which are essential for your success. You've learned how to input and edit data efficiently, ensuring accuracy from the very beginning. The importance of proper data entry cannot be overstated; it forms the basis for all subsequent analyses. Even a minor error can skew reports, impacting everything from client trust to financial forecasting.

As you progressed, essential functions such as SUM and AVERAGE transformed your approach to property analysis. These tools enable quick assessments of potential investments, allowing you to provide clients with timely insights into market trends. Take this example, using AVERAGE to illustrate neighborhood pricing patterns not only reinforces your expertise but also empowers clients with information that supports their decisions.

Moving beyond the basics, advanced formulas like VLOOKUP and IF statements enhance your decision-making capabilities. These tools allow you to cross-reference information seamlessly and adapt dynamically to changing scenarios —skills that are invaluable during negotiations or when tailoring property suggestions to meet specific client needs.

In terms of organization, mastering Excel tables ensures that your datasets remain manageable and visually appealing. By sorting and filtering properties, you can quickly access the most relevant listings for clients while presenting information in an intuitive format. You may have noticed how much easier it is to communicate findings when they are neatly organized; this clarity directly translates into stronger client presentations and greater professional credibility.

Data visualization through charts adds another layer to your analytical toolkit. Creating dynamic visual representations— such as bar charts or scatter plots—makes complex data points more accessible for clients who may not be familiar with analytics. This skill transforms dry statistics into compelling narratives that are essential for persuading potential buyers or investors.

For financial aspects, utilizing functions like NPV (Net Present Value) or calculating mortgage payments equips you with critical information that can influence investment decisions. Understanding how these calculations impact overall returns on properties gives you a competitive edge in discussions with both clients and colleagues.

As you embraced automation through macros, your workflow became significantly more efficient. The time saved on repetitive tasks not only boosts productivity but also allows for more strategic planning and networking opportunities. By prioritizing processes that can be automated, you can focus on nurturing relationships—an essential element of success in real estate.

Your journey through CRM management has also sharpened your ability to track leads effectively. Creating customized templates ensures that no opportunity slips through the cracks while enhancing your follow-up strategies with clients. The tools you've developed will foster deeper relationships built on consistent communication and personalized engagement.

Additionally, recognizing risk management strategies—such as scenario planning—empowers you to make informed decisions that protect both your interests and those of your clients. Being aware of potential risks demonstrates professionalism and a commitment to responsible practices in an often unpredictable market landscape.

Finally, staying attuned to Excel updates and committing to continuous learning will keep your skills sharp as the industry evolves. Engaging with community forums or attending workshops positions you at the forefront of developments, which is vital for maintaining relevance amid ongoing changes in technology and market dynamics.

Collectively, these key learnings lay a solid foundation upon which you can build a successful career as a real estate agent equipped with powerful analytical tools. Each aspect discussed serves not only as a feature of Excel but as a catalyst for achieving success within an increasingly competitive field.

As you reflect on this knowledge, think about how

integrating these skills into your daily practices will enhance client interactions and create new professional opportunities moving forward. You've embarked on a journey filled with potential for personal growth and impactful contributions within the real estate sector—one fueled by mastery over data-driven insights that drive results.

· Implementing Excel Practices

Integrating Excel practices into your daily workflow is more than just mastering functions and formulas; it's about seamlessly incorporating these tools into your real estate operations. This integration can transform how you manage data, communicate insights, and make decisions. By effectively using Excel, you can enhance productivity, streamline client interactions, and improve your effectiveness as an agent.

Start by evaluating your current processes to pinpoint areas where you spend excessive time on repetitive tasks or where manual entries may lead to errors. For example, if you frequently input property details for listings or client interactions, consider creating standardized templates that require minimal effort while maximizing output. These templates should include essential fields like property type, price, square footage, and contact information, making it easy to update and retrieve data quickly.

Once your templates are in place, leverage Excel's functions to automate calculations. For mortgage calculations or investment analyses, setting up a dedicated worksheet allows for instant updates based on changing variables such as interest rates or property values. Using the PMT function, for instance, you can calculate monthly mortgage payments based on principal amounts and interest rates, enabling clients to quickly visualize their potential financial commitments.

To further enhance accuracy, incorporate data validation tools like drop-down lists for property categories or statuses. For example, if you're managing a list of rental properties, a dropdown menu with status options (e.g., "Available," "Under Contract," "Leased") can help prevent mismatches and ensure consistency throughout your records.

Data organization is essential for effective implementation. Utilizing tables in Excel not only makes your data visually appealing but also enables sorting and filtering functionalities that enhance usability. Imagine showcasing available properties to clients; a well-structured table allows you to filter listings based on criteria such as price range or location with just a click—saving time and facilitating informed decision-making.

Visualization techniques can add depth to your analytical capabilities. Charts and graphs transform raw numbers into narratives that resonate with clients who may be less familiar with data analysis. Take this example, if you want to illustrate market trends over the past five years, a line chart showing price fluctuations in specific neighborhoods can provide immediate insight into market dynamics—this clarity can significantly influence potential buyers.

As you become more comfortable with these tools, explore advanced techniques like conditional formatting to highlight key data points. Applying color scales to a dataset displaying property prices can quickly indicate which properties fall below average or exceed market trends at a glance, allowing you to spot opportunities without sifting through spreadsheets manually.

When analyzing larger datasets or generating comprehensive reports for clients, consider using PivotTables. They summarize vast amounts of information into digestible formats, enabling dynamic interaction with your data. By filtering based on different categories—such as property type or geographic location—you can uncover insights tailored specifically to client needs.

Collaboration is also crucial in today's real estate landscape. Sharing workbooks through cloud services like OneDrive or Google Sheets fosters teamwork and maintains version control among colleagues. Real-time updates ensure everyone is aligned, reducing the likelihood of miscommunication during critical negotiations.

While implementing these Excel practices is essential, regularly assessing their effectiveness is equally important. Schedule periodic reviews of your workflows to identify areas for improvement or additional automation opportunities. Staying informed about new features introduced through Excel updates will help you continually refine your processes.

Finally, remember that mastery comes from consistent practice and application of these strategies in real-world scenarios. Start by incorporating one new technique at a time into your routine until it becomes second nature. This gradual approach will solidify your understanding and build confidence as you experience tangible benefits in efficiency and client satisfaction.

Each practice you implement strengthens your position within the industry—enhancing personal efficiency and professional credibility through accurate information backed by solid data analysis capabilities. By fully embracing these tools, you're not just adapting to the demands of modern real estate; you're distinguishing yourself as an agent poised for success in an increasingly competitive environment.

- **Encouragement for Continued Exploration**

Exploring Excel goes beyond merely grasping its functions; it's about unlocking its immense potential to transform your real estate practice. Each tool you master and technique you implement can significantly improve your ability to analyze data, craft engaging presentations, and interact with clients. This journey is not confined to a single training session or a few completed worksheets; rather, it unfolds into a continuous exploration of innovative ways to leverage technology in your daily operations.

To make the most of this exploration, consider dedicating time each week to dive deeper into Excel's capabilities. You might experiment with advanced features like Power Query or learn how to integrate Excel with other platforms, such as CRM systems or property management tools. By committing regularly to this process, you'll refine your skills while discovering new functionalities that can enhance your work. For example, mastering Power Query can automate data cleansing and consolidation from various sources, freeing up hours that would otherwise be spent on manual tasks.

Networking with fellow real estate professionals can also inspire fresh ideas and innovative uses for Excel. Joining local real estate groups or online forums where technology integration is a popular topic can foster valuable connections. Sharing experiences and techniques with peers not only builds community but also opens doors for collaborative projects that streamline practices. Learning from others' successes and challenges can provide insights into effective strategies that align with your own goals.

In addition to community engagement, consider investing in further education through workshops or online courses focused on Excel advancements. Many platforms offer specialized training tailored specifically for real estate professionals, featuring hands-on projects that simulate real-life scenarios. Take this example, participating in a workshop on financial modeling in Excel could equip you with the skills needed to accurately forecast property performance, giving you an edge when advising clients on investment opportunities.

Embrace the challenges that arise during this learning process; they often lead to the most enlightening experiences. If you encounter a complex formula or function, take the time to break it down methodically. Engage in forums or seek mentorship from those who have successfully navigated similar hurdles. Overcoming these obstacles will build your confidence and expertise. Remember, every expert was once a beginner who chose to persist.

Incorporating feedback into your learning journey is equally important. After implementing a new Excel technique, reflect on its impact on your workflow and client interactions. Gathering insights from colleagues or clients about the clarity of your reports and the efficiency of your processes can guide further improvements. This iterative approach ensures that your methods align with industry best practices and client expectations.

Finally, stay open-minded about emerging trends in technology that could influence how Excel is used in real estate. The landscape is continually evolving, and adaptability will keep you relevant. Follow industry publications and thought leaders who discuss innovations like artificial intelligence integration within Excel or advanced data visualization techniques. Engaging in these discussions will broaden your perspective and may inspire you to experiment with features that were previously unfamiliar.

In the end, committing to ongoing exploration within Excel not only equips you with technical skills but also positions you as a forward-thinking professional in the competitive real estate sector. Each step toward mastery empowers you to deliver better service and insights for clients while fostering your personal growth. Embrace this journey wholeheartedly; the rewards will manifest as heightened efficiency and greater success in your real estate endeavors.

- **Final Thoughts**

Mastering Excel as a real estate agent goes beyond simply learning the software; it shapes your career and enhances your relationships with clients. Throughout this book, we've explored various techniques and strategies designed to provide you with practical tools that boost your productivity and improve your decision-making. With this knowledge, you can transform raw data into actionable insights, empowering you to navigate complex markets with confidence.

As you apply advanced functions, organize data efficiently, and create dynamic dashboards, you're not only honing your technical skills but also establishing yourself as a data-driven leader in your field. The ability to interpret data effectively leads to more meaningful client interactions, whether you're showcasing property trends or developing personalized investment reports. In today's market, clients expect transparency and insight from their agents, and utilizing Excel can help you exceed these expectations.

It's important to recognize that the real estate landscape is continuously evolving. As technology advances, it opens up new avenues for growth. Staying informed about these developments is crucial for maintaining your relevance and competitiveness. Embrace ongoing learning as a fundamental aspect of your professional journey. Engaging with resources such as webinars, online courses, and community forums will help you stay ahead of trends that could impact your business practices.

Additionally, your success with Excel will depend on how well you integrate it with other tools and systems in your workflow. Think about how customer relationship management (CRM) solutions or property management software can complement Excel, creating a seamless experience for both you and your clients. This integration facilitates more efficient data handling and client management, ultimately enhancing the quality of service you provide.

Collaboration with peers can also ignite innovative ideas

and solutions. Sharing your experiences not only sharpens your skills but helps foster a supportive network within the industry. The relationships you build can lead to collaborative ventures that leverage each other's strengths, making technology work harder for everyone involved.

View your mastery of Excel not as a final achievement but as part of an ongoing journey toward excellence in real estate practice. Each formula learned and template created acts as a stepping stone toward enriching your professional toolkit. While challenges may arise—whether it's mastering advanced features or reconciling extensive datasets—your perseverance will lead to newfound expertise.

In the end, the goal is to empower yourself and those around you with the knowledge you've acquired. This way, you'll cultivate an environment that encourages analytical thinking within your team or organization. As you share insights gained from data analysis, you inspire others to adopt similar practices, enhancing overall performance in the field.

To wrap things up, mastering Excel is more than just acquiring skills; it signifies a commitment to excellence in real estate service delivery. As you incorporate these strategies into your daily operations, you'll not only develop technical capabilities but also gain a renewed sense of purpose and direction in your career. The world of real estate is ripe for innovation; with Excel by your side, you'll be well-prepared to rise above the competition and redefine what success means in this ever-evolving landscape.

www.ingramcontent.com/pod-product-compliance
Lightning Source LLC
LaVergne TN
LVHW051220050326
832903LV00028B/2183